Versions of Exile Morality
Refugees in Britain, 1790-1845

GOTHENBURG STUDIES IN THE HISTORY OF SCIENCE AND IDEAS

15

ADRIAN VELICU

Versions of Exile Morality

Refugees in Britain, 1790-1845

ACTA UNIVERSITATIS GOTHOBURGENSIS

Abstract

Adrian Velicu. *Versions of Exile Morality. Refugees in Britain, 1790-1845.* Göteborg. (Acta Universitatis Gothoburgensis. 15) Department of the History of Science and Ideas, Gothenburg University.

This study attempts to identify a particular strand of intellectual history characterized by the manner of using ideas and concepts in the extreme situation of exile. The French, Spanish and Italian émigrés in London between the 1790s and 1840s had been expelled or had fled under circumstances that attached a certain guilt to their exile. Their periodicals brought out in Britain contain justifications countering the condemnation implied by banishment and shaping an idiosyncratic kind of moral argument in the process. While there is a level of recognizable political controversy that the opposition might have carried on at home if tolerated, there is another level where the force, which imposed the banishment is answered by rhetoric and by a paradoxical moral justification. Drawing on their own cultural traditions, but also inspired by the British one, the exiles reverse the roles of judge and defendant and claim to be the proper representatives of their peoples. It is a plea forced by extreme circumstances, indicating the need of the émigrés to prove that they were still part of the community. In addition, the way the French exiles employ certain topical concepts indicates the extent to which such ideas lend themselves to being used by opposite camps in a polemic. This fact may point to a method of gauging the precision or the looseness of a concept in a period of transition. The articles written against a background of tumultuous changes convey the immediacy of the refugees' determination to respond to their persecutors, whether by persuasive political argument, idiosyncratic contentions on morality, or just invective.

Distribution:
ACTA UNIVERSITATIS GOTHENBURGENSIS
Box 222
SE-405 30 Göteborg
Sweden

ISBN: 91-7346-399-X
ISSN: 0348-6788

Sättning: Johan Kärnfelt
Tryck: Vasastadens Bokbinderi

Acknowledgements

I owe a debt of gratitude to Professor Sven-Eric Liedman who has followed and supported this work with exemplary tolerance. Professor Liedman has commented on various drafts and made many valuable suggestions, all of which I have given thought to, none of the results being his responsibility. I should like to thank Dr Michael Srigley who has read the final draft, contributing numerous stylistic improvements. I am grateful to the Department of History of Ideas and Science of Gothenburg University and to the Inter-European Research Programme of the Faculty of Arts for financial support. I also wish to thank Dr Johan Kärnfelt who has seen to the typographical matters.

I have benefited from the competence and unfailing courtesy of the staff of the Gothenburg University Library, British Library (both at its Bloomsbury and St. Pancras locations) and New York Public Library. During a very brief but fruitful visit to the University Library of North Carolina at Chapel Hill my work has been facilitated by the particular efficiency and kindness of its staff.

This is a slightly revised version of an earlier text which found its way to a number of Swedish university libraries and departments of history of ideas, receiving its own entry in the respective catalogues (hence this explanation). Apart from minor stylistic changes, I have attempted to clarify the argument in places, added an index, and updated the bibliography.

Contents

1

Introduction

An act of banishment tends to provoke a reaction. A political decision to exile someone, or the sense of fear driving a person abroad presupposes coercion, thus setting up the conditions for a response. This may take a concretely belligerent form—the legendary Coriolanus returning with an army to besiege his native city—or the form of a rhetorical diatribe, ideological argument, or moral justification. In so far as banishment implies attaching guilt to the individual who has to yield to the circumstances there arises the wish to explain and defend oneself. Rousseau had established the connection between exile and being morally flawed; when an individual breaks the social contract he ceases to be a member of the state and consequently "il en doit être retranché par l'exil comme infracteur du pacte, ou par la mort comme ennemi public; car un tel ennemi n'est pas une personne morale …"[1] This measure belonged to the community envisaged by Rousseau, but existing states acted along similar lines. An official decision to exile someone was not always necessary, fear may have decided matters when graver danger loomed ahead. Either way, the exiles have to prove that they do go on being moral persons.

---

[1] "… he has to be removed by means of exile for having broken the contract, or by death as a public enemy; because such an enemy is no longer a moral person." *Du Contrat social* (Paris: Gallimard, 1964) 377. Vol. 3 of *Oeuvres complètes*, ed. Bernard Gagnebin et al. 4 vols. (1957-79).

Therefore even if the émigrés regard their flight as an act of defiance or a tactical step, the accusation or sense of being in the wrong compels some of them to redress the moral balance and counter the condemnation. The need for articulating such an answer leads to a novel way of handling the arguments. The choice, use, and final shape of the ideas and concepts employed for the purpose constitute part of intellectual history, but an aspect that has been neglected so far. This study attempts to identify a particular strand of the history of ideas by looking at the way the émigrés justify their position and establish their moral rightness. An additional aim is to find out to what extent the precision or temporary "looseness" of certain concepts is indicated by the émigrés' resort to such ideas in shaping their arguments. The object of the present analysis is not the strength and validity of the exiles' political arguments as such, but their use for purposes of self-exculpation.

The period examined here stretches from the immediate consequences of the French Revolution during the 1790s to the activities of the increasingly militant nationalists of the 1840s. This was a time when a series of upheavals drove relatively large numbers of people into exile coinciding with an increased facility of bringing out periodicals. Technological and social changes throughout these decades turned the periodical press into one of the customary vehicles for presenting ideas and developing arguments.

The world of exile is vast and fluid. I have confined my discussion to the French, Italian and Spanish émigrés in London.[2] Most of them saw the British political system as a model, and those who initially were not very keen became persuaded after a longer stay. It was in London that the growing habit of conveying information, entertainment or carrying on debates in periodicals was combined with a reasonable—sometimes

---

[2] "Émigré" has been used of the French royalists who fled the country after 1789, then, by extension, for any French person who left because of the Revolution, the implication being that such an "emigrant" was a political refugee. People of other nationalities who went into exile because of political reasons have also been called émigrés occasionally. None of these terms (émigré, refugee, exile) need carry a political dimension, yet they imply it in different degrees (a refugee may need to be qualified as "political," an exile possibly, an émigré hardly). The meanings overlap sufficiently to allow their use as virtual synonyms in a discussion of persons compelled to move abroad due to the political circumstances.

precariously preserved—freedom of expression. Censorship was quite active occasionally, there were abuses, and the British authorities did have certain interests in allowing some of the active exiles to have London as their base (particularly the French émigrés during the conflict with revolutionary and Napoleonic France). On the whole, however, Britain was one of the few places in Europe where the émigrés could voice their arguments, making them, the time, and the place a clearly defined object of study.

Among the texts they produced I have concentrated on the periodicals. Such magazines represent the urgency of the émigrés' point of view better than book-length productions. Following the refugees' efforts to put across their case at frequent intervals tends to convey more faithfully the immediacy of their concerns. Whatever may be lost in profundity may be gained in the spontaneity of the evidence. Besides, it is not clear to what extent the lengthier productions (not numerous) bear the mark of exile. Some were started abroad and completed at home. They may lack the pressures and preoccupations, which can definitely be assumed in the case of the brief texts published regularly. It may well be necessary to state at the outset that this is a different kind of enterprise from the recent valuable work on the French exiles. This is an attempt at a comparative discussion of certain ideas connected with banishment that has entailed a selection of arguments published by several exile groups over five decades.

I understand by an exile a person forced to live outside his (often her) country because of political or social reasons and who intends to return. The flight abroad may be determined by an official decision to expel a particular individual or someone belonging to a particular group (clergy, aristocracy), or by fear of the consequences of having a particular social or political position. A clarification: this discussion does not deal with the decisions of various individuals to leave their countries; it could be argued that in many cases it was a prudential choice, when a choice was possible at all. Again, the analysis deals with the justifications which carry a moral undertone, and with some issues concerning the range of certain topical concepts.

The Characters

It may be helpful here to mention briefly the circumstances that drove the refugees to Britain, the nature of these groups, and to add a word on the editors. Such matters receive a more detailed treatment below, when discussed separately. The first French émigrés arrived already in 1789. These were mainly aristocrats, strongly committed royalists, occasionally called ultra-royalists probably to distinguish them from the constitutional monarchists who appeared in London after 1792. The latter had not opposed the revolution, at least not at the beginning and not entirely. In fact, some of them had contributed to the text of the 1791 Constitution. A stream of clergymen came after 1792, most of them probably belonging to the old-fashioned variety of royalism. On the whole, the newly arrived French in London were hardly a homogeneous group. There was quite a difference between the Calvinist Mallet du Pan (admittedly, a Swiss) and the flamboyant Peltier. They all had in common a dislike of the Revolution or of its development, and later of Napoleon and his regime, but their opposition was expressed in more ways than one, which makes them quite representative of the French voices in Britain.

Spain was unsettled by the French invasion in 1808, but most of the refugees began to arrive after 1812. Political difficulties had earlier driven abroad some active publicists. What brought over the larger number, however, was the Spanish king's refusal to keep his pledge to respect the liberal Constitution. The "liberales" returned to power in 1820 but absolutism was restored in 1823 and more refugees joined those who went back to London. The poet-clergyman, the medical doctor, and the learned historians who edited periodicals offer a variety of attitudes towards exile and the developments at home. They provide examples of commitment without being predictable. Blanco White, a clergyman in search of a faith whose poetry in English was appreciated by Coleridge, or Fernández Sardino, the militant physician who somehow failed to return from exile when conditions were favourable are intriguing individuals in themselves. It is worth pointing out that these periodicals reflect only a part of their personality.

The failure of the 1820 and 1821 revolutions in Naples and Piedmont, respectively, forced a number of Italians to flee their native areas, and quite a few of them headed for Britain. More arrived in the 1830s after further militant actions of an increasingly nationalist nature. Some of them had to leave France in a hurry, their first port-of-call in exile, either expelled or afraid that they would be. Giuseppe Mazzini came to London via France. His way of operating contributed to a certain image of the exile: fiercely dedicated to the cause, ascetic, conspiratorial. Befriended by quite a few people in Britain, Mazzini appears also to have possessed more endearing traits of character. At the same time he was ridiculed by some fellow-exiles for being impractical, and loathed by the authorities of various countries on the Continent for being ruthless.

These are the main groups discussed here, but they were not the only exiles in London at the time. During the 1830s a number of Polish and German refugees came to London. As it happened, they hardly brought out any periodicals (the Italians were not that busy either, but they had one spectacular character who made up for the lack of quantity). For practical purposes I have confined my discussion to the French, Spanish and Italian magazines. They provide sufficient material for analysis as they represent some of the main emerging political ideologies. Although sometimes they have to be mentioned collectively, I do not treat them as groups, but as individuals. More often than not, discussing a periodical means discussing one person's ideas. In common with many early periodicals, the publications of the émigrés were often edited and written by one individual. Sometimes there is evidence of other contributors, and the opinions expressed in their articles may have been shared by other fellow-exiles, but the dearth of information on numbers and internal discussions prevents any generalizations.

The Texts

The importance of these periodicals varies. Apart from reasons of space, I have focused on those whose significance and contents warrant a closer look. Those selected here contain more reflective pieces than other similar publications. There were quite a few more or less ephemeral magazines, above all French ones, simply narrating what happened in France after 1789 with an abundance of details known to that particular author. Usually gory details are interspersed with laments and vituperations. The periodicals discussed here do not spare their invectives either, but at least there is an attempt to understand the situation and to argue a political or moral point.

Among the three French publications discussed here *Mercure Britannique* was considered useful enough by the British government to have each issue published in an English translation. *Mercure de France* carried on a tradition established in France over many years, the only one of its kind in exile. *L'Ambigu* holds the longevity record and its presence cannot be neglected, particularly if it is linked to *Paris pendant l'année...*, both edited by the same person.

The Spanish periodical *El Español* had no competition during the years of its appearance, and so it was the only outlet for the opinions of the Spanish exiles. *Ocios de Españoles Emigrados* and *El Español Constitucional* overlapped occasionally. Those who wrote here were intellectuals and politicians of some consequence in Spain and it has been maintained that during the life of these periodicals London was the intellectual centre of the Spanish-speaking world.

The Italians seemed to have had fewer funds, and, possibly, fewer readers—most of the Italians in London were not given to reading periodicals. Giuseppe Mazzini's *Apostolato popolare* stands out as the only Italian publication of some note at the time in London and the importance of its editor makes it worth discussing despite its modest size in comparison with the others.

The manner in which the émigrés articulate their political ideas does possess some interest. Yet, as political theorists they tend to be marginal and their texts hardly rise above quaintness. These periodicals take on a particular significance when their editors and contributors are regarded as individuals responding to the guilt attached to them by banishment.

The Approach

With the exception of the early chapters of Mazzini's *The Duties of Man* first published in his periodical, most of the material in these magazines is quite unknown. In order to give some idea of what I base my analysis on I present the contents in some detail, while at the same time discussing particular aspects of each publication. In each case I pursue some of the issues in the context of the editor's or contributor's (where known) concerns relating them to the wider disputes and tensions at home and in exile. On the whole, these sections of the analysis follow the texts more closely than the final discussion, which concentrates on those novel elements this study intends to explore.

Philosophical complexity is not the chief characteristic of these texts. Although their authors were all well educated and were used to handle arguments, logical rigour or speculative depth (to name two contemporary aspirations) were not their main preoccupations. Apart from the straightforward political opposition provided from a distance by these periodicals, what is of interest to the present enquiry are the additional features—when they do occur—present in texts produced under such circumstances. These additional elements have to do with an attempt to dismiss the stigma attached to banishment, a defence based on claiming the right to embody and represent one's nation. The polemical use of the ideas of nation, nationality and related concepts are turned by the émigrés into moral assets. This idiosyncratic manoeuvre, whether explicit or not, constitutes a form of moral vindication shaping a particular strand of intellectual history. These claims were articulated in various ways depending on the circumstances of the moment and the émigrés' background. Using and accommodating ideas to one's own framework in this manner helped the exiles to reintegrate themselves—morally, if in no other way—in the political, social, cultural world from which they had been excluded. Turning these notions into moral arguments is done within a polemical frame of mind, not by systematically examining the available concepts and employing them accordingly. Here lies the significance of conveying them through the medium of the periodical press, i.e. repeating them at regular intervals and attempting to keep alive a particular account of events and of their significance.

During what was still a leisurely age the émigrés, with a lot of time to spare, produced sizeable issues. Even a flimsier publication such as Mazzini's has had to be subjected to a rather ruthless selection to make the present analysis manageable. I do describe the contents in each case, but then I concentrate on discussing only a few articles. As a rule, the discussion proceeds chronologically, although where relevant the issues are considered thematically. The final analysis combines a number of elements occurring throughout the periodicals and offers two hypotheses on the significance of using certain concepts in exile, and on the kind of moral justifications put together by the émigrés.

There is not much information on the readership and the circulation of these periodicals. Where known, I mention the details when I discuss a particular publication. A few obvious assumptions can be made: being written in the émigrés' language the magazines were not aimed in the first place at the British readers (apart from *Mercure Britannique* available in the translations organized by the Foreign Office). The readership was made up of fellow-exiles and those who could get hold of smuggled copies in the respective countries. The contents included news items from the press at home reprinted for the benefit of the refugees; then there were pieces containing vigorous opinions, occasionally part of debates abroad, aimed at possible adepts at home, but above all meant as a challenge to the persecuting authorities and as a disculpation to the world at large. As to circulation, there were considerable difficulties. On the whole the authorities kept an eye on such printed matter. Sometimes several numbers were confiscated, others were allowed to circulate for a while and then forbidden, there were cases of piracy (a sign of popularity), while the odd periodical was mentioned by various distant readers.

Previous Research

A review of the earlier scholarly work done on the problems considered here is bound to be lop-sided. The enormous effort spent on the French Revolution, inevitably touching on its émigrés, can hardly be compared with similar historical endeavours concerning the other two groups. However, the earlier and greater event cannot be completely separated from the later upheavals and debates and part of the research on the former may be seen as having some validity for the matters discussed subsequently. Experts on a particular personality, field, period or country may notice omissions. Under the circumstances, an exhaustive review of earlier work would have been unreasonable and possibly unnecessary.

While pursuing the intellectual trajectory of the émigrés, a fine balancing act has been required not to be drawn into the gigantic field of research on the French Revolution. Generally, the pre-1960s studies of the

French exiles have mainly chronicled their deeds and peregrinations, occasionally dwelling on the more exotic aspects such as the ingenuity of various aristocrats when forced to earn a living. The more recent works have looked at the émigrés and their actions as elements necessary to comprehend the wider phenomenon of the Revolution.

Most of the initial, straightforward approaches, have presented the persons, narrated the events and offered extracts from the émigrés' correspondence.[3] Such a study has discussed the émigrés in terms of a particular phase of the revolution. This has limited the period examined to rather brief lengths of time, in some cases not reaching the period when the periodicals discussed here began to appear.[4] A somewhat early work, still much referred to, has looked at the social background and the number of émigrés.[5] An important work in the early 1960s has analysed the ideas of the émigrés, referring however only briefly to the periodicals.[6] A more recent collective effort has explored various facets of the counter-revolution hardly mentioning the periodicals.[7] Closer to intellectual history, there has been a thorough but older work on the circulation of mainly literary ideas, including discussions of fiction and poetry produced in exile. A more recent work has concentrated on political ideas and, while pointing out the marginality of the émigrés' reaction, has emphasized its significance for the development of later political currents.[8] Since the émigrés have been considered part of the counter-revolution,

[3] Ernest Daudet, *Histoire de l'émigration pendant la révolution française.* 3 vols. (Paris: Hachette, 1904-1908). For other similar studies, but more concise and without relying on correspondence, see Margery Weiner, *The French Exiles: 1789-1815* (London: John Murray, 1960); Jean Vidalenc, *Les Émigrés français: 1789-1825* (Caen: Association des Publications de la Faculté des Lettres et Sciences Humaines de l'Université de Caen, 1963).

[4] Emmanuel Vingtrinier, *La Contre-Révolution: première période 1789-1791.* 2 vols. (Paris: Émil-Paul frères, 1924).

[5] Donald Greer, *The Incidence of Emigration during the French Revolution* (Cambridge, MA: Harvard UP, 1951).

[6] Jacques Godechot, *La Contre-Révolution: doctrine et action, 1789-1804* (Paris: Presses Universitaires de France, 1961).

[7] *La Contre-Révolution*, ed. Jean Tulard and Benoît Yvert (Paris: Perrin, 1990).

[8] Ferdinand Baldensperger, *Le Mouvement des idées dans l'émigration française* (Paris: Plon, 1924); Gerard Gengembre, *La Contre-Révolution ou l'histoire désespérante* (Paris: Imago, 1989).

which was active inside France as well, various aspects to do with them (numbers, politics, causes of emigration) have occasionally been placed in appendices of studies on the conditions in France.[9] The biographies of some of the émigrés who edited journals in London do not analyse the texts published in these magazines.[10] Most of the writers have dealt with the military and diplomatic strategies of the émigrés and very little, if at all, with their arguments in periodicals such as those brought out in London (with the exception mentioned below). This is reflected in a work, which sums up most of the research in the field in order to make it available to a larger audience.[11] However, renewed interest in the French émigrés in Britain has resulted in a burst of very recent studies which deserve particular notice here: Simon Burrows' thorough and insightful discussion of the émigrés' newspapers and magazines in London and Kirsty Carpenter's compact and rewarding discussion of the French refugees' presence in the British capital.[12]

One of the main historians who have written on the Spanish émigrés in London has chosen the latter part of the period spent by the "liberales" in Britain, overlooking thus more than a decade in the section dealing with the magazines.[13] This neglect has been partly compensated

---

[9] Patrice Higonnet, *Class, Ideology, and the Rights of Nobles during the French Revolution* (Oxford: Clarendon, 1981).

[10] See Frances Acomb, *Mallet Du Pan (1749-1800): A Career in Political Journalism* (Durham, NC: Duke UP, 1973), and Hélène Maspero-Clerc, *Un Journaliste Contre-Révolutionnaire: Jean-Gabriel Peltier: 1760-1825* (Paris: Société des Études Robespierristes, 1973).

[11] James Roberts, *The Counter-Revolution in France: 1787-1830* (New York: St. Martin's Press, 1990).

[12] Simon Burrows, *French Exile Journalism and European Politics, 1792-1814* (Woodbridge: Boydell, 2000) and Kirsty Carpenter, *Refugees of the French Revolution: Émigrés in London, 1789-1802* (Basingstoke: Macmillan, 1999). See also the shorter studies of Carpenter and Burrows as well as those of Nigel Aston, Philip Mansel and Dominic Aidan Bellenger in *The French Émigrés in Europe and the Struggle against Revolution, 1789-1814*, ed. by Kirsty Carpenter and Philip Mansel (Basingstoke: Macmillan, 1999). All these works became available when the present text had been completed.

[13] Vicente Lloréns, *Liberales y románticos. Una emigración española en Inglaterra: 1823-1834* (Madrid: Castalia, 1968). The same writer includes part of the Spanish refugees' literary productions in *El romanticismo español*, 2nd ed. (Madrid: Castalia, 1989), again, starting in 1824. Rafael Sánchez Mantero deals only with the Spanish refugees in France in *Liberales en el exilio* (Madrid: Rialp, 1975).

for by the interest of other historians in the first sizable periodical published in London and its editor, Blanco White's *El Español*. A biography of this émigré has concluded on the note of his "lifelong struggle against orthodoxy."[14] The pioneering role of *El Español* at an important moment in the history of political ideas in Spain has been the focus of one concise discussion, while more recent articles have concentrated on constitutional ideas as analysed by Blanco White, and by the changes in the constitutional thought of the Spanish exiles, this time paying attention to periodicals published in Paris as well.[15] Even a specialized work on the history of the Spanish periodicals has allowed only brief notices about the London exile publications (Blanco White receives more attention, as usual), although it admits that, for a few years after 1823, London was the real intellectual centre of Spain.[16]

There is an abundance of studies on Mazzini. Yet even one of the recent, scholarly biographies devotes only a few passages to the contents of his London periodical.[17] A history of the Italian periodicals during the *Risorgimento* admits that Mazzini's journalistic work in London was of great importance, particularly as part of the beginnings of the Italian workers' movement but finds no room for a discussion of the texts.[18] Earlier works dedicated to this militant exile do not deal with these par-

---

[14] Martin Murphy, *Blanco-White: Self-banished Spaniard* (New Haven: Yale University Press, 1989) 195.

[15] Manuel Moreno Alonso, "Las ideas políticas de 'El Español'," *Revista de estudios políticos* 39 (1984) 65-106; Joaquín Varela Suanzes, "Un precursor de la monarquía parlamentaria: Blanco-White y 'El Español' (1810-1814)," *Revista de estudios políticos*, 79 (1993) 101-120, and also his "El pensamiento constitucional español en el exilio: el abandono del modelo doceañista (1823-1833)," *Revista de estudios políticos*, 88 (1995) 63-90.

[16] María Cruz Seoane, *Historia del periodismo en España*. Vol. 2. *El siglo XIX* (Madrid: Alianza Editorial, 1996).

[17] Denis Mack Smith, *Mazzini* (New Haven: Yale UP, 1994) 38. Older studies, such as Emilia Morelli's *Mazzini in Inghilterra* (Firenze: Felice le Monnier, 1938) mention the periodical in passing while discussing in some detail other initiatives taken by Mazzini, among them the school he started in London. Margaret C.W. Wicks is equally brief on the matter in *The Italian Exiles in London: 1816-1848* (Manchester: Manchester UP, 1937).

[18] Alessandro Galante Garrone & Franco Della Peruta, *La stampa italiana del Risorgimento* (Roma-Bari: Laterza, 1979) 164. It is the former author who makes these remarks on Mazzini's journalism in Britain.

ticular texts, and neither the new nor the old studies have examined his thought in connection with the moral implications of exile.[19]

On the whole, these studies have concentrated on particular groups of exiles, but have hardly discussed their periodicals in the context of a possible alternative morality. By discussing one group at a time, earlier scholars have been unable to see the émigrés' arguments as shaping an identifiable variety of intellectual history. As the present analysis shows, such a sequence of thought adds an unusual note to the development of political ideologies and the emergence of nationalism throughout the decades in question. The reaction of the émigrés to the implied guilt of exile has also been overlooked at the expense of their exotic presence in Britain and, when mentioned at all, the more striking contents of their periodicals have been taken in isolation. Least of all has there been any attempt to relate the ambit of topical concepts to their use by the French exiles, thus missing an opportunity to evaluate the range of such notions, as shown in the final part of the present work.[20]

Some Forerunners

No history of exile is attempted here but it may be worth mentioning a few significant instances of this phenomenon. Passing lightly over the sense of being ill at ease in the world associated with early accounts of spirit fallen into matter, or with a clearer idea of punishment as in the case of Adam and Eve's expulsion, one of the first historical cases is that of the Babylonian exile of large numbers of the Hebrew population. Exile presupposes therefore a community settled in a particular area in order for an enforced removal of a group or the expulsion of an individual to occur at all. Migratory groups who went in search of new areas to live

---

[19] Gaetano Salvemini, *Mazzini* (1925), in *Scritti sul Risorgimento* (Milano: Feltrinelli, 1961).

[20] Shortly before her death Judith Shklar had given a talk in which she sketched her intention of examining the exiles' situation in a new political context, but she clearly referred to people who intended to settle in a new country, see "Obligation, Loyalty, Exile," *Political Theory*, 21(1993) 181-197. Julia Kristeva's *Étrangers à nous-mêmes* (Paris: Fayard, 1989) 9-62, offers a meditation on the condition of the displaced person who, again, has settled abroad and inevitably remains a stranger.

in without intending to return do not fall into the category of exile as understood in the present discussion.[21]

The ostracism practised in ancient Athens has been distinguished from exile as such, for instance from exile as a form of punishment imposed by the Romans. The former was decided by the citizens' votes and was aimed at those who seemed to threaten the stability of the *polis*; it lasted for ten years and the ostracized person kept his fortune. The latter case emerged in Cicero's time and was much more of a legal measure imposed by the authorities; it applied over an indefinite period and the exiles lost some of their civic rights along with their property.[22] Ovid's banishment to Tomis exemplifies the form that the Roman version could take, although apparently Ovid did not lose his fortune. These varieties of enforced removal from one's familiar area and community have been distinguished from yet another one, deportation where the penal dimension could have been even stricter (the cases of convicts transported to the French Guyana, or to Australia). However, for a person who is forced to leave or to flee, these distinctions may seem little more than fine legal points. Even if the action is voluntary and one can find shelter in exile, the phenomenon has always been associated with punishment, guilt and coercion.

The attachment to a place and belonging to a community have been valued strongly enough to turn the enforced removal into a penalty even if the language and everything that it implies was about the same as in Dante's case. Locke in Holland was in exile, but Voltaire in a French-speaking part of Switzerland or Rousseau in Paris is a more questionable matter. To realize the importance of language it is enough to imagine all the exile periodicals discussed here being produced in English. The impact would have been quite different.

---

[21] Paul Tabori includes the great migrations besides much else of more or less relevance to exile in his *Anatomy of Exile* (London: Harrap, 1972) 66-67. Kristeva's initial reflections are followed by a selective historical survey of varieties of alienation including mythical figures, strangers settling down ("barbarians," "métèques," "guer-tochav"), and exiles proper (61 ff).

[22] On the decisive shift of *exilium* from a "voluntary act" to one imposed on "political offenders" as we know it today, see A.N. Sherwin-White, *The Roman Citizenship*, 2d ed. (Oxford: Clarendon, 1973) 34-35.

These are only a few early cases. One could add examples contemporary with those discussed below, as well as later ones, their number having increased steadily to this day. The émigrés' reasons to flee their countries varied along with the motivation which kept them active: the Poles who came to London after the 1830 revolution thought mostly in terms of nationalist ideals, while the outspoken German intellectuals and militant workers fleeing persecution in the 1830s and 1840s added an international dimension to the proceedings. Even a cursory mention of later groups of exiles, particularly as a result of the world conflagrations and equally fierce local conflicts of our century, would be an unrealistic task here. The complexity of arguments, to look no further than intellectual history, has expanded accordingly, and those discussed below constitute part of the initial phase of a new era.

The Wider Picture

The intensely rational outlook cultivated throughout the eighteenth century began to appear questionable in the 1790s when an incipient preference for the irrational (intuition, the idiosyncrasy of genius) could be noticed. Yet it was not a simple swing of the pendulum. While deductive rigour may have been losing prestige in some quarters, empirical stringency was proving increasingly impressive. The endeavours of someone like Claude-Henri de Saint-Simon, whose rationality was guided by an already determined objective, indicated how the progress of various branches of natural science offered a model for a social science aiming at overall harmonization.[23] To a significant extent it was the development of the biological sciences that inspired some social thinkers. Saint-Simon's secretary, Auguste Comte, would go on and provide an even more systematic theory of the development of humanity. Stringency of a different kind was applied by Bentham in his outlook on a world where reformed legislation and gauging one's actions would merge the individual and social interests. The thoughts developed by Bentham, James Mill and Austin on legislative reform based on utility and taking into account

---

[23] Eric Hobsbawm has suggested that "Saint-Simon is best regarded as a prolongation of the 'enlightenment'." *The Age of Revolution. Europe: 1789-1848* (1962; London: Sphere Books, 1973) 318.

the empirical force of custom dismissed the ideas of social contract and natural law with their metaphorical, and therefore useless and possibly pernicious, dimensions. Thus reason remained linked at this time both with an early, "unscientific" form of socialism, and with a qualified form of radicalism. Bentham's readiness to prescribe legal reforms on a deductive basis anywhere in the world, regarding differences between countries as negligible, would however be rejected by J.S. Mill as a result of the "historical relativism" developed on the Continent.[24]

The effort to understand reality in terms of development may well have been due to the kind of events that affected more than one country throughout these decades: the French Revolution and the Napoleonic wars accompanied by, and then causing, manifestations of nationalism, and then the post-Naponeonic restoration backed by international alliances in stark contrast to the growing militantism as a result of the rapid industrial transformation. These changes along with the attempts to block them showed the sort of radical modification that was possible. Along with the urge to put them into practice the need was also felt to comprehend them. Indeed, most of these radical changes were the consequence of the French and the industrial revolution, and this period has been regarded as dominated by this dual revolution (Hobsbawm 14, 357 & passim). The explanatory force of the concept of development, derived from the Enlightenment idea of progress, contained two different views of how an explanation could be provided, reflecting both the emergence of the Romantic attitude and the survival of the Enlightenment's main features.[25] The contrast here was between an organic perspective on development, a view associated with the reaction against the Enlightenment, and a conviction that development proceeds according to a set of laws, a view preserving the earlier appeal to reason. A distinction has been made between the idea of progress which assumes a universal standard based on reason and the new "historicism" which tends to find its criteria of development inside the growth of tradition resting on a necessity of its own. This was paralleled, once more, by the shift

---

[24] J.W. Burrow, *Evolution and Society: A Study in Victorian Social Theory* (Cambridge: Cambridge UP, 1966) 39-40, 65.

[25] Maurice Mandelbaum, *History, Man, & Reason: A Study in Nineteenth Century Thought* (Baltimore: The Johns Hopkins Press, 1971) 47.

from the concept of the social contract to seeing political entities as the result of people's common characteristics and customs. According to one interpretation, this change in emphasis meant regarding the state as following a purpose of its own rather than developing in accordance with rational intervention. It appeared thus as a national unit grounded in a particular tradition, rather than a universal example of a general standard (Mandelbaum 53, 55-56).

The tension between regarding the world and its history as a unified whole or as divided into separate entities had been resolved in favour of the former by the philosophers of the first decades of the century. Unlike Kant's separation of reason and morality and the cleavage between man and experience, the subsequent German idealist philosophers sought a "higher unity" through their systems (Mandelbaum 31). There was a religiosity about this manner of thought, to be sure beyond the orthodox variety, but recognizable in so far as a form of spiritual or divine immanence was an integral part of the doctrine. The unity and connection of the elements composing a whole could be encountered at the same time in a different strand of thought stressing the organic nature of social development. The reaction against mechanistic explanations led to a reorientation towards organic analogies. What was also being questioned in the process was the constancy of human nature, even if not necessarily as part of the organic outlook on society and history. The ability of an individual to change was seen in different ways, but whether it was due to being part of a process or to being formed by experience and environment, it offered both an explanation and a possibility for action that the rising social science could resort to. The emphasis may have shifted from the historical to the organic view, yet the chief assumption remained that no element can be understood in isolation. A comprehensive treatment of a long sequence of phenomena became relevant for both outlooks.

The highest achievement of the historical development presupposed by the "divine immanence" had a particular moral implication. The component entities are more than a structure of connected elements, they are all part of the final achievement, in a sense they are embryonic manifestations of the "World-Spirit." Hence the irrelevance, or arbitrariness of moral judgement in the case of separate phenomena (Mandelbaum 59). This argument could be applied in the realm of culture, which for Herderians was that of nations, and could maintain the significance and value of each form of expression, considering that each has a role to play in the greater scheme of things. This would be Mazzini's way of looking at the importance of various nations granting moral validity not to separate communities, but to the very fact of constituting a nation, and it would be this absence of moral judgement that the French, and to some extent the Spanish émigrés, would dismiss, ascribing moral weight to their own embodiment of the nation. It was in this respect that a little known strand of thought, going against the grain, added its own contribution to the contemporary outlook on these issues.

In ethics there was a new universalism abroad. An historian of concepts has pointed out that the Enlightenment attempted to put an end to the fragmentariness of morality by cancelling the distinctions between particular states and the international community, and those between the individual and the authorities. This "universality of an enlightened ethic" was part of the criticism of private strategies and the move towards the beginnings of a public sphere of argument.[26] Such claims have been backed by references to Voltaire's remarks that, just like geometry, there is only one morality, and to d'Holbach's conclusion spelling out the same point. This all-embracing feature was still provided by the attributes of natural law, gradually to be replaced by other systems. The same comprehensive range of ethics could be re-discovered in the Kantian criterion of moral action and in the manner of treating the individual suggesting the later doctrine of the rights of man. The contemporary alternative of utilitarianism had universal ambitions of its own, although as mentioned above, less absolute because qualified by deliberation on concrete circumstances.

The dual revolution that characterized this period had its dual effects, aspects of which converged, leading to the emergence of the modern political ideologies. Both the French Revolution with its redefinition of the individual from a subject circumscribed by others' privileges and possibly favoured by limited types of freedom to a citizen with equal

---

[26] Reinhart Koselleck, *Critique and Crisis: Enlightenment and the Pathogenesis of Modern Society* (1959; Oxford: Berg, 1988) 41-42. The quotation is on p. 42.

rights, and the industrial revolution causing increased tension between the new factory-workers and factory-owners led to new accounts about the location of, and way of using, power. These developments are to be encountered more often in the exiles' periodicals than other contemporary arguments.

The incipient conservatism that emerged chiefly as a result of the reaction against the French Revolution stressed aspects such as tradition and the importance of the organic growth of society. Without agreeing with every single word that Burke wrote, certainly not with his favourable opinions on the American Revolution and the militant movements in Poland, some French émigrés and even one or two Spaniards did employ his arguments in support of their own ideas. The subsequent stage of conservative thought with Hegel's emphasis on total subordination to the state was still to come. The revolutionary Constitution of 1791 inspired the Spanish "liberales" when they drafted their own document in 1812, which influenced some of the radical movements in Naples and Piedmont in the early 1820s, reaching even Russia and stimulating the "Decembrists'" rebellion in the middle of that decade. The effects of the two revolutions merged even more obviously in what would become the socialist ideology than in other political ideologies. The ideal of equality proclaimed in Paris and the demands for a more humane and fair treatment arising among the new categories of industrial workers would lead to increasingly systematic and radical theories. But in the early stage the role of the collective, of scientific and technological advances, and of efficient organization produced a number of "utopian" theories. The recognizable signs of socialism in Mazzini's texts were derived from the thought of Saint-Simon.

Mazzini did urge workers to consider their position and educate themselves in order to improve their lot, but only after they became aware of their nationality. Nationalism, not quite a political ideology but not a current of thought as such either, had been emerging with Herder's theory of language and culture a few decades earlier. To the significance of people's expression was added the importance of solving the question of sovereignty within a homogeneous community, an example attempted by the French after 1789. After the stimulus from cultural theories and radical movements, nationalism received a further impulse from the opposition to the Napoleonic invasions. It has been suggested that some of the aspects of nationalism may have to do with a new type of intellectual (philosopher, writer, academic) that was emerging at the time. In contrast with the earlier thinkers who, more often than not, had depended on aristocratic patronage of various kinds or on the Church, a worldly figure with access to salons and moving quite easily within a community which encompassed more than his country, the new kind of intellectual would tend to live frugally on his writing or employed by a university, he would be more introspective, less frivolous, "vaguely prophetic."[27] This earnestness allowing intuition free rein, possibly less concerned with "a sense of the possible" and emphasizing the historical circumstances of a particular environment would have its own impact on political thought.

One half of the dual revolution, the industrial one, would begin to make its effect felt through protest actions after Napoleon was defeated, and through the emergence of the workers' unions in the 1830s, along with a nation-wide movement demanding reforms. The workers' growing awareness of their place in society and potential political impact would have an echo only in Mazzini's periodical. The early exile magazines discussed here were marked by the other half of the dual revolution, the French one. The Revolution had as one of its short-term effects the counter-revolution, and as its medium-term effect the restoration with its dilemma of which parts to preserve from the past. The disputes in this respect led to the clarifications of two general orientations growing into political ideologies in the fullness of time: the ultra-royalists and the liberals.[28] The tension between those who favoured some sort of reconciliation and those who thought of revenge, vaguely echoed by Louis XVIII and Artois (the future Charles X), could be resolved depending on what could be discarded and forgotten and what preserved. The restored French monarchy, watched by politicians and thinkers on the Continent and elsewhere, could contemplate the inheritance of more than one kind of past. The recent one, the twenty-five years of revolutionary and Napoleonic rule, offered, indeed imposed, certain elements

---

[27] John Bowle, *Politics and Opinion in the Nineteenth Century* (London: Jonathan Cape, 1954) 28 ff.

[28] For some of the following arguments, see François Furet, *Revolutionary France: 1770-1880*. Trans. Antonia Nevill (1988; Oxford: Blackwell, 1992) 285-93.

(for example, civic equality); the period immediately preceding 1789 contained other choices, and the more distant period allowed more speculative alternatives. One strong voice from the "liberal" realm of ideas considered an eclectic approach; Madame de Staël, whose contribution to the debate was being mentioned after her death in 1817, would have preserved the initial phase of the Revolution and the kind of monarchy supposed to exist before absolutism when the Estates had been summoned fairly often.

The debate contained a number of more concrete aspects, which reflected political thought on the matter. Questions on the arrangements for an obvious separation of powers as opposed to a vague indivisible sovereignty, a recent ideal, or the advantages of a bi-cameral parliament would also surface in the discussions outside France, as well as in some of the articles printed in the Spanish exile periodicals in London. Calls for freedom of the press in France, with their reverberation abroad, were suggested as a solution to a particular problem as seen after 1815. The "radical individualism" produced by the Revolution, resolved into a presumed common will, ended up in dictatorship in order to avoid the risks of anarchy. A free press was a way of avoiding the perils of centralization and of giving "society" its voice.

The periodicals are discussed in chronological order. Chapter 1 deals with Jacques Mallet du Pan's *Mercure Britannique*. The analysis emphasizes the aspects characteristic of this professional political commentator and constitutional monarchist: a heightened degree of self-reflection in comparison with other French émigré journalists, and the mistrust towards the ultra-royalists. A conflict with the "ultras" is chosen as an example of the tension between the émigré factions showing the role of Mallet's periodical as a space where the future monarch indicated some of his intentions.

Mercure de France is the subject of Chapter 2. This publication is placed in a more extended historical perspective as the only exile magazine among those considered here which had appeared in the home country before resuming publication abroad. The analysis follows the ultra-royalist arguments including issues such as the merits of a foreign invasion in the contemporary European context. This chapter dwells on a long article about the relationship between the royalist émigrés' world and France; this text is presented and commented on in some detail since it is one of the explicit statements where the émigrés reflect on their situation.

Chapter 3 looks at another royalist periodical, *L'Ambigu*. The propagandistic tone peculiar to this publication and its anti-Napoleonic stance are the main aspects emphasized here. I draw attention to the opportunity of reiterating a particular version of events and the significance of this device in the case of an exile periodical of remarkable longevity. The discussion also points out the editor's attempt to readjust the criticism of a revolutionary, or collective leadership (the Directory) to a ruling system increasingly dominated by one person.

The following three chapters examine three Spanish periodicals. In Chapter 4 a more substantial section on the historical background to the period and the particular circumstances of Blanco's exile leads to an analysis of *El Español*. I discuss Blanco White's initial criticism of the Cádiz Cortes and of the Constitution produced by this assembly. My analysis follows those articles by the editor that show his change from a radical position to a rather inconsistent conservatism fading out into political indifference.

Chapters 5 and 6 discuss two Spanish periodicals, which reflect the tensions between the "liberales." *El Español Constitucional*, representing a militant version of liberalism, allows a thematic discussion of constitutional matters and of the significance of factions. I analyse the editor's way of seeing defining aspects of liberalism in relationship to the conditions in Spain and I attempt to outline the implications for the liberals in exile. A controversy between this periodical and *Ocios de Españoles Emigrados* forms part of Chapter 6 where the latter publication's conciliatory form of liberalism is explored in more detail. The appeal to the ancient constitution as an ideal set of regulations to be recovered for the benefit of all is also discussed in the context of the dispute with the more radical "liberales."

Chapter 7 deals with Mazzini's *Apostolato popolare*. I draw attention to the particular circumstances of the states of the Italian Peninsula at the time and the way in which they may have influenced this exile's intellectual priorities. I point out how for Mazzini the importance of national belonging is a preliminary condition for social justice. I outline what

Mazzini considers to be the main advantages deriving from national unity and independence, the opportunity to set up a comprehensive system of education and to reach social justice. The final part concentrates on the way Mazzini sees the virtue of national awareness and its implications for the condition of exile.

The final chapter offers an analysis of the evidence found in the texts. I suggest two conclusions. First, the exiles' moral justification of their point of view rests on an argument, which reverses the roles of the accused and the accuser by claiming to be the genuine representatives of their nations. Second, the manner in which the French émigrés employ certain topical concepts offers a way of determining to what extent such concepts were still "unsettled" at a time of rapid social and political changes.

The first argument is discussed in the context of the various traditions or intentions invoked by the émigrés. The idiosyncratic and paradoxical element of the exiles' claims is not overlooked, but I emphasize how their references to the quality of embodying the nation are connected with their political outlook and contemporary developments. The question of topical concepts is placed in the context of the contemporary debates in Paris. The way in which the French émigrés carried on their discussions indicates to what extent certain current concepts allowed themselves to be used on both sides of a dispute. I try and show how in both cases the manner in which the exiles opted for certain ideas which they articulated in their arguments was aimed at placing themselves in the right.

Chapter 1

A Question of Trust: Mallet du Pan's *Mercure Britannique*

The French ultra-royalist émigrés in Britain managed to be both adamant and inconsistent. One moment they attacked Mallet du Pan for the moderate advice he gave the Count of Provence, the next they appealed to his services. The Count of Artois, the other brother of the executed king Louis XVI, had found refuge in Britain and assumed that the authorities still listened to the advice of the editor of *Mercure Britannique*.[1] D'Artois's entourage had not forgotten that until recently the courts of Vienna and Lisbon paid attention to Mallet's opinions. In his periodical which he brought out for only two years in his London exile (1798-1800) Mallet du Pan carried on his previous work of political commentator which had made him known in Paris almost two decades earlier. He was active in a field where French original work had been increasing as the century wore on.

---

[1] Jacques Mallet du Pan, *Mémoires et correspondance de Mallet du Pan pour servir à l'histoire de la révolution française*, ed. A. Sayous. 2 vols. (Paris, 1851) 2: 369, 390, 401 ff., 502 ff.

A Brief Retrospective

Despite the French contributions to science and literature during the seventeenth century, not a lot was produced on political theory.[2] Bodin and his successors had developed the doctrine of absolute monarchy, which had dominated the pre-1789 France.[3] Meanwhile, the absolutist government of Louis XIV was in visible decline during his last decades on the throne (he died in 1715). Already before the turn of the century an increasing number of thinkers had again become interested in political and social theory. Fresh works appeared on a wide variety of topics in these fields, from histories of ancient French institutions and descriptions of various forms of European governments, particularly England's, to proposals for tax reforms and discussions on the justification of government. Not much of all this was new. There was a tendency to blur earlier theories as they were reiterated in a more eclectic form. The debates on natural rights and the emergence of a new kind of thought were departing from empiricism. In addition, the preoccupation with political and social subjects spilled into literature as well: plays, poems and novels contained their share of the dominating topics.

Locke's ideas were making an impact, as relayed by Voltaire and Montesquieu. But what had sounded fairly mild in England, particularly after Parliament virtually became the sovereign power after 1688 had a more militant ring in France several decades later. One pertinent way of seeing the question would be that in France autocracy was so strongly established that the idea of people's rights was bound to be more abstract than in England, since it had lost to a large extent the concrete possibility of being put into practice. As Locke's ideas began to circulate in France, some of their historical aspects that had to do with belonging to a continuous tradition were being lost. The strong emphasis placed on reason led to the deductive and radical quality of French political thought in contrast with its equivalent across the Channel. This was the context in which Mallet du Pan developed his political ideas in Geneva; he reacted against the "metaphysical chatterers" as he called the "political visionar-

---

[2] George H. Sabine, *A History of Political Thought.* 3rd ed. (London: Harrap, 1964) 542 ff. Some of the subsequent points are based on Sabine's account.

[3] John Morrow, *History of Political Thought* (London: Macmillan, 1998) 258.

ies" in an article of 1782, and opted for a "politique expérimentale" where changes would be based on cautious empirical observations (Acomb 96-97).

The coupling of political and moral elements, as in Montesquieu's conclusion on popular government and public virtue, would re-appear in different forms during the last decades of the eighteenth century, and would prove relevant to Mallet's arguments in exile. This time morality would be linked to international law, which rested on the law of nature, as taught at the time.[4] The fact that Napoleon had erred morally could be shown by pointing out his defiance of international law. Further, Montesquieu's discussion of the separation of powers on the British pattern appears to have influenced the journalist in his preference for a constitutional monarchy.

In contrast with the prevailing contemporary belief in reason, Rousseau brought in the idea of moral intuition as a fundamental component both of the individual human being and society. This moral trait was to be found in the common people where it acquired a decisive force and significance as opposed to the enlightened but individual self-interest, which, in its interpretation from Locke, was assumed to give coherence to society.[5]

The idea of self-interest was seized on by Helvétius as well and worked into a system with strong features that later on would be called utilitarian. Bentham would pick it up in due course, and thus bring back to England, and put to work along radical lines, an idea which more than a century earlier had been doing the opposite job. The Physiocrats were disliked by Mallet on the grounds that their theories were only for the rich. His disapproval was also based on what he considered their unpractical theorizing. It was Adam Smith who attracted his admiration, even if

---

[4] See Knud Haakonssen, *Natural Law and Moral Philosophy: From Grotius to the Scottish Enlightenment* (Cambridge: Cambridge UP, 1996) 286.

[5] In his youth Mallet had taken Rousseau's side when the Genevan authorities decided to burn his works. In the quarrel between Voltaire and the Encyclopedists on the one hand, and Rousseau on the other, Mallet supported initially the former, not least because of his friendship with Voltaire. After 1776 he clearly backed Rousseau, this time partly because his relations with Voltaire had cooled. Nevertheless, a few years later, reviewing the *Confessions* he argued that Rousseau was a defender of the basic truth and, above all, of morality (Acomb 63).

the journalist was not for free trade; but at least Smith was not a "doctrinaire" (Acomb 77-78).

It can safely be stated that after the middle of the century there was a dispute as to the appropriate place where public debates could take place and the persons who would be entitled to participate. The Court at Versailles was losing the battle as more and more pamphlets and other topical publications were being issued in Paris mostly by writers, but also by other participants in the intellectual exchanges often initiated in salons and cafés. An active "republic of letters" had been developing, at first in opposition to the Academies, but then in practice infiltrating them as a result of what seemed a concerted action.[6]

A clear sign that the king was trying to regain the initiative regarding the shaping of "opinion" was Louis XV's address to the Paris parlement in which he asserted the exclusive right of the monarchy to public expression on issues of importance (Furet 16-17). But the authority of the royal court had been growing weaker round about mid-century due to disputes such as the Jansenists' opposition to the established clergy (where people saw monarchy's inability to impose its will), and clashes on financial reforms. The kind of opinion, which the Court tried to influence, was not the "doubtful intellectual judgment" of the *Encyclopédie* definition, but any unlicensed public utterance or exchange, particularly if they were critical or irreverent in any way.[7] Versaille was not too worried about epistemological uncertainties but about the sort of opinion used as a counterweight to absolutism. The fact that discussions could be carried on openly was a contrast, and a challenge, to the secrecy insisted upon by Versailles. A good deal of these debates were hosted by periodicals. Despite the constant battle with the censorship, daring articles, or at least daring passages, did get through.

---

[6] The idea was to incorporate the Academies into a "republic of letters." See Dena Goodman, *The Republic of Letters* (Ithaca: Cornell UP, 1994) 22-24, 46.

[7] See "Opinion" in *Encyclopédie, ou dictionnaire raisonné des sciences, des arts et des métiers* (1751-76): "un mot qui signifie une *créance* fondée sur un motif probable, ou un jugement de l'esprit douteux & incertain." For a discussion of the concept, see Keith Michael Baker, *Inventing the French Revolution* (Cambridge: Cambridge UP, 1990) 167-99, 337-45.

A lot more information was available in the foreign French-language magazines. The best known were *Gazette de Leyde, Courrier d'Avignon* (issued on papal territory at the time), and *Courrier de Bas-Rhin*. There was an uneasy arrangement between the French government and these periodicals. The French authorities could not quite prevent their being smuggled into France, while the magazines could not be as reliable as they were reputed to be without their correspondents being allowed to send their reports from Paris. So the editors toned down some of the criticism and the authorities tolerated the correspondents' activity as well as the circulation of the periodicals.[8]

The tradition of smuggling and circulating magazines would be carried on in earnest when after 1789 the émigrés' publications began to appear. One of the less ephemeral productions was *Mercure Britannique* edited by Jacques Mallet du Pan. Even if sometimes the editor used correspondents as well as other sources such as various reviews, official papers and the home press, as already indicated, the magazine was often edited and written by one person. This was the case here, and therefore it is useful to know something of the man who did the work.

An Editor

Jacques Mallet du Pan (1749-1800) was born near Geneva in a family of the local patriciate. His father was a Calvinist pastor and his mother was the daughter of a syndic, a member of the ruling Councils. While completing his studies in Geneva—philosophy and law—he was introduced to Voltaire whom he started visiting at nearby Ferney. The young man wanted to make a career in letters, although he was also interested in political economy and science. In the end, it was the study of politics that

---

[8] As a rule, the editors were not political exiles. For example, Jean Luzac of the *Gazette de Leyde* was a third-generation descendent of a Huguenot family settled in Holland (see Jeremy D. Popkin, *News and Politics in the Age of Revolution: Jean Luzac's* Gazette de Leyde [Ithaca: Cornell UP, 1989] 15 ff.) On the other hand, someone like Simon Linguet, although not exactly a political refugee to begin with, had increasing difficulties with the authorities at home, so much so that he ended up in the Bastille on one of his unwise visits (see Darline Gay Levy, *The Ideas and Careers of Simon-Nicolas-Henri-Linguet* [Urbana: University of Illinois Press, 1980] 1, 78, 191-92); see also, Acomb (106-144).

proved most attractive. With his first publication Mallet dived straight into the conflict that was tearing the city apart at the time.

About two thirds of the Republic's population called Natifs and Habitants had virtually no political rights and were subject to a series of economic and professional restrictions. The Natifs were granted some minor economic and political concessions in the 1760s, but not the social equality they desired. In February 1770 there was a riot, which resulted in the death of three Natifs. An edict banished without trial some of the rebel leaders and dissolved the Natifs' political circles. In 1771 Mallet joined the fray. His anonymously published pamphlet strongly defended the Natifs.[9] He wrote that Geneva was a despotic state, despite its apparent form of a republic (Acomb 7-8, 14-15).

Yet there was no secret about the writer's identity. When the authorities condemned the pamphlet to be publicly burned, Mallet anticipated further trouble and took advantage of the fact that the Landgrave of Hesse-Cassel wanted a professor for his academy and with Voltaire's help got the job. He was expected to teach French literature, and probably philosophy and history as well. Mallet rapidly tired of the local petty intrigues and the obstacles raised in his path and after six months resigned.

Over the next few years he was increasingly active as a literary and political journalist, mainly in Switzerland. All this time he kept in touch with Voltaire until the philosopher's death. Mallet had been contributing to Simon Linguet's magazine, first published in London and then in Brussels. When Linguet was lured back to Paris, abducted in broad daylight and thrown in the Bastille, Mallet kept the publication going and before long changed its name so as not to have it confused with Linguet's. Now, for the first time he had his own periodical.[10]

---

[9] *Comte rendu de la défense des citoyens-bourgeois de Genève adressé aux Commissaires de Representants, par un citoyen natif* (Genève, 1771). The author provocatively mixes the social categories in his title: "citoyen" was a highly privileged status to which hardly any Natifs could aspire. The right of becoming a bourgeois, a humbler status, could be bought by a Natif only with great difficulty.

[10] Mallet looked after Linguet's periodical *Annales politiques, civiles et littéraires du dix-huitième siècle,* adding to this title "ouvrage périodique, pour servir de suite aux Annales de M. Linguet." He changed its title on 15 March 1783 to *Mémoires historiques, politiques et*

Mallet's articles must have gained a wide readership as in 1783 he received an offer from Charles Panckoucke, probably the most powerful printer-publisher in Paris, to become the editor of the political section of *Mercure de France*. With Mallet on the staff the periodical prospered. The weekly issue of the magazine had to be cleared with the Ministry of Foreign Affairs, a constant source of irritation for the new political editor whose articles were repeatedly censored. Mallet succeeded in antagonizing not only the government, but also the Academicians, the "philosophes" (increasingly the same category), and some of the other journalists.[11] The fact that he kept aloof from the literary and fashionable world did not help either.

During the five years up to the Revolution his ideas went on changing from the authoritarian shade they had lately acquired in Geneva (after his initial militantism) to a somewhat reformist one. Mallet considered that the French government was both despotic and weak, controlled by selfish aristocrats and by ministers without principles. The drought of 1785 caused a lot of suffering and he received many letters from provincial clergymen, noblemen and even some peasant proprietors ("laboureurs") who insistently asked him to let the king know of their difficulties by mentioning them in his articles (Acomb 90).

Without being an out-and-out defender of the British system, Mallet did admire the constitutional struggle of the previous century and its outcome. But he was noticing with disappointment that with the coming of the eighteenth century the parties that earlier had commendably taken part in the battle between the Crown and Parliament had turned into groups competing for the perquisites of power: influence, positions, money. In January 1789 he commented favourably on a fellow-Genevan's work on the English Constitution pointing out that France could learn something from England but that one country cannot copy another's constitution which had developed under its own historical circumstances.[12] Here was one of the many occasions when Mallet pointed

---

littéraires sur l'état présent de l'Europe when Linguet accused him of stealing his magazine (Acomb 116-18, 124).

[11] See letter quoted by Acomb (162).

[12] This was J.L. Delolme's *The Constitution of England or an Account of the English Government* (London, 1772). In the 1760s Delolme had argued in Geneva that the General

out the advantages of the "politique expérimentale," a political system that grows from concrete experience, as opposed to one created by forcing into practice utopian thinking. In his commentary he departed from Delolme's ideas now and then to object to the creed that democracy was an essential condition for liberty. Mallet was for a Parliament made up of people of independent means, so that they would not have to engage in intrigues for financial benefits, and who ideally would possess enough reason not to aspire vainly to public office or high honours. As for the executive power, that belonged to the king. There are indications here of the constitutional monarchist of later years.

In Mallet's opinion, unless a number of reforms were undertaken the French monarchy was doomed. Custom and the slow natural growth of institutions were all very well, but when the ultra-conservative forces became too rigid something had to be done.[13] When the Revolution did come he feared the approach of anarchy. The more violent scenes in Geneva had modified his youthful radicalism. After 1789 he became known as one of the main defenders of constitutional monarchism—the contemporary terms were "monarchien" or "Anglophile," since England was held up as an example.

When censorship was lifted in August 1789, Mallet began to publish summaries of the debates in the National Assembly followed by his own reflections. His commentaries gained the political section of *Mercure de France* a new kind of fame. He followed favourably the work of the first Committee on the Constitution dominated by Mounier, chief theoretician of the monarchists. As the periodical went on supporting Mounier's aims—the right of the royal veto and the establishment of an upper chamber—Mallet started receiving threats. At first, they were aimed at the circulation of the magazine. He did not change his attitude, telling Mounier that having battled against the censorship of the absolutist monarchy for five years he was not going to give in now.

Council was the supreme power, and not the more restricted governing councils because the former included all those who had bourgeois status. This may have contributed to his temporary exile in England. Similarly, he praised England for not having a legislative power based on direct democracy but delegated to representatives (Acomb 198 ff.)

[13] See letter quoted by Acomb (198).

The following year, in April, he made a short visit to Geneva where he had not been for six years. Family matters and a work on constitutional principles seemed to have occupied him, although at the time it was said that he may have left Paris because of threats. In his absence the periodical was edited by Jacques Peuchet whose writing seemed to be influenced by the threats. A note inserted in the magazine on Mallet's return to Paris mentioned his journey to "sa patrie." Mallet was aware, as possibly others were too, that in France he was simply a Genevan working abroad like many of his compatriots.

Back in Paris, he still enjoyed strong support from Panckoucke. Mallet's articles went on in their usual uncompromising vein despite the threats. He was accused of favouring the old regime to which he replied that few enemies of the old regime had been as determined as him. The danger became increasingly worrying. At one point, his house was occupied by about twenty sansculottes. He heard rumours of his impending arrest. So in the spring of 1792 Mallet left Paris.

He headed straight for Frankfurt as Louis XVI's emissary to the anti-revolutionary Coalition leaders. The idea was to persuade Austria and Prussia, and also the military émigrés gathered in Koblenz, to adopt a more moderate manifesto. His draft was rejected and a far more menacing one was adopted under the signature of the duke of Brunswick, the military commander of the anti-revolutionary forces.

Mallet was convinced that he could be of significant help to the allies by gathering and interpreting information about France. He settled in Berne and started sending reports to the British representative in Brussels who passed them on to the Foreign Office in London. The British were pleased with the quality of his analyses (there was also some raw intelligence, but not much), and at their suggestion Mallet began to provide the same kind of material for Lisbon. (In fact, the intention was that Lisbon should function as a sort of letter-box, so that Mallet's contacts with London should be less obvious, but the local government had access to the information.) For about four years he provided advice to the Viennese Court as well, and for a while Berlin also received his comments on French current affairs. The drift of his recommendations can be gathered from a work published at about this time where he was critical both of the allied governments and the émigré world.[14] In his opinion the best thing would have been to return to the Constitution of 1791, but Mallet thought that the greatest obstacle was the émigré court that wanted a return to the pre-1789 arrangements (Acomb 259-61). This did not endear him to the ultra-royalists who did notice that his thoughts were valued by several governments and who later would try to get his help.

After the Fructidor coup (1797) the Directory demanded that Mallet be expelled from Berne. Two of his letters to one of the Directors had been printed in a Parisian newspaper and seemed to have determined Bonaparte, also a member of the Directory, to put pressure on Berne. Bonaparte had been most irritated by the criticism of the French aggression abroad. The Swiss promptly obeyed. In May 1798 Mallet du Pan arrived in London. A lot of his property in Paris had been confiscated or destroyed. Starting a periodical was a way of getting an income and also an attempt to keep his voice heard. He edited *Mercure Britannique* for two years. His health had been deteriorating under the strain of the recent upheavals and in England took a turn for the worse. He died of consumption in 1800 and his magazine ceased to exist. But it was a busy and combative two-year period.

A Periodical

The man he turned to in London was William Wickham who had been the British diplomatic representative in Switzerland and was now an Under-Secretary of State in the Home Office.[15] Wickham had organized an intelligence network, distributing funds to counter-revolutionary groups and relaying information to London about French internal conditions and external actions. Mallet had worked with him in Berne and now contacted him in order to enquire about the chances of starting a periodical. Wickham explained that publishing a political magazine would need se-

---

[14] *Considérations sur la nature de la Révolution de France, et sur les causes qui en prolongent la durée* (Londres, 1793).

[15] See J.A. Hamilton, "William Wickham" in the *Dictionary of National Biography*, 1st ed. (1885-1903).

cret protection from the government, which would be forthcoming, even if funds might not be available (Sayous 2: 359).

The edifying historian seemed to take over from the journalist as Mallet told an acquaintance in a letter that his purpose was to explain the present and the future by resorting to the images of the past in a methodical and consistent manner.[16] Propagandistic intentions were also present, for he added in the same letter that there were a number of misconceptions both in England and on the Continent about the nature, the force, and the success of the French Revolution, which his magazine would try to dispel.

Five hundred subscriptions were enough for Mallet and his family to make ends meet. In the end, the British government would confine its support to buying twenty-five copies of each number for the benefit of the conquered French colonies; although the ultra-royalist *Courrier de Londres* was enjoying financial backing from the authorities, *Mercure Britannique* was not going to get it. The Foreign Office did see to it that an English translation of each issue appeared a few days after the publication of the French one. Soon there were eight hundred subscribers.

The bi-monthly publication offered sixty pages of political commentaries, historical essays, some book reviews and news. To the disappointment of the Foreign Office, there was not a lot of information coming in. Mallet's sources from Switzerland and elsewhere were afraid to write as their correspondence might be opened. Even so, the magazine acquired something of an international reputation. It seemed to have sold on the Continent and it was pirated in France, always a sign of interest. A censored version was being printed in Paris during the 18 Brumaire coup (Acomb 269). The periodical seemed to have had "a secret vogue in the early days of the Consulate" and the French authorities inadvertently stimulated the public's curiosity by announcing that they had seized a number of copies.[17]

---

[16] "[C]'est à grands traits en éclairant sans cesse le présent et l'avenir par des retours et des tableaux du passé que je me propose de composer cette rédaction, en lui donnant une forme méthodique et suivie" (Sayous 2: 367).

[17] Robert B. Holtman, *Napoleonic Propaganda* (Baton Rouge: Louisiana UP, 1950) 58.

A Campaign

In March 1798 France had annexed Mulhouse and Geneva, and turned the rest of the cantons into a republic. The French control was clearly quite considerable: valuable property seized in Berne was used to finance the French military expedition to Egypt.[18] *Mercure Britannique* began to appear in the summer of that year and the early numbers concentrate on these events. The first three issues form a continuous work. Published later as a separate book, "An Historical Essay upon the Destruction of the Helvetic League and Liberty" attacks the Directory's policy of expansion, and discusses the advantages of the Swiss political and social system as a result of its natural development over the centuries. Mallet fulminates against the way the French allegedly misrepresented various injustices in Switzerland to justify their intervention.

One of his chief arguments is that Switzerland has developed its own form of democracy long before France. The slow growth and maturity of its social and political formations are more genuine, Mallet claims, than the abstract principles imposed overnight by the Paris revolutionaries.[19] "La métaphysique politique" is contrasted with "la politique expérimentale" in favour of the latter (1: 21), a recurring comparison.[20] The two phrases stand for an exclusive reliance on reason as opposed to taking into account an accumulation of empirical circumstances, the former constantly appearing at a disadvantage in Mallet's writings which here, if not always, echo Burke's early attack on the Revolution.

The subsequent numbers contain a mixture of analyses and reflective articles on the situation in various countries. The attitude on the Conti-

---

[18] Furet 199; R.R. Palmer, *The Age of the Democratic Revolution*, 2 vols. (Princeton: Princeton UP, 1959-1964) 2: 415.

[19] *Mercure Britannique* 1: 14-15. The variety of ways in which these periodicals were printed prevent the use of a standard system of reference. While attempting to preserve as much consistency as possible, I have provided the necessary information (here, volume and page) to identify the quotes, taking into account the practice of each editor. Unless otherwise specified, all translations are mine.

[20] On what seems to have been a current usage of the word, see Napoleon's note to Marshal Soult in 1805 when he planned to invade Britain: "Let me know whether, within a fortnight, horses, provisions, men and everything can be embarked. Do not give me a metaphysical reply to this question, but go and look at the stores and the different warehouses" (Quoted in Furet 255).

nent towards France is compared with that of Britain and the Continent is found wanting in energy and determination. Historical precedents of oppression and resistance serve to illustrate the inglorious expediency sought by most European nations when faced with aggression. Mallet explains his intention of throwing light on events by resorting to the opinions and behaviour of various states (1: 300), and he resorts as well to scrutinizing the attitude of the French towards political groups in the newly conquered territories. Having occupied parts of Italy, Bonaparte set up the Cisalpine and Ligurian republics after the Campo Formio Peace (1797). Mallet derides the way the French invited the collaboration of the local moderate and conservative elements, avoiding the democrats who were more militant and, one would have thought, closer to the revolutionary way of thinking. The editor of *Mercure Britannique* insists that the French do not really intend to spread the ideals of the Revolution, but simply to make sure of malleable governments in the zones they control.

In addition, there is always the spectre of anarchy, the risk of radical change getting totally out of hand, the meaningless symmetry of abstractions imposed upon traditional rules. Most conquerors have replaced one government by another, one faith by another faith, Mallet writes, but the French invasions are followed by "néant en matière de religion, & d'abstractions chimériques en législation."[21] In an analysis of the foreign policy of the Directory he compares France with ancient Rome arguing that France had already started its campaign of conquests as a young republic, whereas Rome had begun its own campaign in earnest only when republicanism was decaying into imperial rule. France began where all great republics ended, "par les crimes hardis, & par les guerres extérieures."[22]

True to his initial intentions, Mallet goes on showing that France is not as powerful and influential as it appears to other countries which, intimidated, fail to form a proper coalition against the Directory. The country has been weakened by the general chaos caused, among other things, by the "fanatisme *philosophique* qui a remplacé celui de la religion

---

[21] "... nothingness in religion, fanciful abstractions in legislation" (1: 357).
[22] "... by impudent crimes and wars of conquest" (1: 406).

..."[23] He had mentioned earlier the citizens who were condemned to do evil by the imposition of theory on their daily lives. His article turns to the revolutionaries' demands for freedom of opinion on which they insisted as long as their own were not the dominant ones. Once in power, they tyrannize both spirit and body, stretching humanity on the dissecting table in order to reform its anatomy (1: 412). The image of tampering with a natural organism harks back to the idea of the gradual development of a community as the best way for the growth of its political institutions.

Once more, theory falls victim to Mallet's criticism, this time by means of a rhetorical device that binds it inextricably with crime as its consequence. The former subjects of the French king, more recently turned republican patriots, invent "des théories pour leurs crimes, des crimes pour le succès de leurs théories."[24] This argument is linked to their dogmatism as they claim, in Mallet's opinion that the British live in a state of servitude while the French enjoy equality of rights. He also contrasts the revolutionaries' concern for a hypothetical individual's "droits de l'homme" with scant attention being paid to the real people's "droits des hommes." This may have well echoed Burke's evocation of Parliament's words to Charles I on inheriting freedom not abstractly "'as the rights of men,' but as the rights of Englishmen ..."[25]

Political freedom based on the separation of powers and property inspires fear in France, Mallet argues. The Directory dislikes the British Constitution since it limits the power of the executive and allows a certain amount of power to the monarch. The "monarchiens" like himself would have granted even more power to the king in the system they advocated for France. This was at odds both with the republicans' ideas and with the intransigent line of the ultra-royalists.

Mallet was not only criticizing the French invasion of Switzerland, he was attacking the wider policy of the revolutionary authorities. Having turned Holland into a submissive "Batavian Republic" and absorbed

[23] "*The philosophical* fanaticism, which has replaced the religious one ..." (1: 412).
[24] " ... theories for their crimes, crimes for the success of their theories" (1: 442).
[25] L.G. Mitchell, ed. *Reflections on the Revolution in France* (Oxford: Clarendon, 1989) 82. Vol 8 of Paul Langford, ed. *The Writings and Speeches of Edmund Burke*, ed. Paul Langford. 8 vols. to date (1981-).

Belgium the Thermidorians had launched "a foreign policy destined for far-reaching repercussions which they could not gauge ..." (Furet 162).

Little is known of Mallet's sources of information inside France. Most probably one of them was Jacques Peuchet, his old colleague from *Mercure de France*, and the man who succeeded him as political editor after 1792. Under the Directory Peuchet worked for the Ministry of Police where he was head of the department dealing with litigation connected with émigrés, priests and conspirators.[26] His position may have well facilitated access to further confidential information and with his contacts as a former political journalist Peuchet would have been a useful correspondent. Mallet also used open sources and could write about a clear improvement—from his point of view—in the French "opinion publique" (1: 456). The change consisted in the citizens' beginning to realize that the conquests had more to do with avarice than with the idea of the Revolution. It was the parliamentary purge of the 18 Fructidor, when for the first time the army had been used instead of the sansculottes, the misfortune of Switzerland, as well as Britain's military victories that had opened people's eyes, Mallet claimed (1: 457). Placed at a distance from the rapidly unfolding events, he combined in this case internal with external developments and selected the more obvious changes that suited his opinions. However, there was a difference between the tone of *Mercure Britannique* and that of the other two French periodicals discussed below. Irrespective of Mallet's degree of bias, he was aware that such a problem arose in the émigrés' writings. This awareness, apart from other circumstances, may have made him reluctant to back the royalists' claims of embodying the nation, choosing instead to prove his rightness by considering infringements of the international law as moral errors. As a chronicler of contemporary events, as he saw himself, the question of bias in exile must have been a permanent worry.

---

[26] Acomb 259. Yet after the coup of Fructidor (September) 1797 Peuchet had to go into hiding which must have limited his ability to collect and pass on information, assuming that Acomb is right and he did help Mallet.

A Suggestion

A possibly genuine letter to the editor asked what advice Mallet du Pan would give to someone who embarked on producing a history of the Revolution. Not only was it too early, Mallet replied in December 1798, but the evidence, such as it was at the moment, was unsatisfactory (1: 533 ff). The article develops into a series of reflections on writing history and the difficulties of doing it in exile. Many factors that make up the specific character of the French Revolution are finally summed up in the "contraste éternel entre les principes & les actions, entre l'empire des idées & celui des intérêts ..."[27] The editor warns against the historians who first build their system and only afterwards substantiate it by means of distorted reports. They write history in order to suit their theory instead of the other way round (1: 538). There are many elements which have led to the Revolution and could explain its unfolding, he goes on, but so far most writers have simplified things out of ignorance or sensationalism; each faction has had its own defenders and liars, it is hard to see who can judge between the various groups, both inside and outside France (1: 543). And next Mallet touches on a paradox that may be one of the keys to understanding his state of mind as a political thinker in exile.

Above all, the prospective historian is warned not to use information provided by exiles. The factions who lost the political fight and had to flee start babbling as soon as they cross the border, he writes, but from all that one can only glean a few facts already known and even those drowned by invectives (1: 544). And then he quotes approvingly Machiavelli: "*Il ne faut jamais croire aux rapports des proscrits.*"[28] Among the sources one should beware of there are those who send reports about public opinion and private views, "des mémoires instructifs sur l'opinion & les opinions," to various European Courts (1: 544). Mallet himself had been banished from his country, he had provided advice to various governments, and considered himself a chronicler of contemporary events with a view to using the material as an historian. Now the editor of an exile

---

[27] "... everlasting contrast between principles and actions, between the realms of ideas and interests ..." (1: 537).

[28] *"One should never believe the exiles' accounts"* (1: 544, ital. in the original.)

periodical no longer consulted by governments and royal courts, he was still clinging to a modicum of prestige and influence. But to what extent was he believed? His credibility was essential to his crusade against France. Although his warnings may have referred to others, he did fit his own description far too well not to experience self-doubt.

Mallet du Pan's willingness to appear credible would be bound to have an impact on his manner of thinking and of putting across his beliefs. It could be argued that he needed a persuasive angle, which would lend trustworthiness to his ideas. He could do that by bringing in moral values. Unlike most of the other exiles discussed below, the French-speaking Swiss did not attempt to assume the role of representative of his nation. There was nothing proprietorial about the earlier invocation of the commendable Helvetic political tradition. His criticism was aimed at the foundation of the French revolutionary system; he regarded expansion abroad or terror at home as symptoms of morally discredited principles. By implying that the outward behaviour of revolutionary France compromised its moral basis he would do more than just condemn the invasions (removing in the process the need of arguing the truth of particular details which may be questioned as coming from an exile). If morality and politics could be seen as closely interconnected, he could let the flaws of one reflect on, and weaken, the other. This connection was not new, but during the eighteenth century a new kind of international community had been emerging, increasingly regulated by legal agreements still based on natural law regarded as "part of universal morality" (Haakonssen 286), as pointed out above.

The link between politics and morality had been assumed in a good deal of recent texts on political and cultural matters. In his *Contrat social* and earlier writings Rousseau had linked the growth of morality with that of the social, and by implication, political life.[29] Several decades later Robespierre was placing the activity of politics on the foundations of morality in his addresses to the Convention in February and May 1794.[30]

---

[29] See, for example, Rousseau (3: 364-65). On the connection between republicanism and morality, but also virtue and terror, see Palmer (2: 124-29).

[30] See, for instance, "Rapport sur les principes de morale politique qui doivent guider la Convention." Quoted in Palmer (2: 124-25). See also Gengembre (58): "... la Révolution se place d'emblée sur un plan moral."

Henri Grégoire's report to the Convention in October 1794 argued for government intervention in cultural activities; he backed his proposal by linking morality and culture, but also civic virtues and classical republicanism. By not leaving the artists and intellectuals to their own devices, the government not only would create opportunities for the increase of virtue, but would also ensure the political strength of the country.[31]

Whatever the merits of Grégoire's suggestion, morality was indeed time and again coupled directly or indirectly with politics. In addition, the link was established even more authoritatively in the article on "moeurs" in the *Encyclopédie*. The suggestion of ethical choice is located in the main definition of the word: people's free actions, whether good or bad. "Moeurs" did carry the wider connotations of customs or manners. Later in the article the reader is told that in order to find out more it is necessary to look at various ways in which people are governed, and a brief review of republics, despotic monarchies, and other forms of government follows.

This was what Mallet was trying to imply, that the deficient morality of the system could be read in its actions. If in the search for rightful authority the effort of transforming obedience into duty becomes brutal persecution, then the values of the system could be shown to be flawed. Besides, once France imposes its rule on other countries the plain injustice of an invasion further reveals the questionable moral basis of the whole enterprise, and the system becomes even more discredited. Mallet's way of shifting the blame onto those who banished him differs from that of most of the other émigrés discussed here. He does figure in the final chapter but his example shows the difficulty of generalizing about matters of exile argumentation and his contribution cannot be omitted.

The caution urged by Mallet when it came to relying on exiles' accounts might well have been reinforced by his witnessing the rigidity of the extreme royalists. However, this rigidity was not compact. The disputes discussed in the following two sections constitute an example of the difficulties in bridging the gap between the intransigence abroad and the mood at home.

---

[31] Carla Hesse, *Publishing and Cultural Politics in Revolutionary Paris, 1789-1810* (Berkeley: University of California Press, 1991) 140-41.

The Malouet Controversy

As a result of several French military defeats in Italy in 1799, hopes were being raised among the monarchists inside and outside France that the restoration could be close. A Parisian "gazette" had mentioned the possibility of a "roi constitutionnel" and the name mentioned was that of the Duke d'Orléans, later king Louis-Philippe.[32]

In 1798 Mallet du Pan had received two private letters from Jean-Étienne-Marie Portalis, a lawyer, former member of the Council of the Ancients, which together with the Council of the Five Hundred had the legislative power under the Directory. He had fled abroad after the coup d'état of 4-5 September 1797 (17-18 Fructidor) when some of the Directors purged the two Councils of the royalists who had been increasingly dominating them after the swing to the right in the April-May elections of 1797. Portalis had met Mallet before, and now from his brief exile in Germany was expounding his ideas on how a future king should act in case he found himself back on the throne.[33]

Portalis claimed that the French people were tired of deliberating and that there was no need for any proclamations to turn them into royalists (Sayous 2: 394 ff). The king should appear as the head of the entire nation, not only of a faction, not as "le chef d'un parti, mais comme le chef de la nation" (Sayous 2: 394). Also, the monarch ought to respect the results of the "force des événements et des choses," a phrase which must have appealed to Mallet since it was one of his favourite explanations of the course of history.

The lawyer warned against any unwise return to the old order: "Tout retour aveugle ou passionné à des institutions usées qui n'ont pu se soutenir elles-mêmes compromettrait la sûreté de la nouvelle monarchie."[34] In addition, those things that the reinstated monarch would want

---

[32] A. Sayous, ed., *Mémoires et correspondance de Mallet du Pan* (Paris, 1851) 2: 392. Sayous is more than an editor, linking Mallet's letters and fragments of diary by substantial passages of his own.

[33] Portalis would return to France after Bonaparte's coup d'état on 9 November 1799 (18 Brumaire), would become a member of the State Council, and one of the main authors of the Napoleonic Code.

[34] "Any blind or fervent return to worn-out institutions which had not been able to survive would compromise the safety of the new monarchy" (Sayous 2: 394).

to bring back must not be re-established by means of explicit laws; the king should rely on people's memory and customs which have not faded out as some believe, "il faut s'en rapporter à la mémoire, au souvenir des hommes et à leurs habitudes qui sont encore moins effacées que l'on ne pense" (Sayous 2: 395). For example, the reinstallation of the aristocracy by law would destroy its dignity; it would be better to pretend that it had never been abolished.

Portalis linked the safety of the throne to the freedom of the people. Neither of them needed a constitution the length of a book. One guarantee only was necessary: "L'inamovibilité des juges si nécessaire à la liberte individuelle du citoyen, et le concours d'une Assemblée délibérante pour les impôts et pour les lois."[35] Portalis saw the various political groups (not yet fully-fledged political parties) as destructive factions, and there should not be the impression that the nation was subjected to only one of them. All such "partis," as he called them, should cease their activity for the general good of the nation.[36]

In his second letter Portalis made a distinction between the act of re-establishing and that of regenerating; a future king should concentrate more on human beings than on things in order to create, as it were, "un nouveau peuple" (Sayous 2: 397). Again, there was no need to worry about any loss of dignity if a monarch failed to bring back the old institutions. Pragmatism rather than theories would be required, Portalis added. He explained in passing that, as it happened, he was an objective judge of the situation, not having joined any faction, or emigrated. He considered that it was absurd to leave France in order to save it, and to place oneself in the foreigners' service in order to solve a national conflict.

Mallet sent some relevant extracts to a member of Louis's court in exile who passed them on to the future king. Apparently, Louis was impressed by them and suggested or at least approved the publication of a

---

[35] "Permanently appointed judges, so necessary to the individual freedom of the citizens, and the cooperation of a debating Assembly for taxes and laws" (Sayous 2: 395).

[36] Sayous 2: 395. Diderot and d'Alembert's *Encyclopédie* defines "parti" (in its sense used in modern history) as "une faction, intérêt ou puissance que l'on considere [sic] comme opposée a une autre," and there is a cross-reference to "faction."

letter by Pierre Victor Malouet in *Mercure Britannique*.[37] Malouet sent the letter to Mallet enclosing a private note which included a few lines from Louis's chief of staff who let him know that the king was grateful to him, and mentioned the rough draft of a text whose final form, and also content, were left to Malouet's discretion. It appeared that Louis was acquainted with the text since he suggested that it should be tightened up, assuming that Mallet du Pan, as editor, would add his own reflections.

Malouet's letter begins with the rumours that the monarchy might be restored but with a change of dynasty to suit the authorities in France. Like Portalis, he sees a close connection between the people and the king, and the question is to re-establish the legitimate rights of both. Malouet doubts that the king would want to return to the pre-1789 system, if only because so many people that would make it possible have vanished. Further down, he refers somewhat effusively to Louis's commendable character that would prevent him from exercising an arbitrary authority. Caution is also needed because one does not quite know what the nation wants since it had been forced to make its ideas known "par l'organ des Jacobins" (3: 425), an unspecified but, as far as Malouet is concerned, clearly unreliable means of communication.

The people and the monarch would have to help each other if the country wants a return to normality, which would include regaining "la liberté civile" (3: 426). This mutual help is needed since "Ce n'est plus avec des courtisans, c'est avec des hommes dont le caractère & les talens commandent la confiance, qu'un Roi peut gouverner la France."[38] Such remarks were probably not welcomed by d'Artois's entourage, as was shown by the royalists' criticism of *Mercure Britannique*. And Malouet clarifies his point, in case anyone missed it, that the king would need virtuous and able people "pour en recomposer l'esprit public & la puissance de son gouvernement."[39]

---

[37] Sayous 2: 395. Malouet had been a member of the National Assembly where he was known as one of the monarchists' leaders. He had escaped to England after the September massacres of 1792.

[38] "It is not with courtiers, but with men whose character and talent inspire confidence that a king can govern France" (3: 426).

[39] "… in order to recompose the public interest and the power of the royal government" (3: 426).

A change of dynasty would certainly lead to civil war, and Malouet appeals to the French to get rid of its tyrants whose inability to govern without resorting to the sword shows "la Nécessité de revenir au sceptre paternel & national" (3: 428), a curious phrase to which I return below.[40] He makes the additional point, certainly dear to Mallet's heart, that France in its present political circumstances presents a danger to other European states. And the letter ends with the assertion that the peace of Europe would be safe once France has a proper government and a wise monarchy (3: 432).

The editor's comment appeared in the following number of the periodical (10 August 1799). Mallet deplores the endless speculations on hypothetical political systems in France, and strikes a more international note by arguing that the disputes should be settled, above all, with an eye to "l'intérêt général de l'Europe" (3: 472). In such uninformed discussions the exception is generalized, and the perspective on French affairs is coloured by the "coterie" to which one happens to be attached, he adds. "C'est en France qu'il faudra parler à la France," but the lack of calm and lucidity prevents those interested from following such debates wherever they might be carried on.[41]

Mallet points out that his comments are not meant as a criticism of the letter and suggests that the author had no other intention than being the spokesman of Louis's fatherly feelings, "l'organe des sentimens paternels de *Louis XVIII* " (3: 475, ital. in the original). He drops the hint that if only Malouet quoted the authority behind his statements all critics would be silenced. And the editor judges that it ought to be the king himself or his ministers who openly present such controversial ideas. Then Mallet turns to the irritation caused by Malouet's letter among certain émigrés in England, and points out that they will not hear of a "gouvernement légal" (3: 476), or of the king's aversion to arbitrary power since they only understand rule by force. Mallet singles them out as a handful of privileged persons who want to have the final word concerning both the monarch's attitude, and the fate of the monarchy in general. And, referring to their extremism, he launches one of the choicest insults

---

[40] "… the need to return to the paternal and national sceptre" (3: 428).
[41] "It is inside France that one will have to address France" (3: 472).

he can think up calling them "ces bonnets rouges déguisés" (approximately, "these disguised revolutionaries") which must have incensed the émigré courtiers up and down Britain. Also, he makes a distinction between them on the one hand, and the true royalists together with the great majority of the émigrés on the other.

A good deal of the subsequent comment is spent on the presumed mood in France and the possible support that the royalists abroad might expect. The editor argues that Malouet attributes too much importance to factors such as the people's fear of the government when he tries to explain the citizens' reluctance to support the monarchy more openly; one must not forget the exhaustion of those who have lived through a decade of relentless upheavals often leading to despondency and indifference (3: 487). Referring to the complications of outside intervention, including the difficulty of knowing from a distance the exact situation in France, he ridicules those who try to hold courses in French history "au télescope" (3: 486). Whoever may be longing for the return of monarchy would not want the reimposition of feudal privileges, but a monarchy that would agree with such changes (3: 488).

Jean-Gabriel Peltier, the editor of a series of French-language periodicals, which represented the ultra-royalists' views, attacked *Mercure Britannique* and all those associated with it. He concentrated on Mallet whose comment and sarcastic remarks had provoked at least as much outrage as the letter. The outcome of all this was that d'Artois invited both Mallet and Malouet for a friendly chat, possibly as a hint to the ultra faction to calm down. Later the journalist was informed in a letter that d'Artois's initiative had not been a spontaneous gesture but that it had been suggested to him; the implication was that the only one who could have done this was his elder brother.[42] But what is the significance of this controversy?

Assumptions and Expectations

Mallet returns often to the difficulty of understanding the developments and deciding on the right approach to political problems from a distance.

---

[42] The letter was sent by a certain Count Sainte-Aldegonde (Sayous 2: 445).

Under the circumstances, both political journalists and future kings were forced to rely on assumptions. It could be safely argued that, at least in the case of those who intended to seize power, the main assumptions were formulated in connection with the nature of changes that had taken place in France and the extent to which they should be accepted. Not everybody saw things in the same light. For instance, d'Artois was not unduly troubled by the niceties of political dilemmas vis-à-vis the dynamics of change. He simply wanted an army to restore the monarchy so that everybody could return to the way things were before 1789.[43] Other émigrés' intentions were less clear-cut.

Louis's opinions, as they were indirectly presented by Malouet, did seem to countenance a number of changes: "Tout est changé depuis dix ans tant au dedans qu'au dehors," Malouet wrote, hinting that the king was aware that these external and internal changes during the last decade prevented a return to the old ways. Above all, there is the puzzling phrase used by Malouet when he mentioned the "sceptre paternel et national." When a symbol associated by definition with the monarchy receives such a different attribute it can hardly be a question of a straightforward return to the pre-1789 times. In a text that clearly enjoyed the favour and the approval of the hopeful monarch the sceptre is suddenly no longer royal but national (the "paternel" is completely overshadowed by the unexpected "national").

It has been pointed out that during the early stages of the revolution, before Louis XVI was executed, the motto of the ancien régime, "un roi, une foi, une loi," was replaced by "la nation, la loi, le roi." Gradually, everything that had been "royal" (the navy, etc.) became "national."[44]

---

[43] See d'Artois's letter to Mallet soon after the journalist's arrival in Britain (Sayous 2: 502 ff.). The Count thought that Mallet would have frequent contacts with the British government who would follow his advice. His requests were clear: "il faut que le gouvernement britannique, calculant noblement ses plus grands intérêts, remette entre les mains du roi de France une armée ..." (Sayous 2: 504-505). He expected great things from Mallet: "Parlez, tonnez, ne craignez pas d'en trop dire à un cabinet qui sait apprécier votre opinion ..." (Sayous 2: 505). There was only one way to return: "Ce n'est qu'en rentrant dans ses droits par la force des armes que le roi pourra conserver l'autorité nécessaire pour gouverner un grand peuple ..." (Sayous 2: 505).

[44] See Jacques Godechot, "The New concept of Nation and its Diffusion in Europe," in *Nationalism in the Age of the French Revolution*, pp. 14-15. Cf. also Keith Mi-

This usage was not unusual in France, but it was highly surprising in a text by an exiled constitutional monarchist who was indirectly putting across the opinions of a member of the royal family hoping to return to the throne.

It may be that Louis wanted to make this very point in a published text. However, his thinking seemed different in his private letters to his brother where he worried about the political soundness of d'Angoulême, d'Artois's son. Freshly arrived from England, d'Angoûléme kept suggesting that on his return to France the king ought to consult the people on possible changes to the constitution.[45] The young man's argument was that the people would obey more willingly a constitution of their own choice and that "l'opinion générale" wanted a representative government. Louis concluded this part of the letter stating that he simply did not believe in "cette pretendue opinion générale" (Daudet 2: 322), and that in any case such a government was not suitable for France. This letter must be from 1799 (Daudet omits to date most of the letters he reprints) since that was when d'Angoulême came from England to Mitau for his marriage.[46] It was the same year when he was concurring with Malouet in hinting at the monarchy's willingness to assent to the developments in France.

So, a closer look suggests that Louis was shifting his ground. He may well have done it with a clean conscience since he could claim that he had always been inclined to pay attention to the wishes of the Third Estate. In 1788 when he was still Count of Provence he had been willing to see an increased representation of the Third Estate, while his younger brother, d'Artois, had been against it.[47]

---

chael Baker, *Inventing the French Revolution: Essays on French Political Culture in the Eighteenth Century* (Cambridge: Cambridge UP, 1990) 9-10: "With the Revolution, the sacred center was symbolically refigured; the public person of the sovereign was displaced by the sovereign person of the public; *lèse-nation* was substituted for *lèse-majesté*."

[45] Extracts from these letters are reprinted by Daudet (2: 321-22).

[46] Mitau (Jelgava), about 50 km south of Riga, was at that time part of the Russian Empire. After moving from place to place across Europe, Louis and his entourage had eventually ended up as the guests of the Tsar.

[47] See Peter McPhee, *A Social History of France: 1780-1880* (London: Routledge, 1992) 31. On d'Artois's tiny exile court being "even more reactionary" than Louis's, see Furet (179).

Ten years later Louis was aware of the importance of the image projected. In a text written probably in 1799 for the edification of young d'Angoulême, his advice was that "[l]e meilleur, le véritable moyen de plaire à la nation Française, c'est de paraître Français dans vos discours, dans vos actions, enfin dans toutes vos manières."[48] It is not inconceivable that he himself was equally aware of the way he was perceived and of the expectations he managed to create, however difficult they were to disentangle.

It may be the case that Louis was willing to accept a number of changes but, somehow, maintain a privileged position for the monarchy. Either way, the matter was not spelled out in public. The differences between the two brothers would be amplified and would become more visible in 1816 when Louis XVIII dissolved the Chamber and held new elections. The moderates won against the "ultras" (d'Artois's faction) and one historian has seen here the virtual clash of two parties (Furet 288).

Mallet du Pan's image of busy émigrés trying to influence things from a distance, as if using levers whose effect cannot be gauged (3: 472), brings up one of their chief difficulties: reconciling their political views with the wide variety of transformations at home. Here there is a difference between intellectuals such as Mallet or Portalis who realize the complications that distance creates but need not turn thought into action, and someone like Louis whose role compels him to act, despite being aware of such difficulties. Much more than the political observers, the future king is consequently forced into various assumptions on which to base his initiatives. There is an interplay here between such assumptions and the anticipations (fears, hopes) of people in France. The émigrés constantly endeavour to respond by finding values or symbols which would harmonize their own ambitions with the people's wishes. If only reliable information were available those exiles keen on power would know which fears to appease, which hopes to cultivate. Under the circumstances, the new values and symbols have to be picked up as they emerge and be responded to as appropriately as possible. It is

---

[48] "The best and most genuine way of appealing to the French nation is to appear French in your speech, actions, in a word, in your entire behaviour" (Daudet 2: 325).

here that invoking the "sceptre national" might help. Some hints of the anticipations at home are given by recent émigrés such as Portalis. A legal expert, apparently without an axe to grind but known in Paris as a moderate royalist, Portalis seemed sufficiently trustworthy. Obviously, his reflections had their own bias, but he was free from the distorted images shaped by years of idle speculation abroad.

Once more, just as there were expectations on the part of the potential leaders in exile regarding the state of the country and the people's mood, so there were fears or hopes among the French at home concerning the restoration of the monarchy. The anticipations in France could occasionally be estimated and explained—with inevitable biases—by intellectuals like Portalis who found themselves briefly in exile. Meanwhile, any émigré who intended to work for the return of the monarchy but did not want to turn the clock back had to distinguish between what they themselves assumed was necessary for the country, and what the people thought would happen after a possible restoration. Apart from sheer military force (the extremists' option), the persuasive approach was the main alternative. Thus, the exiles' assumptions had to fit the anticipations inside France, turning fears into hopes where necessary. The task was virtually unmanageable. Therefore, in the vague realm where the gap remained stubbornly unbridgeable one solution would be the expression of commendable moral intentions. Neither the exact information was available, nor the proper feel for the latest mood at home in order to formulate precise promises. But an acceptance of change implied in a "monarchien's" letter to the editor, and then confirmed by the journalist himself in a well-known exile magazine may have carried the desired moral reverberations and bridge the gap.

A development that few émigrés reckoned with was the arrival of Bonaparte on the scene. In the article occasioned by the coup d'état of 18 Brumaire Mallet pointed out that by concentrating a lot of power in his own hands the general could control the factions better, and would also be able to increase the possibilities of doing good or evil. Mallet observed that the intentions of new governments impelled them to distance themselves from the "revolutionary tyrannies" and that was why this new government promised so many things, making statements in favour of peace, property and freedom. The article also mentioned the suppression of the oath of hate towards the monarchy, not because of any pro-royal feelings as some optimists abroad believed, but in order to remove a formula associated with Jacobinism. And all the time Mallet referred to Bonaparte's takeover as a new revolution.

"[L]es nouveaux arbitres de la France," as the editor calls the general and his entourage, see their enemies among extremists, be they republican anarchists or ultra-royalists, "les Républicains anarchistes & les Royalistes absolus …" (4: 355). Once more, Mallet du Pan's sarcasms are accompanied by a more serious political point. While ridiculing the stampede of the opportunists for positions, honours, and favours ready to be re-distributed by a new government, Mallet conveys concisely his image of the political spectrum in France and his opinions of its various shades. A tame version of republicanism is offered by the "Républicains mitigés" and a moderate form of royalism is provided by the "Royalistes d'opinion" who, contrasted with the absolutist ones, indicate the lack of conviction, which is here attributed to "opinion." Between them Mallet places several categories including "gens à théories, d'ambitieux & d'intringans [sic] sans férocité …" (4: 355). These "theoreticians" and "schemers lacking in ferocity," the former always a nuisance for Mallet, the latter significantly placed next to them, are added to the crowd of "modérés" who would accept the new "tyrannie du pouvoir" (4: 356). Surprisingly enough, the constitutional monarchist known for having avoided political extremes (even if not remaining neutral) seems here to have an implicit sympathy for the intransigent groups, not necessarily because of their political convictions, but because only they could have provided some opposition to Bonaparte. To be moderate meant in this case to be a supporter of the new government. Mallet's hostility towards Bonaparte remained constant, altering occasionally the light in which he regarded the Jacobins and the ultra-royalists.

Without any noticeable trace of irony Mallet claims that this "revolution" seems as fundamental as that of 1789. He sees entirely new means being used, and anticipates quite different results from those of the previous commotions. He finds a dominating military element in this case, which permeates even the language, and which would lead neither to a republic, nor to a restoration of the monarchy, thwarting the illusions of both camps. Yet, Mallet refrains from speculating on the expansionist ambitions of the new leader. The magazine subsequently offers mostly news from Britain and the Continent. There are news items about France, but *Mercure Britannique* hardly comments on anything. The editor was already very ill and had only a few months to live. So had the periodical.

When Mallet died, Louis, who had not much liked the man because of his independence, did regret the loss of a defender of the monarchy (Daudet 2: 429). The future monarch wanted the satirical writer Antoine Rivarol to take over this role. Louis still had his own indirect manner of passing on messages: a courtier was asked to write to Rivarol and explain that on Mallet's death the king drafted a note, as it were for himself, and left it to the courtier to use it in any way he pleased. The note said that now that Mallet was dead Rivarol, referred to in very flattering terms, may like to dedicate his efforts to cure "the ills of the country" (Daudet 2: 430). Mallet would be missed, Louis went on, but the good and the damage he had done through his writing balance each other: "Mallet du Pan était pour la royauté a peu près comme Jean-Jacques pour la religion. Son recto était la profession de foi du plus pûr royaliste; son verso semblait être l'oeuvre d'un des auteurs de la Constitution de 1791 ..."[49]

With Napoleon as the new leader of France, and an awkward defender dead, there was perhaps a need for new ways of adjusting the assumptions from abroad to the expectations in France. Circumstances were changing and the émigrés needed to evaluate not only the citizens' hopes, but also the intentions of the new leader. After 1800 the voice of the French constitutional monarchists was less and less heard in exile. Many returned to France where some were given responsible positions. Those who stayed abroad hardly contributed to the few surviving exile

---

[49] "Mallet du Pan's attitude towards monarchy was a bit like Jean-Jacques's towards religion. One side of him showed the convictions of the most genuine royalist, the other seemed to be the work of one of the authors of the 1791 Constitution ..." (Daudet 2: 429-30).

periodicals. As for the ultra-royalists, they carried on their journalistic activity abroad devising a kind of self-exculpation made possible by the particular tradition they drew on. These claims were articulated by the next two periodicals discussed here, but it was *Mercure de France* that offered a distinctive justification meant to dismiss the offence implied by exile.

—

Chapter 2

The Sound of an Uprooted Journal: *Mercure de France*

The reorganization of the Church in France after 1789 meant the aboli-tion of most of its privileges, and the nationalization of its property. These measures, included in the Civil Constitution of the Clergy (initiat-ed by a decree of the Constituent Assembly in August 1789, but voted through a year later), transformed the churchmen into state employees and brought in requirements such as pastoral experience for bishops, thus facilitating the promotion of poor priests. Some people welcomed the changes, but there were also doubts, controversies about the auto-nomy of the French Church versus papal authority, and riots. By the summer of 1791 hardly more than half of the humbler priests had taken the obligatory oath to the Civil Constitution, and only very few bishops. At this point, whoever refused was expected to retire with a pension.

The question of the oath has been seen as one of the main crises of the Revolution because it offered the counter-revolution a popular base.[1]

---

[1] See D.M.G. Sutherland, *France 1789-1815: Revolution and Counterrevolution* (London: Fontana, 1985) 97; also, William Doyle, *The Oxford History of the French Revolution* (Ox-ford: Clarendon, 1989) 143-44, 146. Also, Nigel Aston, *Religion and Revolution in France, 1780-1804* (Basingstoke: Macmillan, 2000) 166-79.

For the first time since July 1789 those who had accepted the initial changes were pushed into making choices they would rather not contemplate. The significance of the revolutionary anti-clericalism escaped those peasants whose parish priest had grown up among them and shared their hardships.

By 1792 those who had not taken the oath—now in a new version— were given a fortnight to leave the country, except the prelates who were over sixty and ill. It was at this time that a wave of clergymen emigrated, following the earlier waves of aristocrats in 1789, and officers in 1791. Among the clergymen who arrived in Britain there were also the editors of the London edition of *Mercure de France*. It appears that they did the job on a voluntary basis, along with any available bits of paid work. There is no evidence, as in the case of *Mercure Britannique*, of financial support from the British authorities.

The younger of the two editors, Pierre Vinson (1762-1820), was born in a poor family, became a priest, refused to take the oath, was imprisoned, fled to Spain, and from there to Britain where he taught astronomy. His co-editor, Jean-Marie, Abbé de Chateaugiron (1750-1803), had taught at a "college" (a kind of secondary school establishment) in Rennes, fled to Jersey and then came to London where he published various unsigned works, and funeral orations for Louis XVI and Marie-Antoinette.[2]

---

[2] Vinson returned to France in 1814. Having been against the Concordat (Bonaparte's treaty with Pius VII), he published in 1816 "Le concordat expliqué au roi ...", was accused "d'avoir donné des alarmes aux acquereurs des biens nationaux," found guilty, and sentenced to a short prison term and a light fine; see *Biographie Universelle*, 1st ed. (1811-28). On Chateaugiron, see, M. Prevost & Roman d'Amat, ed., *Dictionnaire de Biographie Française* (Paris, 1959-). There is no mention in the latter work of Chateaugiron co-editing *Mercure de France* which may mean that his younger, and possibly more energetic fellow-editor dealt with most of the work; the mention that he did share the work can be found in Abel Dechêne, *Contre Pie VII et Bonaparte: Le Blanchardisme, 1801-1829* (Paris: Firmin-Didot, 1932) 142. See also the list of French clergy and the relevant notes in Dominic Aidan Bellenger, *The French Exiled Clergy* (Bath: Downside Abbey, 1986) where Vinson appears as "scientist and entertainer" (280).

A Periodical with a Past

When Vinson and Chateaugiron left France one of the most influential periodicals in Paris, *Mercure de France* was still coming out, albeit under increasing difficulties. This was one of the oldest magazines in France.

Paris had a publication called *Mercure français* already in 1611.[3] These were early days for the periodical press: news of the latest comets and floods jostled with erudite pieces. The impact that a printed work of this kind could have on its readers soon became obvious to Cardinal Richelieu who put one of his close collaborators in charge. In 1662 the title was changed to *Mercure galant*, the tone was lighter and the variety of items increased. The publication followed the arts world more systematically, it reviewed the latest plays (Racine was taken to task for his style), and it took sides in topical debates (in favour of the Moderns in their quarrel with the Ancients).[4]

Some of the main contemporary writers were not left indifferent to it: Boileau and La Bruyère ridiculed it but kept reading it. Imitations began to appear in the provinces and abroad. There were further brief interruptions, and the periodical surfaced in 1717 as *Nouveau Mercure*. Finally, seven years later, it was baptized *Mercure de France*, by now enjoying royal favour. Besides the lighter fare, the reader was also offered more substantial matter such as political news, essays on geography and thoughts on the legal system. The magazine in its new shape still divided opinions: some considered it essential reading, others dismissed it.

The decades after Louis XIV's death (1715) were a period of some renewal for many institutions. New laws encouraged the domination of one field by one periodical. Thus, *Gazette de France* was given a virtual monopoly of political news, *Journal des Savants* concentrated on science, while *Mercure de France* acquired a quasi-monopoly in the literary area.

Mercure attempted to be impartial, as it announced early on. Despite its literary orientation, there was the odd excursion into science, particularly under Marmontel's editorship after mid-century. The "philosophes"

---

[3] Claude Bellanger et al., ed. *Histoire générale de la presse française*. 5 vols. (Paris: Presses Universitaires de France, 1969-76) 1: 78.

[4] Bellanger, ed. 1: 139. For subsequent information on *Mercure de France* see 1: 207-219.

were discussed at length, risky works by Bacon and Bayle were also presented, and the first volumes of Diderot's *Encyclopédie* were welcomed.

The intention to be impartial was reinforced by Voltaire's "advice to a journalist" (November, 1744). In fact, this aim was becoming something of a commonplace among those who tried their hand at history, whether historians proper or not, and perhaps an example to writers on current affairs. This was part of the effort of turning history writing into a science. The "philosophes" endeavoured to do it, even Voltaire, despite sacrificing detachment for the sake of wit or in order to advocate a particular cause. Voltaire praised Hume's *History of England* precisely for its lack of bias (as it appeared to him), a novelty in the history writing of Britain, until then marred by partisanship.[5]

The year 1778 was a turning point in the existence of the periodical. It was bought by Charles-Joseph Panckoucke, printer, successful businessman and friend of the "philosophes." He merged it with another publication and thus provided it with a political supplement. The Foreign Minister, who was in charge with controlling publications, granted him the monopoly of political periodicals (the *Gazette* was still dominant among the dailies). Despite such preferential treatment, and the subtitle ("dédié au roi …"), now and again there were clashes between the censors and some of the editors.[6] In its extended form the journal appeared every ten days, and the recent addition practically turned it into the leading periodical in Paris enjoying considerable sales.[7] The success of the publication continued even after 1789 when historians have placed it "dans la presse conervative, mais avec des nuances" (Bellanger, ed. 1: 463). For instance, *Actes des Apôtres* edited by Peltier was considered more virulent and right wing, to use an almost anachronistic term. The difference between Mallet and Peltier would remain constant even in

---

[5] See Peter Gay, *The Science of Freedom*. Vol. 2 of *The Enlightenment. An Interpretation.* 2 vols. (London: Weidenfeld and Nicolson, 1967-69) 2: 378-79.

[6] On Panckoucke not interfering with his publications, and on the *Mercure* editors having more freedom than others, see David Kulstein,"The Ideas of Charles-Joseph Panckoucke, Publisher of the *Moniteur Universel,* on the French Revolution," *French Historical Studies,* 4 (1966), 306.

[7] In 1778 *Mercure de France* had 995 subscribers in Paris, about 700 in the provinces (Babeuf being one of them), while eight subscribers could be found at Versailles among the royal family. By the late 1780s it was coming out weekly and had 15,000 subscribers.

their London exile. It is worth anticipating here that *Mercure de France* under its exile editorship would virtually become much more "ultra" than it was in Paris between 1789 and 1791 where its political editor kept it on the constitutional monarchist side. The periodical preserved its prestige during these turbulent couple of years through Mallet's "analyses judicieuses" and "prévisions souvent justifiées par les événements" (Bellanger, ed. 1: 464). It all came to an end in August 1792 when *Mercure de France* was banned together with other "journaux aristocratiques"; nuances did not help. A few journalists and printers were arrested, some went into hiding or escaped abroad, and the equipment was confiscated.[8]

Crossing the Channel

Unlike all the other periodicals discussed here, *Mercure* had a past and would even have something of a future once back in Paris (it ceased publication in 1825). When it was issued as an exile magazine in London it had already a distinctive personality, which the editors abroad could choose to maintain or alter. The two clergymen tried to preserve it, at least outwardly. The format remained the same, while the contents showed the same approximate balance between literary topics, lighter items (riddles, comic poems, word-puzzles), political news and the occasional editorial. The articles were not signed, except for the rare initials. It appeared every ten days for about sixteen months. There is hardly any information on its circulation or readership. The assumption is that its past prestige did attract a fair share of readers.

As at its re-launching almost a century earlier, *Mercure* was announcing from London that impartiality and royalism would be some of its guiding principles, in itself a revealing failure to see the contradiction.[9] Impartial

---

[8] Bellanger, ed. 1: 501-502. A version of the magazine would resume publication in Paris in July 1800 with interruptions, amalgamated with other periodicals for a while, and with a much-changed profile as a result of Napoleon's control.

[9] "… exempts, autant qu'il est possible à l'humanité, de toute influence de parti, nous nous prescrivons rigoureusement la plus sévère impartialité; mais en même tems nous serions désolés que par ce mot on entendît une froide indifférence. Nous sommes François, Catholiques, francs Royalistes, dévoués jusqu'à la mort aux intérêts de l'autel et du trône: quelques-uns d'entre nous sont consacrés aux autels, quelques autres sont gentilshommes, et tous partisans zélés de la justice, des moeurs et de la vérité" *Mercure*

but not coldly indifferent: although the editors would distinguish between persons and opinions in reporting controversies, they stressed their commitment as French Catholic royalists. Thus the point was made that the present series would not break with tradition. Besides, the London *Mercure de France* would not compete with other French publications abroad, each having its own style and scope (10 April 1800: 4-5). The editorial intention of being impartial could be encountered in connection with other fields as well. A quarter of a century earlier the influential Panckoucke had put Simon Linguet in charge of the *Journal de Bruxelles*; Linguet, otherwise known as a fierce polemicist, had promised "[d]ans la politique, exactitude et clarté; impartialité et modestie dans la littérature …"[10] Less impartial in real life, as his quarrel with Mallet showed, Linguet was only one of a long line of journalists and historians who considered that they ought to proclaim impartiality as their aim, irrespective of the campaigns they were involved in.

The editors may have been emboldened in their enterprise by the British government's recent insistence on the inclusion of the restoration of the monarchy in France among the conditions for a peace treaty. The political climate in Britain may well have been favourable to starting an exile periodical, but fears of militant action had resulted in harsh measures affecting some of the local population.

A new radicalism had grown in the early 1790s, mainly among middle-class dissenters who found inspiration in Locke's political theory. Several radical "societies" emerged, with a network of provincial branches, and systems of printing and exchanging information, somewhat on the pattern of the French Jacobin clubs. Parliament had suspended the

---

de France, 10 April 1800: 4 ("… unaffected by the influence of any faction, as far as this is humanly possible, we aim rigorously at the strictest impartiality; at the same time we would be sorry it this word were understood as cold indifference. We are French, Catholic, openly Royalists, devoted until death to altar and throne: some of us are ordained, others are gentlemen, and all strong supporters of justice, customs and truth"). And in the same issue there is a mention of "la déclaration formelle que nous faisons de suivre exactement le plan de l'ancien *Mercure* …" ("… our formal declaration to follow exactly the plan of the old *Mercure* …"). Cf. "L'impartialité sera le premier de nos devoirs," quoted in Bellanger, ed. (1: 207). I have not modernized the spelling in my quotes from the London *Mercure*.

[10] Quoted in Bellanger, ed. (1: 296).

Habeas Corpus Act in 1794, and consequently those suspected of political agitation could be held without trial. Soon afterwards large meetings were forbidden, public lectures held outside universities needed a licence and official supervision, the legal definition of treason was made more comprehensive, and by 1799 anything resembling union activity among workers was seen as conspiracy and could be punished promptly.[11] The country and the political system set as an example by Montesquieu and Voltaire were no longer quite the same. England was changing partly due to the French Revolution, but to a larger extent due to its own growing tensions that would lead to increasing social conflicts during the next century.

The new law prescribing the magistrate's supervision of the newspaper publishers need not have worried the émigré editors who, while the two countries were at war with each other, would argue for an invasion of France followed by a change of its political system. In urging this action, the émigrés would resort to rhetoric but also to political theory; however, the immediate circumstances they referred to were the constitutional developments in France.

By and large the same parliamentary majority had been in power since the declaration of the Republic (September 1792), through the various clashes that culminated with the execution of Robespierre (July 1794), and continuing under the Directory. An occasional coup d'état would occur when things got out of hand—as in the autumn of 1797 after the swing to the right in the spring elections; or the voting results would be tampered with when the electorate favoured the Jacobins a year later. Further internal and external difficulties of the Directory were going to be solved by yet another coup. Bonaparte was the obvious person to deliver military backing—the use of the sanculottes or other militant civilians was by now out of the question.

The 18-19 Brumaire (November 1799) coup was followed by a constitution, which maintained the system of two chambers, where one debated the bills and the other did the voting. This was the brief period when the "idéologues" supported Bonaparte. Destutt de Tracy had in-

---

[11] See J. Steven Watson, *The Reign of George III: 1760-1815* (1960; Oxford: Clarendon, 1985) 357-363.

troduced the word ("idéologie") and the attempt to establish a science of ideas by emphasizing the physiological characteristics of sensations. This empirical foundation of the formation of knowledge inspired a number of initiatives in the field of education and the "idéologues" were in great favour with the Directory. One of the chief ideologists, Georges Cabanis, drafted a pamphlet that appeared to justify the Brumaire action.[12] The new constitution was seen here as democracy without any of its inconveniences.[13] He noted approvingly that it prevented the "ignorant classes" from having any influence on law making or government, and that everything was going to be done for the people in their name (Cabanis 2: 475). But the cordial relations between the "idéologues" and Bonaparte were not to last. This could be anticipated by a close reading of Cabanis's text where he also listed several objections to the new document, the first one being against the "force immense" of the executive power (Cabanis 2: 485).

Cabanis was writing this in December 1799. *Mercure* discussed the new constitution in April 1800 pointing out that it excluded the people from the process of law making and that its sovereignty passed into the hands of a military despot.[14] These objections were hardly raised because of the émigrés' concern with people's rights. Any criticism of the system voiced in Paris, such as Cabanis's warning remark, could be used abroad to strengthen the case for monarchy.

The situation seemed unclear both for those who tried to estimate it from a distance, and for those closer to the events. The Jacobins' lamentations about the First Consul's blocking their return to power competed with the royalists' cheers for a hopeful restorer of the monarchy, the

---

[12] Maxime Leroy, *Histoire des Idées sociales en France*. 3 vols. (Paris: Gallimard, 1946-54) 2: 157 ff.

[13] "Quelques considérations sur l'organisation sociale en générale et particulièrement sur la nouvelle constitution" in Claude Lehec et Jean Cazeneuve, ed., *Oeuvres philosophiques de Cabanis*, 2 vols. (Paris: Presses Universitaires de France, 1956) 2: 475.

[14] "Ainsi le Peuple François n'a plus aucune part à la confection des loix: il n'a plus de mandataires, de représentans véritables: sa prétendue souveraineté se trouve concentrée dans les mains du Premier consul, qui n'est lui-même qu'un despote militaire, environné des formes trompeuses du républicanisme" (10 April 1800: 36).

journal remarked, baffled and cynical at the same time.[15] The periodical
was confused here by further changes in France; the émigré journalist
was wondering why a number of refractory priests (those who had refused to take the oath) seemed to be openly active, while known royalists
appeared to live unharmed in Paris, indeed some even being given responsible positions. The journal found the explanation in the mixture of
fear and hope that dominated the early reign of the First Consul.[16] The
fact was that Bonaparte was gathering whatever able people he could
find, be they former revolutionary leaders or undisguised royalists.[17] The
somewhat puzzled guesses of the anonymous commentator of *Mercure de
France* can be contrasted with the forceful image conveyed by Mallet confronted with the same spectacle. The revolutionaries were welcome as
long as their republicanism was attenuated ("mitigé"), while the royalists
could join Bonaparte's administration provided they only called themselves so but did not act accordingly.

The place of the people in relation to power had lately been pondered
on by Germaine de Staël and Benjamin Constant. They were at the centre of the intellectual world in Paris, and even if their work was published
much later, it is reasonable to assume that they frequently discussed the
topic at the time. Madame de Staël's manuscript, heavily annotated by
Constant, took up one of the main ideas mentioned in connection with
the 1795 constitution: the sovereignty of the masses had replaced the
king's sovereignty, namely absolutism, which had nevertheless been recreated under a different form. The purpose in 1795 had been to avoid a
"legislative dictatorship," hence the establishment of two chambers with

---

[15] "Ah! malheur à nous, disent les Jacobins qui conservent encore l'espérance de
régner bientôt après l'avoir détruit, malheur à nous, s'il raisonne en sage et agit en
héros! Victoire et gloire immortelle au Premier Consul, disent les Royalistes de leur
coté, si son bras courageux devient le restaurateur du trône et des autels, et le sauveur
de la patrie!" (20 April 1800: 138-39).

[16] "Pourquoi le culte catholique y est-il publiquement exercé dans les campagnes, où
les prêtres, qui n'ont fait ni *serment* ni *promesse*, célèbrent et chantent publiquement
l'office divin? Pourquoi tous les chefs des armées royales ... sont'ils à Paris tranquilles
sous la protection du gouvernement républicain? ... La réponse à toutes ces questions
paroit simple et réduite à ces deux mots: *la crainte et l'espérance*" (20 April 1800: 139).

[17] See Georges Lefebvre, *Napoléon*. Trans. Henry F. Stockhold, 5th ed. 2 vols. (1965;
New York: Columbia UP, 1969) 1: 79.

different roles (Sutherland 273). Germaine de Staël and, probably, Constant argued that sovereignty could not be possessed as an indivisible right by the entire population (dismissing Rousseau's point in the process), and therefore had to be delegated. The nature of representation is not put in Burke's terms, but there is a similar tone about the representative not having to be the direct spokesman of the (mostly) uneducated citizens. Various institutions (the two chambers, the Directory, a commission checking the constitutionality of law) would do various jobs ensuring the freedom of the people by exercising sovereignty in its name. In a passage reminiscent of Cabanis' "ignorant classes," Germaine de Staël mentioned the need to wait for a new generation educated in the spirit of liberty; meanwhile certain authoritarian methods had to be preserved.[18]

The Case for an Invasion

The extent to which such a system of allocating power should stay intact formed the main subject of an article that revealed particularly well the émigrés' way of thinking by showing what kind of concepts they resorted to and how they used them. The analysis started from the reaction in Paris to several French military defeats. The monarchists living in France were distressed, *Mercure* remarked, and the periodical went on to explain why in fact the Coalition's victories were a good thing.[19]

---

[18] Madame de Staël, *Des circonstances actuelles qui peuvent terminer la révolution et des principes qui doivent fonder la république en France*, ed. Lucia Omacini (Genève: Droz, 1979) 158-60.

[19] "… nous attendons encore avec la plus vive impatience le moment où les Puissances coalisées déclarent ouvertement au Peuple François qu'elles ne sont armées ni contre sa liberté, ni contre son territoire, mais pour la conservation de l'un et de l'autre sous la forme de son ancienne et paisible monarchie: à l'indispensable nécessité d'un pareil manifeste, on oppose communément cet axiôme du droit de gens, que *nulle Puissance ne doit s'immiscer dans le gouvernement intérieur d'une autre Puissance, ni lui en prescrire la forme*. Mais si ce principe est incontestable en lui-même, il nous paroit au moins inapplicable à la circonstance présente." ("… we still await most impatiently the moment when the allied Powers will announce to the French People that they have not armed themselves against its liberty or territory, but for the preservation of both under its ancient and peaceful monarchy. The indispensable necessity of such a declaration is usually opposed by the axiom of international law according to which *no Power should*

The article admitted that the principle usually invoked was that a foreign power should not intervene in another country's internal affairs and change its political system. But the validity of this principle depended on the social pact between people. In a passage appropriating for the moment Rousseau's idea on the kinds of freedom lost and gained when forming a political community, *Mercure de France* states that no external intervention would be justified in a society where people surrendered their "liberté naturelle" for "la liberté civile" to establish a new state.[20] However, when "une horde de factieux" takes over and upsets the arrangements agreed by the community, the principle of non-intervention does not apply. It is significant to see how far afield the émigré writer strays in order to find arguments against Bonaparte. The émigrés return the accusation of guilt by writing about the "usurpateur" who has placed himself "par la force ou par la corruption, sur le trône de son Prince" (10 May 1800: 321). The moral flaw can be corrected here by means of a foreign invasion. But the argument needs the distinction between the legitimacy of an initial, voluntary pact with its subsequent hierarchy, and the aberrant sudden emergence of a new leadership repudiating the initial covenant. The importance of the proper kind of contract becomes an argument in a discussion of the rights and wrongs of a foreign invasion. Here it is the *pacte d'association* that is commendable, and there is only a hint of the subordination to a king (when the divine right of the kings is to be defended the emphasis shifts towards another version of the contract: the *pacte de soumission*).

It may well be the case that *Mercure de France* was trying to exploit the idea circulating in Paris about sovereignty being vested in powerful institutions and not in the people. The royalists implied that in that case sovereignty could just as well reside in the monarchy. The initial consent of the people would have granted the monarch the right to embody the country, this time inclining towards the *pacte de soumission*. Therefore, the

---

interfere in the internal affairs of another Power, or impose a form of government on it. But if this principle is incontestable in itself, it seems to us that it can not apply at all in this case" [10 May 1800: 319]).

[20] 10 May 1800: 321. See also *Du Contract social*: "Ce que l'homme perd par le contract social, c'est sa liberté naturelle ... ce qu'il gagne, c'est la liberté civile ..." (Rousseau 3: 346). I have kept the spelling of the title used in this edition.

reasoning went, a change forced from the outside need not worry anyone as long as its aim was the restoration of the voluntary, previous agreement. From the propriety of such a covenant derives the ruler's legitimacy, a recurring term contrasted at every step with the various aspects of "usurpation." The foundation of this particular kind of legitimacy is evident from the association of terms when the restoration of the "ancienne et légitime forme" of the state is required (10 May 1800: 322). The idea of "legitimacy" would dominate even more the discussions following the Restoration fifteen years later. Opinions on its meaning differed: the Bourbons referred to tradition backed by the Holy Alliance, while in their own exile periodicals the Spanish liberals also invoked legitimacy, but in a context of popular representation. In 1800 the French émigrés were supporting their argument for invading France and "restoring" its proper leadership by referring to Grotius's statement on the right to attack a bellicose nation which troubles its peaceful neighbour (10 May 1800: 323). In the long run "le silence et l'inertie d'une neutralité approbative" would turn out more destructive than immediate action (10 May 1800: 322). Some of the concepts deployed in these arguments were given different meanings in Paris, a fact on which I concentrate in the final part of the present work.

The author of the article probably counted on the appeal, such as it was, of the *thèse royale* during the past two centuries in its opposition to the *thèse nobiliaire*. These were two rivalling claims as to whether France had originally been a constitutional monarchy where the feudal lords had various powers, including the legislative one, or whether the king had possessed them all along. The former had been supported by Montesquieu (wrong on facts, rhetorically persuasive, eager to justify the aristocratic judiciary), and the latter by Dubos (right on most things, but having an ulterior motive to legitimize Louis XIV's actions against the aristocracy).[21] *Mercure* could even claim support from an unexpected quarter—all his life Voltaire had argued in favour of the *thèse royale*. More

---

[21] See Gay (2: 466-470). Jean-Baptiste Dubos (1670-1742), clergyman, literary critic and historian.

than three decades earlier he had written to d'Alembert that "the cause of the king is the cause of the philosophes."[22]

The justification of an invasion was also seen in terms of a European federation of monarchies that had achieved a balance of sorts. When upset, this equilibrium must be redressed by forceful action from the outside including, where necessary, the restoration of a monarchy. Here, too, the royalists' position was at variance with the course of thought back home. France had been in the process of defining itself as a particular entity in Europe, breaking with the post-Utrecht agreement among monarchies, and, in its crusading revolutionary spirit, expecting other peoples on the Continent to follow suit. Before the doubts about the location of power raised during the late 1790s, its place had been clearly specified in the Declaration of the Rights of Man and Citizen: "Le principe de toute souveraineté réside essentiellement dans la nation."[23]

Mercure de France was both restricting the sphere of sovereignty by placing it within the monarchy, and at the same time extending it by regarding the monarchy as part of an overall European federation, not a particularly un-orthodox thought before the development and impact of nationalism. An émigré's point of view from London needed to perceive Europe as a more or less homogeneous coalition of monarchies embodying the traditional values to be restored in France. Meanwhile, the political developments at home had to be conveyed as an aberration to be put right by other powers. "La France révolutionnaire" was contrasted with the "sociétés civilisées," the latter word being given a recent meaning. As late as the 1760s, "civiliser" was defined in the *Encyclopédie* as transferring a trial from the sphere of criminal law to that of civil law. By the closing decades of the eighteenth century the meaning of improvement through social development came increasingly into use, and the word could be applied to those societies where "civil" liberty had emerged as the result of the initial contract between their members. The subsequent gain due to the process of historical change could be seen in

---

[22] Quoted in Gay (2: 471).

[23] J.M. Roberts, ed. *French Revolution Documents* (Oxford: Blackwell, 1966) 1: 172. Cf. also art. I of the draft of the constitution submitted to the National Assembly in October 1789: "Tous les pouvoirs émanent essentiellement de la nation ..." (1: 173).

their social, political and cultural characteristics.[24] The fact that the words appear in several articles of this periodical only reinforces the point that the recourse to these terms was not accidental.[25] The message was backward-looking but some of the key terms were quite up-to-date.

The image of perpetual order as well as a one-sided view of the hypothetical contract, as seen above, needed to be recreated to an anachronistic extent in order for the defence of a foreign invasion to be justified. In addition, the credibility of such an argument hung on political developments in Paris where it appeared that the latest constitution was confining the newly-won sovereignty of the people to an increasingly powerful executive body and, in time, to one person.

Bonaparte's ascension, "un étranger, un Corse, un vil insulaire" (30 May 1800: 459), was followed with intense disapproval. He had abandoned his soldiers in Egypt in order to return to France and to look after his own interests (30 May 1800: 460). The idea of a ruler's legitimacy was never far from the mind of the *Mercure* writer—by his action Bonaparte was preparing "sa nouvelle usurpation." The enthusiasm with which he was received was due to the fact that people saw in the new government the image of monarchy, whose true presence they actually desired. In the same spirit *Mercure* deplored the peace following the battle of Marengo (10 July 1800: 253). The new "funeste" peace would only grant additional legitimacy to an undesirable state of things imposed earlier by sheer boldness and persistence (10 July 1800: 254-55). Yet the author had his

---

[24] "... la politique, dans plus d'un Cabinet de l'Europe, semble combattre et ruiner ses plus chers intérêts, au lieu de les servir; qu'elle considère, mais à tort, cet injurieux défi, ce combat á mort livré par la France révolutionnaire á toutes les sociétés civilisées, comme une guerre ordinaire entre des Gouvernemens réguliers; qu'elle se livre à des spéculations d'accroissement, et d'avantages particuliers, au moment d'un écroulement général ..." ("... the policy of several European Governments seems to oppose and ruin their most important interests instead of looking after them; they wrongly consider the abusive defiance, the fight to the death started by revolutionary France against all civilized societies as an ordinary way between normal Governments; this policy toys with speculations about expansion and particular gains at a time of general collapse ..." [10 June 1800: 40]). On "civiliser" see *Dictionnaire historique de la Langue française*. On "civilisation" being used for the first time in the 1750s see Albert Soboul, *La civilisation et la Révolution Française*. 3 vols. (Paris: Arthaud, 1970-83) 1: 18-19.

[25] See, for example, an article from 30 July 1800 (401) where "chefs des nations civilisées" are urged to die nobly, sword in hand, rather than by "la ciguë révolutionnaire."

suspicions: the Continental Powers seemed more interested in weakening France, rather than defeating the present government (10 July 1800: 260-61).

The fickleness of "la volonté générale" is suggested by calling it "la volonté humaine," a force easily manipulated by the legislator's own greed. He who claims to represent the people and to pass laws in its name does it on the basis of a "prétendu contrat" (20 Aug. 1800: 104). And the discussion turns, yet again, to the problem of legitimacy: "Il faut une base à l'autorité qui réprime; cette base je ne puis la trouver dans la volonté d'un autre homme."[26] By now the general will has become the will of one person. The solution would be to have the divine authority as a proper foundation. Reason (accompanied here by force) is not enough to enlighten human beings on their duties towards themselves and towards one another, the writer insists. The overall tension in the realm of ideas between tradition and reason throughout the preceding decades is once more confirmed here (see also Lefebvre 2: 9-20).

The views of *Mercure* on the coalition of outside forces were spelled out in a series of articles starting on 30 June 1800. In the 1770s Europe could be considered "une République fédérative" regulated by various documents guaranteed by most states, *Mercure* explained. All this made up a code called in this analysis "droit publique de l'Europe."[27] This was not a proper legal system, but a number of alliances, agreements and family connections. Even here one encounters a hierarchy with its own ranks. The term "republic" combines here one of its contemporary connotations of a community of like-minded members but of varying degrees of importance (e.g. Kant's republic of monarchies, or "republica christiana") with the later, exclusively egalitarian connotation: the article does argue that the smallest member would have a say in the general

---

[26] "The repressing authority needs a foundation, and I cannot see it in another person's will" (20 Aug. 1800: 104).

[27] A section with the title "État de l'Europe avant et après la Guerre d'Amérique. C'étoit une République fédérative" starts as follows: "Au moment où le Roi Louis XV ferma les yeux, l'Europe pouvoit être regardée comme un corps fédératif, composé de divers membres, dont les propriétés, les rangs, etc. étoient clairement et distinctement réglés par des titres écrits, reconnus et garantis partous. L'ensemble de ces titres de propriété constituoit un code auquel on donnoit avec justice le nom de *Droit public de l'Europe*" (30 June 1800: 215).

arrangements and could maintain its independence. The virtue of this order was that it had grown naturally and, consequently, everyone had an interest in preserving it, as this also meant preserving one's freedom and "existence."[28]

The unity of Europe was also based on a presumed common front made in former times against Arab and Ottoman conquerors at either end of the continent.[29] The political purpose and cooperation must have played a significant role within the more official, religious aims, the periodical argues. Later, common action was taken against those states that endangered the peace. Therefore, there were precedents based on a "droit public" which France recognized and benefited from.[30] Unlike the argument based on the social contract, the one resting on the "droit public" of disciplining this or that state was put together *ad hoc* by gathering various events and arranging them so that they could serve a particular purpose.

This was the European framework, as seen by the periodical. The principle against outside intervention had injudiciously been launched by Louis XVI's Minister of Foreign Affairs, and later used by various groups, factions, and governments up to the present moment, the peri-

---

[28] "Sous les auspices de cette sage combinaison d'engagemens, de garantie et de puissance, le plus petit État jouissoit de sa liberté, et de sa propriété, de son indépendence.

Il y avoit donc un ordre réel établi, et par consequent chacun avoit un intérêt réel à le maintenir; et comme cet intérêt étoit celui de la liberté et de l'existence, il en resultoit nécessairement le droit d'employer tous les moyens possibles pour empêcher la destruction de cet ordre" (30 June 1800: 216).

[29] "Dans des tems reculés on avoit vu l'Europe entière alliée contre les Arabes et l'Empire Ottoman, qui avoient conquis l'Espagne au midi et la Grèce au Levant; et certes, quelqu'eloquentes qu'aient été les déclamations prodiguées contre les croisades, il est bien difficile de se persuader que la politique n'ait pas eu plus de part que la religion dans ces ligues mémorables ..." (20 July 1800: 357).

[30] "Il résulte de tous ces exemples, qu'on se crut en droit, dans tous les tems, de s'unir contre ceux qui troubloient ou même, paroissoient prêts à troubler le repos de l'Europe, et se ménager des forces suffisantes pour forcer les peuples à changer domination.

Les alliances ou les lignes des diverses nations contre une d'elles qui menace le bonheur commun, sont donc fondée en exemple comme en principe. La France a, de tout tems, reconnu ce droit comme une des bases de droit public, et de tous les États de l'Europe; elle est celui qui en a tiré les avantages les plus réels" (20 July 1800: 358).

odical points out reproachfully (30 June 1800: 214). This principle, discussed earlier by the journal in terms of a social contract, was now being discredited by the image of a would-be harmonious European "federation." In the former case the reference was to a historical tradition of the covenant that was easy to recognize, while in the latter case the image invoked had a more debatable and a less obvious pedigree.

To what extent was *Mercure* trying to give currency to a newer, more striking idea as an additional argument in its efforts to justify a corrective invasion of France? The various treaties and agreements that the article hints at when it mentions the recent European consensus are palpable acts, as opposed to the hypothetical social contract. Yet, there is an implication that the two things are similar. They both presuppose consent and, therefore, a binding agreement.

At a time when the importance of natural law was declining in favour of utilitarianism in the ethical thought of the century, the royalists relied insistently on the former, choosing to see in it an agreed hierarchy rather than the challenge of reason. The emphasis on the moral implications of contract allowed a stronger ethical case for an outside intervention. One witnesses here a clash between two interpretations of the natural law. The revolutionaries (with whom the Directors and Bonaparte were lumped together) assumed that the relations after the contract had gradually degenerated and a return to an uncorrupted stage was imperative. The aim of the Declaration of August 1789 was to state "les droits naturels, inaliénables et sacrés de l'homme" (Roberts, ed. 1: 171). On the other hand, the royalist émigrés considered the Ancien Régime a mature set of norms that should be observed.

By the third sequel of the article on the "European interests" the discussion moved on to a "théorie générale" on the right of other nations to act against another country in the name of the overall balance. This theory was based on various types of interests and *Mercure* decides to take into account mainly the territorial and commercial ones.[31]

---

[31] "Mais commes les intérêts eloignés, quelques grands qu'ils puissent être, sont moins frappans pour le bonheur commun des hommes que les intérêts immédiats, nous appuyerons notre théorie générale par des preuves tirées des intérêts territoriaux et commerciaux de chaque nation.

A quick sketch conveys first the general image of an ordered society based on laws bequeathed by one's ancestors, borrowed from abroad, or proclaimed by kings or proper legislators. The chain of authority is made up of various classes ranked hierarchically.[32] A distinction is made between similarity and equality—the former can be applied to all human beings but not the latter. *Mercure* wonders whether the two have become synonyms ever since Marat and Brissot maltreated the language in their respective periodicals. This distinction is clarified by pointing out the various personal qualities with which people are endowed (30 July 1800: 421).

The drift of this particular part of the discussion is that acquiring and owning property has led to an economic and social hierarchy that is interconnected with the political one. Tampering with one would mean tampering with the other (30 July 1800: 423). The implied point is that, left to their own devices, people would naturally find their own level according to their personal abilities.

Des formes assez simples et trés sages étoient assez communes à tous les Gouvernemens de l'Europe avant la révolte des François. De la Suède à l'Espagne chaque peuple étoient gouverné suivant un code qu'il avoit en partie reçu de ses pères; en partie tiré des codes étrangers, et en partie reçu de ses Rois ou magistrats. Par-tout on distingueroient ceux qui gouvernoient, la règle suivant laquelle ils gouvernoient, et ceux qui étoient gouvernés.

Ceux qui gouvernoient étoient par la nature des choses en nombre proportionné à ceux qui étoient gouvernés; et les premiers étoient, comme les derniers, subdivisés en diverses classes, dont la subordonation mutuelle formoit une chaîne d'autorités graduées.

Afin d'empecher cette chaîne de flotter au gré du hasard dans le tems et dans l'espace, nos ancêtres en avoient fixé l'extrémité aux marches du trône de l'Auteur de la nature; et la religion l'imposoit avec une auguste impartialité son joug sévère sur le col des Rois et sur celui des bergers" (30 July 1800: 420).

[32] The Romans divided the population in classes by economic criteria, but the word seems to have temporarily lost this meaning towards the middle of the eighteenth century, at least in French. The usage in connection with hierarchical superiority is noted in 1680, first about writers, then about people in general. Quesnay used it in 1758 in a social context, but the *Encyclopédie* registers first the taxonomic sense in natural science, then its meaning in education, and finally a naval meaning. If the political and economic meaning had not been generally revived by 1800, it may mean that *Mercure* was trying to emphasize the organic characteristics of society by the way it used "class." See also *Dictionnaire historique de la Langue française.*

The Burkean reverberations of the idea of a slowly maturing social order justified by its very existence are perhaps less surprising when encountered in *Mercure*. The analysis had started—a few articles ago—in a somewhat different key, possibly reminding the reader of Rousseau's contract. Indeed, it has been argued that there are more similarities between Rousseau's and Burke's basic concepts than meet the eye (Sabine 617-18). From these texts it appears that this *Mercure* commentator was comfortable with both thinkers' outlook regarding the importance of the community.

Reversing the Roles

In March 1800 the lists of émigrés were closed by decree. The authorities' declaration that there were no more French émigrés was seized on by the royalist exiles of *Mercure de France* who concluded a first brief comment by stating that, indeed "[*i*]*l n'y a point d'Émigrés François*, et c'est sur cette proposition simple que les François royalistes eux-mêmes n'ont pas bien conçue, ne semblent pas avoir examinée [sic], que s'appuyent tous leurs droits et tous leurs devoirs."[33] This rather cryptic ending must have intrigued a reader who sent a letter to the editor signed "D.F.D.V.P." (unless the message was planted), asking him to enlarge on the matter (20 Sept. 1800: 396). A long analysis follows in the same number explaining how the émigrés had seen their condition throughout the years. This argument with its references to the royalists' general outlook on history and culture has a different tone from many other articles full of invectives and vituperations. Its effort to reverse the role of accuser and defendant displays significant evidence of the émigrés' thought.

Once more, the émigrés need to make distinctions in order to seize and employ one convenient aspect. The geographical place of one's birth is contrasted with a set of customs and traditions within which an individual is brought up: a prosaic "lieu" is set against "les usages, les moeurs,

---

[33] "*... there are no more French émigrés*, and what the French royalists have not grasped and do not seem to have thought about is that all their rights and duties rest upon this very simple statement" (30 Aug. 1800: 178, ital. in the original).

les coutumes *des nos pères*; qui sont devenus pour nous la vie même."³⁴ Having established this difference, the writer attaches the term "patrie" to the relationship with the ancestral customs and laws ("avec les habitudes *de nos pères*, avec leurs loix ..." [20 Sept. 1800: 397]). This shift from the importance of a place to that of a tradition assimilated by a person implies here a shift of loyalty as well. The entity that is worth resorting to when an individual defines himself turns out to be not so much the native region as the set of traditional values that have shaped his personality. They have been handed down by one's ancestors ("pères," "patres," forefathers) and make up the proper "patrie."

The idea of contract is brought up again. Here it becomes a virtual pact between this set of traditions, which guarantee and defend the inherited rights on which society is based and the person who undertakes to respect and maintain them. This "contrat mutuel et obligatoire" prescribes the conditions on whose fulfilment rests "l'amour de la patrie" (20 Sept. 1800: 398). According to this version of the royalist argument with appropriate Burkean echoes, the implicit agreement between tradition and the individual presupposes rights granted by the former and duties incumbent on the latter. The course of the disquisition heads towards one of the key terms required by the émigrés to prove their point, the inviolability of these rights because "c'est sur leur inviolabilité que se fondent nos devoirs" (20 Sept. 1800: 398). And one must constantly bear in mind that these rights are part of a tradition and a covenant identified with "la patrie."³⁵ As long as the circumstances facilitating the existence of these conventions remain unchanged, or the modifications occur properly within the "pacte sociale," the duties of the individual also remain unchanged. In so far as these conventions are embodied in, and represented by, one person (the monarch), the mutual obligation and loyalty ("contrat mutuel") suggested above take on a concrete quality. (It should be added that this mutual loyalty does not necessarily place the monarchy in a flattering light: "traditional kings who abandoned their

---

³⁴ "... the practices, the manners, the customs of *our ancestors* which have become for us life itself" (20 Sept. 1800: 397).

³⁵ A similar point is reiterated later in the article: "Quand a commencé ce qu'on appelle émigration? Au moment où il n'y a plus de patrie, où le contrat social a été entièrement violé" (20 Sept. 1800: 406).

peoples lose the right to loyalty" [Hobsbawm 86]. It was after the king's attempted flight abroad that the appeal of republicanism increased among the population at large.) So far the article has established the points needed to proceed to the effects and significance of any upheaval.

Considering the ultra-royalists' outlook on contemporary developments, it is not difficult to anticipate their opinions on the dislocation of tradition. When "la majorité réelle ou supposée déchire violemment le contrat, et annulle toutes les dispositions, toutes les formes antérieurs ... tous les devoirs cessent, la société est ramenée à ses premièrs élémens, et chaque individu rentre dans ses droit primitifs et individuels."[36] The purpose of the initial contract has been defeated. It is worth noting that the regress leads to an individual state of things implying a loss of the collective achievement of a sequence of customs. Later, the Spanish liberals in exile would dismiss the traditional values vindicating a strong monarchy, and would find virtue in the very individual possibility of opposing royal absolutism.

The counter-accusation against the revolutionaries is that in breaking the contract they have also withdrawn "la protection de la loi à une portion de citoyens" (20 Sept. 1800: 399). This reference to certain citizens left without the protection of the law is a reference to the stream of anti-émigré laws passed during the 1790s, and possibly to the decree of September 1792. According to this legal decision, the parents of the émigrés in France, regardless of their political attitude, were to be considered as "mauvais citoyens." The result was that some individuals were less entitled to the protection of the constitution than others, as one historian has pointed out (Higonnet 100). The émigrés themselves were qualified as "bad" *tout court* since they had ceased to be citizens after their flight. Subsequent legislation would declare them "dead as civil persons" (Higonnet 126). The flawed moral status of the exiles defined by Rousseau was thus confirmed by legal measures as well. The émigrés' arguments, the royalists' above all, were bound to possess the tone and intention of self-exculpation.

---

[36] "... the real or supposed majority violently destroys the contract and cancels all the provisions and previous forms ... all duties cease, society returns to its initial stage, and each individual recovers his primitive and individual rights" (20 Sept. 1800: 399).

A further distinction follows, between the physical and moral needs which society, as the result of the contract, undertakes to fulfil. Therefore, "la patrie" is defined as "des moyens de satisfaire aux besoins physiques et moraux que nécessite la conservation de la société" and a whole apparatus with strong economic and social components is shaped in the process.[37] But once this system disintegrates, so does "la vraie patrie." The note introduced here by the mention of the true, genuine "patrie" leads finally to the gist of the article. This internal disintegration does not mean that the real "patrie" cannot continue its existence elsewhere.

These émigrés against whom laws have been passed, whose goods have been confiscated, whose status has vanished make here a claim meant to erase the condemnation and guilt attached to them by social changes and legal pronouncements. It is a bold attempt to reverse the situation of exile: "Quant au moment de cette rupture, une portion de citoyens conserve religieusement ces formes, y tient fermement, veut les conserver; c'est là que reste la *patrie* ..."[38] The author of the article does raise the question of the status of the French in France, "[d]ans cet état, que devient la majorité même restée sur le sol où se trouvoit la patrie? Tout ce qu'on voudra ..."[39] This inimitable answer is further clarified by a quick retrospective view of the emergence of the main social groups. As the result of the initial agreement, called here "contrat primitif" (20 Sept. 1800: 409), two (unequal) groups emerged, "ceux qui n'étoient appelés qu'à faire la masse de la nation, et ceux qui l'étoient à la defendre au dépens même de leur propre intérêt."[40] The latter are further divided according to their functions, including the clergy. The purpose of summoning this image is to identify the composition of the "patrie" with a particular group and its various roles. (In this section of the argument "nation" is suddenly spelled with a capital letter to emphasize its separa-

---

[37] "... means to satisfy the physical and moral needs necessary to the preservation of society" (20 Sept. 1800: 402).

[38] "When after such a break a number of citizens religiously preserve these forms, clinging firmly to them, will preserve them, that is where the *patrie* finds itself ..." (20 Sept. 1800: 402).

[39] "In this situation what becomes of the majority itself left on the soil where the fatherland used to be? It's up to them ..." (20 Sept. 1800: 403).

[40] "... those only destined to form the mass of the nation and those destined to defend it even at the expense of their own interest" (20 Sept. 1800: 407).

tion from the bulk of the people who are only "la masse de la nation.")
The recent radical changes desired and undertaken by the nation have
nothing to do with the Nation. The author of the article states that, as
demonstrated above, the Nation "se compose du Souverain, des pro-
priètaires, des corps administratifs militaires, religieux, judiciaires; et rien
de tout cela ne prit part à ce bouleversement, et c'est-là ce qui constitue
le corps de ce qu'on appelle l'émigration."[41] The terms are not always
used consistently, but at this point *Mercure* resorts to a medieval sense of
the "nation" made up of the aristocracy (including the monarch) and the
higher clergy; consequently, the persons whose lineage is well known
("nobilis") constitute the nation and embody a particular sequence of
customs proclaimed as the relevant tradition, the rest are "the people."
Since most of the former find themselves abroad, that is precisely where
the nation is. This was what *Mercure* meant by the statement that there
were no longer French émigrés. And to crown the paradox, the author of
this commentary argues by implication that the émigrés are not those
who have stayed constant to the defining set of traditions, but, if anyone,
those who have shamefully forsaken themselves, i.e. their identity ("turps
est deserere se" [20 Sept. 1800: 410]).

In the issue of 30 April 1801 there was a brief announcement to the
effect that the publication of *Mercure de France* was becoming increasingly
hard due to the cost and communication difficulties. This was also the
last number of the series to be published in London. The more emphatic
anonymity of this periodical in comparison with the clearly personal
voices of Mallet and Peltier in their respective publications lends a note
of finality to the arguments presented here. The unembarrassed way in
which the explanations are put together take on the authority of general
statements on behalf of most émigrés, rather than one editor's comments on an isolated event.

The royalists hoped for a change of political system as a result of outside intervention. That never happened, yet, ironically, France's military
expansion would lead to a temporary return of the monarchy in 1814.

---

[41] "… is made up of the Sovereign, [land]owners, military, clerical and legal bodies;
none of them participated in the commotion, while it is they who constitute the body
of the emigration" (20 Sept. 1800: 409).

But in the meanwhile circumstances were changing. It was becoming obvious that the restoration of monarchy was no longer prevented by a revolutionary government, however diluted, but by a military leader with imperial ambitions. The targets were changing and an editor of satirical magazines known in Paris in the early years of the Revolution would take over the task of carrying on the royalist argument in his own polemical manner.

Chapter 3

Persisting: Peltier's *L'Ambigu*

After the Brumaire coup of 1799 France found itself governed by a tri-umvirate of consuls. True to tradition, it became obvious soon enough that only one really mattered. And the First Consul wanted a fresh start. In 1800, and again in 1802, the new leader granted amnesties to most French émigrés who returned in rather large numbers. Several categories were excepted, and, naturally, they kept their distance: those who were closely connected with the Bourbons, others who had been highly-placed in the émigré military forces, and the clerics who disapproved of Bona-parte's way of treating the Church both before and after the Concordat (his pact with the Vatican ratified in April 1802).[1] Of those who did re-turn some were promptly integrated into the new administrative system together with the royalists (and Jacobins) who had kept a low profile in France. The number of French exile publications diminished considera-bly. But there was the odd new periodical launched after the shift of power in France. Probably no émigré magazine outdid *L'Ambigu* (1802-1818) in longevity, and when it comes to oppositional stamina few jour-nalists rivalled Jean-Gabriel Peltier.

---

[1] Geoffrey Ellis, *The Napoleonic Empire* (London: Macmillan, 1991) 29.

A Journalist in Business

Born in Bretagne in 1760, Peltier studied the classics and, unusually for that time, French and history at the Oratorians' teaching establishment in Nantes (Maspero-Clerc 2-4). The Oratorians were known at that time for promoting "advanced" ideas, while in Nantes the revolutionary spirit was rather strong as witnessed by the English writer Andrew Young during his travels. So were the Freemasons on whose lists Peltier's name could be found. He moved to Paris and after the Revolution became the editor of *Actes des Apôtres*, a monarchist satirical magazine (Maspero-Clerc 26-28, 29). In 1792 Peltier started a new publication, *Correspondance politique*, but later that year he decided to flee to England. Immediately after 1789 he had supported the "monarchiens;" by 1798 he broke with the constitutional monarchists and practically became the spokesman of the "royalistes purs" (Maspero-Clerc 26). It is worth pointing out that despite Peltier's more ardent monarchism compared with Mallet's qualified constitutional variety, when the future Louis XVIII wanted to air some of his opinions (with the help of Malouet) he did not choose one of Peltier's exile publications.

In London Peltier brought out several short-lived periodicals, some hardly more than a bulky volume of anecdotes, personal recollections, diatribes and panegyrics. In 1795 he started *Paris pendant l'année…* which carried on in the same vein until replaced by *L'Ambigu*. Prolific, if not particularly profound, an energetic satirist if not always witty, Peltier went on criticizing the ruler who had replaced the Directory. Having been an increasingly fierce enemy of the French Revolution, he became a tireless critic of Bonaparte's Consulate and, in the fullness of time, of Napoleon I's Empire, although his initial reaction to Bonaparte's rule was positive.[2] Following the attacks aimed at a collective leadership new arguments had to be found against a forceful individualistic ruler. This relentless criticism went on for over a decade. After the Restoration Peltier failed to obtain any satisfactory position. Consequently, Louis XVIII became the next target of the former monarchist's jibes as Peltier

---

[2] Throughout nearly two decades Peltier insisted on spelling the man's name "Buonaparté," emphasizing his Corsican origin.

returned to editing his journal in London until 1818. My discussion stops at the early 1814 issues when the editor ceased to be a political exile.

While in Britain, Peltier supported himself both by journalism and a range of other activities, including business. He did odd jobs for the British government such as printing a volume of memoirs about the war in the Vendée region (where the revolutionary authorities encountered strong local resistence), or translating correspondence to do with French prisoners of war. The receipts and letters dealing with these transactions are filed among similar documents under Secret Service payments provided by William Huskisson, Under-Secretary of State in the War Office.[3] Huskisson coordinated the intelligence, military and propaganda operations undertaken mainly by the French émigrés against revolutionary France. On the whole, it may be assumed that Peltier's contacts stretched beyond the known world of politicians and businessmen.

A less usual source of income became available in 1807 when Peltier was appointed Haitian consul in London. Britain established diplomatic relations with Santo-Domingo only in 1825, but that did not prevent Peltier from attempting to represent Emperor Christophe's interests. He was paid in bags of sugar and coffee, which he had to turn into cash (Maspero-Clerc 201-108).

When Mallet du Pan started his *Mercure Britannique* the Count of Provence's representatives and the British authorities tried to propose Peltier as one of Mallet's colleagues. The incompatibility between the "Calvinist and liberal Genevan" and the inflexible royalist became visible rather rapidly (Maspero-Clerc 93). The differences between the editors of various exile periodicals were increasingly obvious by 1798. Peltier was close to the ultra-royalists while Mallet du Pan remained a constitutional monarchist along with several former members of the National Assembly living also as refugees in London. The mention of a programme of a "mild monarchy" in case of restoration, a possibility aired in a pamphlet published in Paris in 1799 and then discussed in Mallet's magazine was enough to send Peltier into fits of furious criticism. Peltier's biographer

---

[3] Receipt sent by Peltier, 19 May 1796 (British Library, Add. mss. 38769); Peltier's letter and receipt to Huskisson, 26 February 1801 and 26 May 1801 (British Library, Add. mss. 38736).

considers that the journalist was the "faithful interpreter of the political ideas of Monsieur's (Comte d'Artois) entourage, rather than that of Louis XVIII's" (Maspero-Clerc 141).

In France the Directory had been battling with financial problems and political crises. Sieyès, one of the Directors, decided to use a military man to impose order once and for all. Bonaparte was not his first choice but the Corsican's popularity decided the outcome. Sieyès assumed that he could manipulate the rather unworldly soldier, but once the deed was done, the Director was covered in honours and financial rewards and removed from the political stage in no time.[4] Briefly out of his depth, the general quickly found his bearings and France had a new leader who assumed the title of First Consul.

These events created confusion and raised some hopes among the émigrés. Initially, Peltier welcomed the Consulate. As soon as Bonaparte spurned Count of Provence's approaches, the journalist became critical. Peltier's name began to appear in the French police reports (Maspero-Clerc 140, 141, 147).

Hardly was *L'Ambigu* launched when the French and the English signed a peace treaty at Amiens in 1802. At the time the British had a Tory government. The decision to sign the pact was far from enjoying unanimous backing in the party. There were some Tories who thought that this respite would allow the French to rearm. Some of the newspapers were controlled by the Conservatives and in the sustained war of words with the French press Peltier was, in fact, helping the Tory rebels through his continuing criticism of Bonaparte. During this short period of good Anglo-French relations Bonaparte asked London to put Peltier on trial for slander. After a while the British government obliged (February 1803). The pretext was an article about Hortense de Beauharnais's marriage.[5] The former recipient of Secret Service payments was now

[4] The fierce revolutionary of 1789 became a "count of the Empire" in 1808 and a "*grand officier* of the Legion of Honour." At an imperial ceremony which Sieyès attended in court dress someone ironically said: "Avez-vous vu Sieyès? *Qu'est-ce que le Tiers-état?*" (Higonnet 262).

[5] Hortense de Beauharnais (1783-1837), Napoleon's stepdaughter, married Napoleon's brother, Louis; one of her children became Napoleon III.

accused of activities for some of which he may have been discreetly rewarded earlier on.

Bonaparte was sensitive to what the British and German papers were saying about him and, clearly, worried about the émigré magazines as well (Holtman 72). Aware of the growing importance of the press, the First Consul had closed down sixty newspapers in Paris, and out of the remaining thirteen some would cease publication during the following years. The few survivors would practically be official organs. A number of provincial dailies were closed down as well.[6]

It was something of a mystery how Peltier could afford one of the best and most expensive barristers to defend him.[7] Despite the official peaceful relations, an acerbic dispute between the British and the French press was going on, and it was against this background that the trial took place. There is hardly any direct evidence, but it would be reasonable to assume that some of the journalist's influential backers had not abandoned him entirely. The defendant was found guilty and sentenced to a small fine. The British press followed the proceedings closely. It would all turn out to be good publicity for Peltier. Soon Britain and France were at war with one another again, the journalist was back at work, and the increased circulation of his periodical covered the fine.

"Outrageous Miscellanea"

It seems that the British government was more generous towards Peltier than towards other exile editors concerning the cost of the press for his information (Maspero-Clerc 274). The French papers in particular could be very expensive in Britain. When the editor was not defending himself in court or arrested for dubious business transactions (as it happened in 1811 and 1816), the periodical appeared every ten days.

---

[6] Bellanger, ed. 1: 550, 552. See also Holtman (44). The harsh measures against the press would continue and *Histoire générale de la presse française* concludes: "From the point of view of freedom the situation of the French periodical press was worse in 1814 than in 1788" ("En 1814, la condition de la presse française est, du point de vue de la liberté, pire qu'en 1788") 1: 567.

[7] This was James Mackintosh, the author of *Vindiciae Gallicae*, one of the replies to Burke's *Reflections on the Revolution in France.* Mackintosh had welcomed the French Revolution but by 1800 he had changed his mind.

The subtitle of the first numbers was "outrageous and amusing miscellanea, a journal in the Egyptian manner."[8] Bonaparte's hurried departure from Egypt in 1799 in order to reach Paris, leaving his troops behind, constituted the object of prolonged mirth in Peltier's magazine.

The first editorial promised a wide variety of materials; anything in the everyday life of his readers striking the editor as worth including would be found here: songs, riddles, political stories, secret reports, literary reviews (1: 2). The first number commented on a topical event, the promulgation of the new Constitution in August 1802. It was the second document of this kind since Bonaparte had seized power. It had been accompanied by a referendum, which resulted in Napoleon being appointed Consul for life.[9] Just as the 1799 Constitution lacked a declaration of the rights of the people, so did that of 1802. The First Consul's powers were increased considerably and the text began to display the traits of a monarchist constitution (Godechot 164).

Peltier briefly describes the contents and then imagines the remarks of a group of observers. They contrast moral honour with judicial or military honour: the former is about to fade away because of the new Constitution and, therefore, would lead to the disappearance of "des moeurs et des opinions Françaises" (1: 10). The implication seems to be that an outsider is tampering with the local tradition, and that a massive administrative structure was being erected leading to the extension of the official sphere about to encompass everything else.

There is a reference to "the true rights of the nation" that need to be placed on a solid foundation. It is not clear whether this is the kind of nation meant by the royalists of *Mercure de France*, but there is a similarity in so far as ancient customs and the nation's rights have a common origin; in this context the emergence and preservation of customs are usually associated by royalists with those whose lineage is well-known, the nobles. This foundation ought to be provided by "un gouvernement paternel fondé sur les habitudes anciennes, les besoins, et les anciennes

---

[8] "... variétés atroces et amusantes, journal dans le genre egyptien" *L'Ambigu* 1: 1. References are given to volume and page numbers.

[9] See Jacques Godechot, ed. *Les Constitutions de la France depuis 1789* (Paris: Garnier-Flammarion, 1970) 163, 167.

affections du peuple Français."[10] Now that the word "rights" is missing from its usual place in the constitution, Peltier brings it up and attempts to give it a different connotation, by associating it with a sequence of customs whose unbroken survival would invalidate the radical changes since 1789. The editor attempts here to develop an argument in a Burkean vein. The revolution caused an unnecessary disruption because what appeared as conflicting interests had in fact a common foundation. By selecting particular elements on which the government should base itself, Peltier tries to suggest that an equal validity characterizes both the ancient customs and the needs of the people. The implication that the affections of the French people are directed at those who are in exile, and who would provide an equally affectionate government, the royalist editor manages to insert a note of consolation for those who see themselves as the embodiment of ancient customs.

In a later commentary the new constitution is seen as a suspension of hostilities between the various factions who are after power (1: 97). In the same text Peltier mentions the attack in the *Moniteur* against the *Times* and against a couple of exiles. The editor claims that the article was dictated by the First Consul himself, something difficult to prove but not hard to believe considering Bonaparte's close interest in matters of propaganda.[11] It was soon after this exchange that the French would persuade the British authorities to prosecute Peltier, but for a while he could give free rein to his satirical talents. Peltier derides the Consul's indignation that his enemies are allowed to walk about freely and conspire against him in foreign capitals. Peltier points out that a number of English refugees, active against the British government, find shelter and support in Paris. There has to be some fair play here, he adds mischievously, but Bonaparte is not willing to observe it.

There are reviews of Necker's *Dernières Vues de Politique et de Finance*, not well received, the entire family is ridiculed as an endlessly scribbling clan, mainly a reference to Necker's daughter Germaine, better known as Madame de Staël (1: 116), and of Louis de Bonald's *Législation primitive*

---

[10] "... a fatherly government based on ancient customs, on the needs and the ancient attachments of the French people" (1: 10).

[11] On Napoleon writing anonymous pieces in the *Moniteur* or amending articles, see Bellanger, ed. (1: 557).

..., the latter signed by Chateaubriand and most probably reprinted from *Mercure de France* which by then had resumed publication in Paris; the poet praises Bonald's work (both being conservative thinkers), but takes issue with him on the origin of language and its role in the development of reason. This was the kind of piece that shows the difficulty of filling an émigré periodical. Literary or theatre reviews printed at home could re-appear in an exile magazine to inform but also, when possible, to reinforce the line pursued by the exiles.

A series of letters addressed to William Cobbett on the restoration of "Louis XVIII" are signed "A Continental Observer," and dated in Hamburg throughout 1803. Cobbett had just started his *Political Register*, a periodical that he would go on editing until his death thirty-three years later. He was still a Tory supporter, although in time he would associate more and more with radical circles. The letters in *L'Ambigu* return to one of the permanent subjects of discussion among the French émigrés: how many of the revolutionary changes should be preserved after the restoration of the monarchy taken for granted by the author (3: 5-9). The opinion of the Hamburg contributor is that the present political, administrative and military institutions should be kept for a while (3: 7). As the years were passing and those whom Peltier saw as able to provide a "paternal government" were still in exile, the idea of a compromise was returned to increasingly often. When Mallet had given space in his *Mercure Britannique* to a tentative exchange on a less than intransigent restoration Peltier had replied violently. Now, still a most committed royalist, Peltier allowed himself space in his periodical for suggestions concerning some kind of compromise. These were however only glimpses of a somewhat more conciliatory attitude.

Addressing the Faithful

In an exile periodical that comes out for almost two decades there is time and room for a special kind of piece. This is usually meant to appear as a comprehensive analysis or commentary. In fact, it turns out to be a re-telling of the main events and a re-stating of the author's, or a particular group's, chief ideas. For instance, an article such as "Ambition du Gouvernement révolutionnaire de France, et Moyens d'en arrêter les dan-

gereux Progrès" ("The Ambition of the French revolutionary government and ways of halting its Advance" [3: 23-38]) seems to state a problem and offer a solution. An analysis of the text would nevertheless yield
very little; what is more significant is the very presence of such a text and
its role. Peltier makes the usual royalist points (the "philosophes" have
destroyed religion and Burke is quoted on the resulting damage [3: 24-
25]), doubtful events are repeated as well-established facts (Louis XVI's
son was poisoned in captivity [3: 25]), and the habitual accusations are
re-voiced (corruption and brutality have eclipsed any other consequences
of the Revolution [3: 23-24]). All in all, no fresh distortions are produced, the opponents are not assailed by new invectives; the reader
would fail to spot any original angle. The informational value and the
analytical worth of the piece are negligible. So what is its purpose?

I would suggest that such a text has something like an incantatory
value. The same material, re-hashed at approximately regular intervals,
repeats a version of events and their interpretation in an attempt to make
it the accepted one or, at least, to maintain it as a sufficiently strong can-
didate in competition with other versions. Without taking the analogy
too far, a certain state of things is in fact wished into being, and a particular sense of community is summoned up in the process. In addition,
it could be argued that *L'Ambigu* was countering the constant stream of
opinions articulated at home with those of its own; Lynn Hunt has
pointed out that "[i]n the absence of a common law tradition or any acceptable sacred text of reference, the voice of the nation had to be heard
constantly."[12] The presence in exile of such texts as those produced by
Peltier helps to reassure a particular readership that the reasons and explanations that define them have not changed. Sharing the author's convictions—or the convictions of those he represents—serves to maintain
the coherence of such a temporary community.

At the same time, the members of a particular camp are counted once
more, as it were. Those who react critically to such a reiteration of the
creed, occasionally even from inside the group, are noticed and pigeon-
holed accordingly. The rest re-confirm their bonds. But the preservation

---

[12] *Politics, Culture, and Class in the French Revolution* (Berkeley: U. of California P., 1984)
21.

of a particular sense of a shared purpose is just one aim, and only a temporary one. Once this goal loses its importance, for example when the group returns home from exile, what remains significant is the survival and the imposition of that particular version of events as well as a specific interpretation.

Peltier encountered an additional problem as a long-term French exile journalist. He had to integrate in his much-repeated story of the revolutionary developments the course taken by events under Napoleon. The periods before and after the coup of November 1799 are linked by calling Emperor Napoleon I's country "revolutionary France" ("la France révolutionnaire" [7: 129]). It is a moot point whether Bonaparte was the product of the Revolution and whether Napoleonic France was a break with the revolutionary France or not. The idea of "ending the Revolution" had been present in various debates almost from the beginning, and not always as an initiative of the opposition. Some moderate reformers assumed that the Revolution was over after the abolition of the feudal privileges in August 1789. The 1791 Constitution was then talked about as an attempt to end the Revolution. Madame de Staël and Benjamin Constant considered that the revolutionary process was completed with the post-1795 constitutions, while Napoleon confessed to his brother Joseph that he had "always intended to end the Revolution by the establishment of the right of inheritance" (qtd. in Furet 238-39). The discussions would go on and further dates would be offered as the final point of the 1789 Revolution (1830, 1848, 1989, etc.). Either way, *L'Ambigu* needed a continuous sequence in order to paint everything with the same brush; no break should be allowed between the Revolution and the Empire.

As far as "Buonaparté" was concerned, it was also a question of establishing a particular image at an early stage. From the point of view of Peltier and his royalist readers it was as the usurper and the aggressor that Napoleon should be remembered. Not too difficult a task, since some of Peltier's contemporaries, the Jacobins or even some members of the Directory, none of them royalists, would agree that the new leader's legitimacy was doubtful.

Meanwhile, the number of the faithful was diminishing, quite a lot of émigrés were returning to France. Once home, many kept their distance from the authorities and only a few rushed to serve Napoleon (Ellis 75). This was probably also a readership that Peltier had in mind. The chronicle of events offered again and again by *L'Ambigu* may have prodded their royalist conscience and tempted them to re-examine their intentions and loyalties. Towards the end of the article "Ambition du Gouvernement révolutionnaire …" the journalist wrote that among the émigrés who returned some still wanted the restoration of monarchy, while others feared it (3: 37). Among the latter there were the clergy who had accepted the Concordat, and whom Peltier considered "égoistes, êtres à peu près nuls dans les grandes crises politiques." An erroneous political choice is seen as the reflection of moral inadequacy because "leurs âmes ne sont pas assez fortes pour se laisser échauffer [sic] par l'enthousiasme de la vertu …"[13] It was among such former fellow-exiles that this article attempted to separate the keen from the indifferent ones.

It could be argued that Peltier's possible goal of achieving an effect by repeating his account at regular intervals resembles, with some qualifications, Joseph de Maistre's understanding of one of the causes of the French Revolution. The conservative thinker argues that one of the causes was the expectation that some abstract words, re-defined and repeated often enough, would lead to concrete changes.[14] Under very different circumstances, Peltier is also re-defining whatever terms he needs (loyalty, sovereignty), and by invoking them frequently enough he hopes to bring about their concrete equivalent.

Aspects of Opposition

France's agreement with the Vatican according to which the Pope recognized the right of the First Consul to appoint bishops, and accepted the sale of Church property had caused a lot of the clergy to stop supporting the royalist and the counter-revolutionary cause. (This support would be regained by the royalists in 1812 when Napoleon considered the Concordat as null and void [Lefebvre 2: 185].) Paradoxically, by his treaty

---

[13] "… selfish beings, quite worthless in great political crises …"; "… their spirit is not sufficiently vigorous to experience the enthusiasm of virtue …" (7: 37).

[14] See Jack Hayward, *After the French Revolution: Six critics of democracy and nationalism* (New York: Harvester Wheatsheaf, 1991) 52.

with the Vatican in 1801 Napoleon antagonized those who were far less religious-minded. While Chateaubriand, back from exile (some of which had been spent in London where he knew Peltier), was publishing *Le Génie du Christianisme* under the benevolent eyes of the authorities, a large number of former anti-Catholic militants had to dissimulate. There were also other reasons for joining the opposition.

Napoleon was tightening his control over the expression and circulation of uncomfortable opinions. In January 1803 the Class of Moral and Political Sciences of the "Institut National" was closed down. When the Directory had established the Institute in 1795 as a substitute for the royal academies, the purpose was to combine theory and practice while improving the sciences and the arts so as to serve the Republic.[15] The new Class of Moral and Political Sciences was meant to perpetuate the values of the Enlightenment. It contained the Section of the Analysis of Sensations and Ideas and this is where the philosophers gathered. Besides developing a "science of ideas" based on physical movement and resistence, the "idéologues" also discussed political problems, so the purpose of suppressing the entire Class was plain: "political theory could not be tolerated in a state where politics was not" (Kennedy 104). The Tribunate and the Senate were purged of those who could have formed an open opposition (Cabanis, Daunou) in March 1802. Others, such as Destutt de Tracy who did disagree with the First Consul were only allowed to stay on for a few years because they kept quiet. What they wrote privately and would publish after Napoleon's fall was another matter, as Tracy's commentary of Montesquieu's work would show.

Madame de Staël was not allowed to live in Paris, and Chateaubriand was ordered to leave the capital in 1807 after comparing Napoleon with Nero in an article published in *Mercure de France*—the magazine was promptly closed down. It is surprising that the remark passed unnoticed by the censor because already in 1805 new restrictions had been placed on all printed matter. For example, book printers needed a licence and had to take an oath of loyalty (Lefebvre 2: 171).

---

[15] See Emmet Kennedy, *A Philosophe in the Age of Revolution: Destutt de Tracy and the Origins of "Ideology"* (Philadelphia: American Philosophical Society, 1978) 42-43.

An internal opposition was growing. Its members continued some of the debates of the late 1790s in the salons of Helvétius and Condorcet's widows, as well as Madame de Staël's, discussions which took place within the Institute and its periodical (*La Décade philosophique, politique et littéraire*). One of the chief topics was the role of the people and the location of sovereignty, the implication being the proper level at which power could be exercised legitimately. The "idéologues" seemed to react against Robespierre's equating the "people" with the least educated citizens, and also against his position, as Daunou expressed it, that "no one had the right to be wiser than the people" (qtd. in Hayward 35). Daunou was one of the authors of the 1795 Constitution, and in his opinion the solution was restricting popular control in general, and granting more power to an educated, enlightened and propertied elite. Such an attitude explains the ideologists' efforts towards educational reform, and also the crystallization of a social scientism advocated at this stage particularly by Cabanis, Condorcet's disciple, and developed by Saint-Simon and Comte.

In the context of shifting sovereignty and, implicitly, power moving away from the mass of people towards representative bodies and initiated elites, it was not difficult for the royalist exiles to use the momentum of the argument and place sovereignty even further away from the people. The émigré writers in *Mercure de France* had done this by invoking the principle of the divine right of the king and locating sovereignty within the monarchy. (It is not clear whether the principle was employed here in Bossuet's more absolutist sense or Bodin's slightly more circumscribed one.) Peltier tried to gather evidence from various quarters to prove that sovereignty should be vested in the king and, in addition, to argue for a hierarchy of forms of government which would support his thesis.

In 1806 one could read in *L'Ambigu* a substantial piece called "On Politics and Morality" ("Sur la Politique et la Morale" [12: 78-91]). Peltier was here in a philosophical mood and reflected on the increasing complexity of science and society. What struck him was that this complexity could be conveyed in an increasingly simple manner (12: 78-79). Peltier points out that an example of such concision is Rousseau's statement that governments start out as democratic, turn aristocratic, and finish as monarchies (12: 79). This is a real "formula" of political science, on a level with Newton's binomial theorem, Peltier argues. The journalist chooses to concentrate on the phrase "natural tendency" ("inclinaison naturelle") displayed by governments as they move from one stage to the next, and thinks that in the *Contrat social* Rousseau tried the impossible by attempting to reverse the normal order.

Peltier goes on to define politics and morality. Politics is a set of rules that guide governments' behaviour towards one another and towards their citizens. Morality guides people's behaviour towards one another (12: 81). Peltier sees a similarity here. The former deals with the "social body" ("corps social"), the latter with the individual—politics orders matters on the general level, morality on the particular one. The terms can change places as in an equation (12: 81-82). Peltier apologizes in a note for being so scientific, and thus being forced to break the rules of stylistic elegance.

Trying to simplify the issue, Peltier calls them "la grande morale" and "la petite morale" (12: 85). They may be similar but they are not identical. What works on one level may not do so on another level. Governments hold their power from God (Peltier supports his point here by referring to Rousseau's third stage, the monarchy, without referring to the expected authorities Bossuet and Bodin), and cannot stray from their duties in the name of a morality, which would be valid on the individual level. Thus, for instance, Peltier justifies capital punishment. As he sees it, the danger is that one term, politics with everything that it implies (duties, etc.) is re-defined and, consequently, the harmony in which politics and morality have developed up to that point is destroyed. Peltier prefers to interpret "the natural tendency" of governments to develop into monarchies as an irreversible development. One cannot do violence to the equation by altering parts of it, for instance changing the manner of governing in order to return from monarchy to democracy. This way of justifying the role of the monarchy, emphasizing in the process its incongruous presence in exile, differs from the defence of royalism developed by *Mercure de France*. As Peltier addresses directly political and moral issues, he avoids any reference to exile as such and sees himself as delivering a rational demonstration of a proper political development with its implicit moral dimension.

As mentioned above, the relations between Napoleon and the "idéologues" were not good. That included Destutt de Tracy who was allowed to keep his official position, although by 1806 he was less and less active in the Senate. He was concentrating on producing a commentary on Montesquieu's *Spirit of the Laws*. Destutt de Tracy was hardly thinking along Peltier's lines, but there was an attempt to explain things in terms of a hierarchy of forms of government based on their chronological development, somewhat in the way Peltier perceived Rousseau's statement.

About half way through his commentary, Destutt de Tracy sums up Montesquieu's first twelve books and what he himself has to say about them. On the principles of various governments and their consequences regarding laws, judgement and punishments (discussed in Book VI), the "idéologue" writes that his own conclusions are more generous.[16] His subsequent explanation is based on the progress of the human mind: the first forms of government are "democracy and despotism," a subsequent degree of civilization is characterized by an aristocratic form of leadership, while a further stage is reached by means of a representative form of government. Destutt de Tracy clarifies his point adding that force and ignorance reign during the first stage, then, as opinions begin to be shaped, religion dominates the second, and reason prevails during the last one.

The aim of the commentary at this point is to demonstrate that in the first two cases the laws are framed under the sign of revenge, while in the last case the purpose of the laws is to prevent the occurrence of evil. Even if he was not making speeches in the Senate, Tracy was constantly meeting people and was talking about his work. The émigrés were not unfamiliar with the intellectual debates in Paris and they may well have learned of, and referred to, the idea of the hierarchy sketched by Tracy where representation was placed above democracy. The exiles could interpret the concept of representation in various ways and narrow it to coincide with the monarchy.

---

[16] Destutt de Tracy, *Commentaire sur l'Esprit des Lois de Montesquieu* (Paris, 1819) 222-23.

It should again be added that in matters of morality Destutt de Tracy and Peltier did not see eye to eye. In an earlier brief essay (1798) reprinted in the same volume with the *Commentaire* the philosopher linked evil and ignorance and considered that the way to improve people morally was through education. Peltier saw the preservation of morality in terms of the sanctity of property and of the maintenance of the status quo. He did not see morality as something that could be improved, but as something given and, lately, in danger of deterioration.

In his own way, Destutt de Tracy was also in opposition. When commenting on Book XI he warned against giving too much power to one person (de Tracy 138-39). There was no question of bringing the book out in France. It was first printed in Philadelphia (1811), and in Paris only in 1819, after Napoleon's fall. The philosopher was marginalized by the Emperor who tried to block the spreading of his work. According to Destutt de Tracy, a good government should not prescribe the elementary books to be used in schools and should not increase the censors' powers to "protect what it thinks to be the truth."[17] Two years before writing these lines (1804) Napoleon's librarian, Barbier, had omitted Destutt de Tracy's *Éléments d'idéologie* from the catalogue of a model *lycée* library, although Barbier himself did not think it a bad book (Kennedy 138). Some of the tenets of liberalism seem to loom in the philosopher's manuscript of 1806 at a time when Benjamin Constant kept alive the debate about similar values. In the context of censorship and combating the "inequality of knowledge" by means of the free circulation of ideas, Destutt de Tracy writes that "when opinions are free, it is impossible that with time, truth will not emerge" (qtd. in Kennedy 175). Although both were Napoleon's adversaries, their outlook on essential questions of morals and politics diverged widely.

A Change of Tone

The references in *L'Ambigu* (7: 129, 131, 132) to restoring harmony in Europe and a "droit public de l'Europe" ("a European civil code") may have been a way of responding to Napoleon's perception of his own role

---

[17] Quoted from de Tracy's manuscript in Kennedy (175).

on a continental scale. It has been argued that by assuming the title of emperor instead of king, the French leader "implied something of European dimension" (Lefebvre 1: 207). The only emperor at the time had been both the heir to the throne of the Holy Roman Empire and the "theoretical head of Christendom" (Lefebvre 1: 207). The proclamation of a French emperor challenged such claims. It is possible that Peltier considered that his own arguments against Napoleon had to be pitched at the same level. The set of rights and concepts mentioned by the journalist should concern a European sphere, not only a national one.

Depending on whom people believed, Napoleon was either robbing other countries of their works of art, stamping out the local opposition and imposing French military rule, or was bringing in the ideals of the Revolution and gathering together the nations according to the universal goal of the previous century. Napoleon's "conception of a universal civilization" (Lefebvre 2: 253) was in contrast with the expanding contemporary ideas of the irreducible diversity and ultimate validity of national cultures, and therefore national entities. Peltier was among the critics who were intensely sceptical about the benefits of Napoleon's "universalism." The editor could choose to polarize the argument by resorting to ideas supplied by Romanticism and related currents of thought, or by invoking a European legal system and a balance of power tinged by pre-1789 values.

Where suitable, the Emperor's local difficulties were related by Peltier to the developing ideals of the period. Discussing the opposition encountered by the French forces in Spain during 1808, and the statements in which the Spaniards defied the invaders, the journalist argued that "the national conscience is all there, it inspires the censures and threats aimed at Napoleon" (22: 8). Further on, Peltiers wrote that such qualities helped nations to stand up to those who endangered their "physical and social existence" (22: 8, 10).

Peltier was quick to apply his own definition to the conflict in Spain. What was basically a defensive war against an invader, the first considerable resistance from irregular groups of fighters, is called by the journalist "the Spanish counter-revolution" (22: 11). This article from July 1808 must be one of the first press reports to mention the low-level war waged by irregular troops against an army, later known as "guerrilla."

The editor was trying already to subsume the latest events and the wider phenomenon emerging in Spain within his general chronicle offered periodically to the reader. Peltier's point of view prevented him from seeing any resistance against a non-monarchic France as anything else but a counter-revolution. A number of assumptions were somewhat inconsistently being made here: that Napoleon, earlier much cursed by Peltier for crowning himself as emperor, was in fact now a revolutionary, and that the attempt to place his brother on the Spanish throne was also a revolutionary act. The editor of *L'Ambigu* draws a veil over the liberal values emerging in Spain in connection with the War of Independence. Blanco White would start his own exile periodical in 1810 but there does not seem to have been any contact between the two émigrés.

In a discussion about the contrast between "politesse" and "civilisation" the journalist saw once more a number of changes, both superficial and fundamental on a European level (31: 489). The first term has to do rather with the development of arts, the second with good laws, the reader is told (31: 491). It is the legal system that ensures the quality of morality in a country. Peltier attempts to prove this by claiming that the difference between the two is that "the progress of the arts is relative, while the perfection of law is absolute" (31: 491). He adds that there can hardly be a question of progress in a field where there is no clear point of reference. The arts change rather than advance. In legal and constitutional matters progress can be observed because there is a decisive criterion to which people can refer: natural law (31: 491-92). From this "fixed point of departure" which is common to all people, are deduced "the secondary laws." These man-made laws, imposed in particular cases and in specific countries, these "positive laws," indicate the degree of improvement of a particular social order. This is how a people's degree of civilization can be established. Further on, Peltier links this legal (constitutional) process to morals as a means of judging the latter. By December 1810 when this article appeared it would have been obvious for an émigré reading his copy of *L'Ambigu* in London, or for a police official perusing the text in Paris to realize what the editor was driving at. The changes that had occurred in Europe over the past two decades had resulted in losses in the sphere of civilization and gains only in matters of "politesse" (31: 499). The method of persuasion by repetition is replaced here by an attempt at demonstrating the consequences of the Revolution and of Napoleon's rule by what seem to be philosophical and historical arguments. The connection between the "legal will" ("la volonté legale," for example, of property owners) and "moral force" is made once more two years later in connection with the rights of the Emperor and the rights of the Bourbons (38: 516). Peltier commented on these matters in September 1812 when Napoleon was about to enter Moscow and was waiting in vain for a sign from the Russians that would confirm his conquest. After Napoleon's setbacks in Spain and during what looked like a highly unwise venture in Russia, Peltier was drawing attention to the moral claims of the royalists by linking them to issues of legitimacy sanctioned by tradition. The Emperor was beginning to appear less than invincible and the chances of a monarchist restoration seemed that much more realistic.

Peltier offers yet again one of his syllogisms that would justify the restoration of the monarchy. He equates rights with moral capacity. Unless surrendered or transferred expressly, the individual cannot be deprived of either of them. The Bourbons have not surrendered or transferred their rights. Therefore, the Bourbons still possess them (38: 516). This piece of reasoning rests on the assumption that there is an earlier, permanent order, which cannot be questioned or modified. Peltier chooses to concentrate on the loss or preservation of (the monarch's) rights, and does not scrutinize how they have been acquired, apart from mentioning their divine origin.

Since 1807 the Count of Provence had settled in Britain putting an end to his wandering about the Continent. Napoleon's position was beginning to show signs of weakness, starting with his difficulties in Spain; the restoration of the monarchy in France seemed again a realistic proposition. Simply repeating the favourite royalist chronicle of facts and their significance was no longer enough. Evidence that seemed more respectable intellectually had to be provided and Peltier was doing his best. When the monarchy was indeed restored eighteen months after the article on rights and morality appeared, and the journalist returned to Paris after an absence of over twenty years to reap the rewards of his militant loyalty nothing was available for him. Back in London, with fresh reasons for bitterness, he went on editing *L'Ambigu* for another four years, this time including the French king among the targets of his sarcasm.

In the meanwhile, apart from Blanco's publication, a second Spanish exile periodical was being brought out in London. Even if the French monarchist and the Spanish "liberales" may have known of each other, no dialogue seems to have taken place. It is not surprising: while Peltier gathered arguments in favour of royal absolutism (although toned down and confused after being spurned in 1815), the Spaniards strained to put across a convincing case against absolutism. This shows again the difficulty of elaborating a theory valid for all exiles. In this case there are similarities when it comes to arguing against the guilt implied by being banished. Yet, the "liberales" would attempt to base their self-exculpation on different grounds.

Chapter 4

Self-imposed Exile: Blanco White and *El Español*

As many French émigrés were returning home, some to reinforce the Napoleonic administration, others just to find their bearings in a changed society, the Spanish refugees began to arrive in London. They were associated with liberal reforms and with opposition to the French invader and most of them had been driven into exile by the consequences of the military occupation of 1808 and by the monarchist reaction against the 1812 Constitution. Once in London, the Spanish exiles edited a number of periodicals, and I have chosen to discuss those dealing with politics and history. In addition there is a consensus that these were the main Spanish exile publications judging by their contents, contributors and impact at home (Cruz Seoane 2: 53-57, 110-12). *El Español* (1810-1814) was edited by José María Blanco White who is still quoted by modern historians who need a concise opinion about Spain at the time. *El Español Constitucional* (1818-1820, 1824-1825), and *Ocios de Españoles Emigrados* (1824-1827) contained the journalistic productions of the main "liberales" in London, and represented the two chief directions in which Spanish liberalism developed after 1814. The editors and contributors to these publications had been educated at a time and in a world where new ideas arrived with some difficulty in a country tentatively interested in economic reform, and not too keen for other sweeping changes.

This chapter contains a more detailed background to the period discussed here, while further information on the context is provided as the discussion of the Spanish periodicals proceeds. This preliminary section is followed by a presentation of Blanco White and his periodical. Unlike the other Spanish exiles, he fled before 1812 and therefore had the possibility and reasons to criticize the Cortes of the liberal Constitution. In analysing the contents of his magazine I have concentrated on this criticism as well as on his other political remarks, comparisons between the Spanish and the British political systems, and his gradual move towards Burke's ideas.

Encouraged by the Golden Age

The notions of the Enlightenment did reach Spain, but their impact was restricted. Anticlericalism and the fierce belief in reason were much less emphatic than, for instance, in France. The modifications that appeared to preoccupy the small educated groups were illustrated by the manner in which the Economic Societies were founded and by their aims: these Societies were approved by the government (with the exception of the Basque one), and they concentrated on promoting "popular industry."[1] The common feature of the reforms envisaged was utility. Any seeds of emancipation contained in these attempts at improvement would only develop several decades later.[2]

It is not clear to what extent the official encouragement of the Economic Societies was meant to counteract the possible impact of the latest ideas. The informal gatherings of educated people from which the Societies emerged debated subjects from physics to philosophy. Yet when the Societies took concrete form interest concentrated almost exclusively on useful sciences and solving practical problems. Their name ("Sociedades de Amigos del País") shows that their object was above all local and not universal emancipation. Generally, the Spanish Enlightenment did not

---

[1] R.J. Shafer, *The Economic Societies in the Spanish World* (N.p.: Syracuse UP, 1958) 11; 13 on aims; 48-52 on the authorities taking the initiative.

[2] Raymond Carr, *Spain: 1808-1939* (Oxford: Clarendon, 1966) 38.

possess the radical characteristics encountered elsewhere.[3] The attacks against scholasticism could find support, but even if there was a wish to reform the Church there was no sign of a general offensive against it. Atheism and materialism did not really make any inroads in Spain.[4] For historical reasons, mainly to do with the struggle against the Arabs and subsequent suspicion towards non-Christians, the Spanish Catholic Church had a stronger position vis-à-vis the authorities and a more influential one among the population than the Church in other Catholic countries. During the latter part of the eighteenth century any anti-clerical criticism was still directed against the spirit of the Counter-Reformation and not the Church as such (Abellán 3: 428).

The desire to improve agriculture and develop manufacturing had a patriotic undertone, possibly because of the state in which Spain found itself at the end of the eighteenth century. It had been a powerful empire, it had enjoyed a golden cultural era, and a lot of wealth had been brought over from its colonies. Most of that lay in the past. There was an acute sense of lagging behind the main European countries, of being treated as a secondary power.

A controversy during the 1780s indicated the degree of national sensitivity and suggested the chief issues characterizing the contemporary intellectual background. Charles Panckoucke, the wealthy Parisian publisher, decided to edit an even more comprehensive encyclopaedia than Diderot's, although perhaps not as critical.[5] Three hundred subscribers were found in Spain. The first volume on geography appeared in 1783 and contained a critical article on "Espagne" by a certain Nicolas Masson de Morvillers. The author decried the country's ignorance and idleness, its incompetent government and bigoted clergy whom he claimed to be, to a large extent, the cause of its backwardness. The text provoked a scandal in Madrid. Carlos III read it and demanded an apology from the publisher, censorship (grown slack of late) was revived, and a number of

---

[3] José Luis Abellán, *Historia crítica del pensamiento español.* 5 vols. (Madrid: Espasa-Calpe, S.A., 1979-91) 3: 484.

[4] Enrique Martínez Ruiz, Enrique Giménez, José Antonio Armillas, Consuelo Maqueda, *La España moderna* (Madrid: Istmo, 1992) 471.

[5] Richard Herr, *The Eighteenth-Century Revolution in Spain* (Princeton, NJ: Princeton UP, 1958) 220 ff.

Spanish authors replied belligerently to Masson. The authorities encouraged rebuttals of the infamous article, while the Spanish Academy offered a prize for the best defence of the nation's cultural and scientific progress.

A literary polemicist, Juan Pablo Forner, regarded Masson as a representative of the *philosophes* and attacked what he saw as the useless speculations of the modern age, rejecting in the heat of the argument the most recent scientific developments in Spain. The controversy went on in the Spanish periodicals as some of the local intellectuals dismissed Forner's criticism and defended the latest cultural and economic advances.

This debate showed that there were two ways in which the Spaniards regarded the contemporary difficulties and conceived the solutions. For some, Spain's former greatness was superior to the latest work of the fashionable *philosophes*, and therefore there was no need to pay attention to them. Others admitted the glorious past of the nation but argued that it had been followed by two centuries of decay and it was necessary to catch up with other states, which had been developing during that time.

The use of the past in debates on contemporary issues and priorities did not occur only in Spain. The invocation of medieval values, neglected during the centuries that had extolled classical values, was part of pre-Romanticism in Spain and elsewhere.[6] But due to the local social conditions this device acquired a particular significance in the absence of a counterbalancing element. For example, only a decade later in Britain the constitutional debate among the radical intellectuals would be conducted both in terms of historical precedent and of purely rationalistic natural-rights theory.[7] There was a surviving tradition from the sixteenth century of limiting the king's power by means of a constitution. The revival of interest in history in the earlier part of the century had resulted in the transformation of a committee compiling a "diccionario histórico-crítico" of Spain into the Royal Academy of History (Herr 337 ff).

---

[6] Ángel Valbuena Prat, *Historia de la literatura española*, 8th ed., 3 vols. (Barcelona: Gustavo Gili, 1968) 3: 116-17. For the revival of medieval themes in Spanish literature at the turn of the century and the following three decades, see E. Allison Peers, *A History of the Romantic Movement in Spain*, 2 vols. (Cambridge: Cambridge UP, 1940) 1: 123 ff.

[7] James A. Epstein, *Radical Expression: Political Language, Ritual, and Symbol in England, 1790-1850* (New York: Oxford UP, 1994) 4-5, 10.

Throughout the century an "enlightened" interpretation of history had been developed which linked the decline following Fernando and Isabella's death with the destruction of the medieval constitution, Spain's "proper form of government."[8]

Forner, for instance, wrote on the need to teach elements of the national constitution. Even if his essay remained unpublished at the time, his opinions were part of a two-century old tradition in Spain that blamed the decline of the country on the Habsburgs. The nationalistic undertone was accompanied by the idea that there were laws that even the monarch had to observe (Herr 344). One of the early Spanish writers on political theory, the Jesuit Juan de Mariana, had stated this point in 1609 deriving the king's authority from the consent of the citizens, a text where he also justified tyrannicide.[9] In the discussion leading to the 1812 Constitution the argument based on a mythical past would become increasingly evident.

The Masson controversy was taking place at the end of Carlos III's reign. Among the Bourbons who had taken over the Spanish throne after the Habsburgs as a consequence of the War of Succession, Carlos III (r. 1759-1788) showed more ability and interest in reforms than his predecessors. University education was one area that benefited from his attention. The Jesuits dominated teaching at all levels in Spain and their expulsion from the country in 1767 left a gap that facilitated a series of changes. Two years later the central authorities asked the universities to put forward new plans. The intention was to raise standards and to include new subjects, paying more attention to science and emphasizing its practical applications.[10] As part of these reforms the Council of Castile, one of the country's chief governing institutions, organized a competition for the best textbook on philosophy to include specifically the ideas of Descartes, Malebranche and Leibniz. The winner was a Capuchin friar whose compilation became compulsory at those universities not using the equally accepted *Institutiones philosophicae* by the mathematician and physicist François Jacquier (Herr 169-70). The modified syllabus meant

---

[8] Herr 341. See also Carr (74).

[9] Bernice Hamilton, *Political Thought in Sixteenth-Century Spain* (Oxford: Clarendon, 1963) 9, 41-42.

[10] John Lynch, *Bourbon Spain: 1700-1808* (Oxford: Blackwell, 1989) 285.

that scholasticism was losing ground, while modern science, helped by new chairs in mathematics and physics, received increased attention. Besides, the teaching of Natural Law was introduced in order to diminish the influence of the canon lawyers (Carr 76).

The efforts at modernization decreased during the rule of Carlos IV (r. 1788-1808), a mediocre character compared to his predecessor, and as the reaction to the French Revolution resulted in various restrictions. The aim of the monarchy was to prevent the spread of ideas from France. Customs officials watched out for French periodicals, the censorship of the internal press intensified and non-governmental journals were closed down. But as French publications kept being smuggled into Spain, representatives of the Inquisition were attached to the customs in order to check more carefully the printed matter (Lynch 378-79). On the whole, it was a question of keeping people in ignorance by means of total silence, rather than of engaging in debates against the Revolution: in 1796 the Spanish Inquisition forbade the translation of Burke's *Reflections on the Revolution in France* simply in order to prevent any talk about the event even if the writer condemned it (Herr 297-98).

Not that the masses appeared very interested. The Spaniards' religiosity and monarchism fanned from the pulpit did not constitute fertile ground for the few militant ideas that trickled down from the north. France's declaration of war against Spain added the fervour of nationalism to the earlier resentment against France and its unsettling development (Lynch 380, 389).

There were tensions within the Church between traditionalists and a few daring clergymen. Yet the latter only wanted to bring the institution somewhat up-to-date, for example on censorship.[11] This conflict took shape due to the wider one between the regalists (a term used by historians writing in English) and the clergy, a conflict, which encompassed issues of power and property. The secular authorities resented the papal jurisdiction over questions such as marriage, and were willing to pursue a programme of reforms. Pressed by financial needs, the government looked to Church property for a quick solution (Lynch 401). But the

---

[11] William J. Callahan, *Church, Politics, and Society in Spain: 1750-1874* (Cambridge, MA: Harvard UP, 1984) 82.

economic difficulties were not much attenuated by the massive sales of Church land between 1798 and 1808. The social tensions were not lessened either when it turned out that most of the purchasers were powerful landowners and not modest farmers as, somehow, had been expected (Lynch 416). However, in their conflict with the Church the secular forces had strengthened their position. This dispute meant also that foreign events were exploited according to need. For instance, a French radical measure against the Old Regime such as the Civil Constitution of the Clergy (1790) was re-cast in terms of the local dispute: the crown supporters opposed to the economic, educational domination of the Church saw it as a "piece of thoroughgoing regalism" (Carr 69). Thus the test of the French clergy's loyalty to the revolutionary regime in Paris was wilfully misunderstood and reinterpreted in Madrid for use in the local ongoing controversy.

It has been argued that Carlos III's regalism, and to some extent Carlos IV's, left a decisive legacy to liberalism (Carr 61, 68-69). In several incidents during the 1790s the liberals referred to regalist principles while the traditionalists invoked the privileges of the Church (Lynch 402). During this decade most liberal deputies of the assembly, which proclaimed the 1812 Constitution were still at university learning that reforms presupposed cooperation only with the enlightened clergy (Callahan 96).

But a decade earlier, there had already been a group who had rejected both Church and monarchy, however reformist the latter tried to be (Lynch 261). Out of this group emerged the liberals who wanted to go beyond the reforms of Carlos III and his officials. They had in mind more fundamental changes and did have their say in 1812.[12] Despite all the economic and social problems it was foreign politics that brought matters to a crisis.

---

[12] Some historians see a continuous line from Carlos III's reformist administrators to the later, comparatively radical liberals: "there is no practical reform of the nineteenth century, no reforming attitude of mind, that cannot be traced back to one of the servants of Charles III" (Carr 61). This quote is mentioned approvingly by Adrian Shubert in his *Social History of Modern Spain* (London: Unwin Hyman, 1990) 170. Shubert quotes a later edition.

The rise of Godoy, the royal favourite, was watched with hostility by a number of courtiers and politicians who formed a faction round the heir to the throne, the future Fernando VII. The 1807 treaty between Spain and France was aimed at the joint conquest of Portugal to complete the continental blockade against Britain. Godoy, now chief minister, encouraged this strategy with an eye to his personal interest (Lynch 406). Godoy's and the rival factions were at daggers drawn, and Napoleon who was in touch with both decided to rely on neither. The French troops on their way to Portugal were dispersing about Spain instead of heading straight for their destination. A riot in March 1808 resulted in Godoy's fall from power, Carlos IV abdicated in favour of his son, and Fernando VII entered Madrid triumphantly. A month later Napoleon replaced Fernando with his brother, Joseph Bonaparte. Carlos and his son realized that they were practically being kept hostage in France, while the rest of the Spaniards discovered that most of their country had been invaded.

Spain was more difficult to occupy and control in its entirety than Napoleon had thought. During the War of Independence (1808-1814) the French were constantly harrassed by small irregular armed groups beginning the modern tradition of guerilla fighting. Meanwhile, the regular troops, helped by the British forces, engaged the invaders in more traditional warfare. All this time the authorities were made up of local assemblies ("juntas provinciales") with a lot of autonomy and a central council ("Junta Central") without too much power at the initial stage. The need for unity strengthened the case for a national assembly ("Cortes") causing a debate on the fundamental conditions of political life that Spain had known.[13]

Under the difficult circumstances of war, a complicated system of voting resulted in an assembly, which met at Cádiz, in unoccupied territory, to draft a constitution. The "Cortes" was dominated by reformists whose ideas had their origin in the radicalism of the 1790s. One of the principles that guided the deputies gathered in September 1810 was the sovereignty of the people. The debates leading up to the final text were influenced by Montesquieu, by the standard discussions of natural law in

---

[13] Carr 93. See also 94-97 for the background to the debates on the constitution.

the eighteenth century, by the recent reformist attempts in Spain, and by Bentham's work. There were also references to the ancient constitution of Spain, but mainly by way of making the new one acceptable to the conservatives.

The Constitution was issued in March 1812, as Wellington was successfully fighting along the Spanish army against the French, and as Joseph left Madrid. The French troops withdrew the following year. This Constitution was directed against regional, guild, ecclesiastical and aristocratic privileges, taking further the work of Carlos III's modernizers, but now couched in different terms: "civil equality, personal liberty, the rights of property, and freedom of contract" (Carr 98). However, the document would hardly be tested in practice.

Fernando VII had promised to respect the new Constitution, but on his return to a liberated Spain promptly abolished it. Once in Madrid, the king's brief doubts as to his course of action concerning the liberals were dispelled by the evidence of military support and by the petition of a group of deputies who condemned the 1812 Constitution: several prominent liberals to whose cooperation the new king partly owed his return to power were imprisoned. The Cortes building was sacked by groups of citizens who found themselves in agreement with the king, with the military, and with the conservative deputies. There were similarities between this coup d'état and that of 1808, the same elements were involved: "Ferdinand, the army, the mob" (Carr 119).

Clergyman and Journalist

By the end of the eighteenth century Seville had become an intellectual centre where the study of the humanities claimed a tradition of several centuries (Valbuena Prat 3: 110). In 1793 a few students and teachers at the University set up a cultural society regarded at the time as the most significant undergraduate activity.[14] The aim was more literary than political, but any academic unofficial initiative could have aroused suspicion even if, lately, the subversive tendencies in the academic world seemed to have faded away.

---

[14] Herr 362. See also *Iglesia. Pensamiento. Cultura* (Madrid: Alianza Editorial, 1988) 453. Vol. 3 of *Enciclopedia de Historia de España* (1988-93).

One of the students was José María Blanco y Crespo (1775-1841). He was ordained in 1800, served for a while in a newly opened Pestalozzian school in Madrid. This was a military college trying to function according to recent pedagogical advances. After the French invasion Blanco moved to Seville where as co-editor of a periodical he was in charge of the political section. This magazine had been started by the poet Manuel José Quintana who was also a secretary of the Junta Central. The council wanted to transform the periodical into its own organ, but Blanco refused, saying that he "would not serve as an instrument for deceiving the people."[15] He criticized the re-establishment of known royalist representatives in the Cortes.[16] Despite threats that the magazine would be silenced, Blanco went on attacking the authorities for being afraid of summoning the Cortes. The periodical was closed down in 1809. It has been suggested that one of the consequences of the clerical conflict between traditionalists and reformers was the emergence of a radical type of clergyman, an unusual character in Spain earlier on (Lynch 401). It may be argued that Blanco can be placed in this category.

The following year Blanco fled to England and slightly modified his name to Blanco White. One of his grandfathers was Irish and he was familiar with the English language. While still in Spain he had been appointed to draw up a report on a possible constitution and he carried on his interest in the matter in a periodical launched in London. It was partly distributed by the British government "which, however, did not dictate [Blanco's] politics."[17] His growing doubts about Roman Catholicism determined him to qualify as an Anglican clergyman after studying theology at Oxford, but during his last years he abandoned Anglicanism and joined the Unitarians.

The first number of the monthly *El Español* appeared in April 1810. The editor had in mind a Spanish readership as he explained later in his

---

[15] Raquel Asún Escartín, "Blanco White, José María," in *Diccionario biográfico*. Vol. 4 of *Enciclopedia de Historia de España*.

[16] Albert Dérozier, *Manuel Josef Quintana et la naissance du libéralisme en Espagne*, 2 vols. (Paris: Les belles lettres, 1968-70) 1: 494.

[17] "White, Joseph Blanco," in *Dictionary of National Biography*, 1st ed. (1885-1903). See also *Diccionario biográfico* and Ramón Ezquerra, "Blanco-White Crespo, José María," in *Diccionario de Historia de España*, 2nd ed. (1986).

autobiography: "I continued the periodical work *El Español* till the return of Ferdinand VII to Madrid in May 1814. But when Ferdinand had abolished the Constitution of the Cortes, and subjected the country to his despotic government, the introduction of my work became impossible; and I stopped it."[18] Clearly, Blanco saw his magazine as a contribution to a continuous debate and not as an isolated voice trying to keep alive a set of principles. By his own account, *El Español* gained influence and circulated in Spain. The British ambassador at Cádiz knew it and was asking for copies (Thom, ed. 1: 191, 202, 205-206). Blanco's critical articles made him unpopular in more than one quarter back home. The anti-French material displeased the invaders, while his analyses of the Spanish authorities' policies were sufficiently noticed by them in their temporary headquarters at Cádiz to consider it worthwhile slandering *El Español* later on.

The periodical had a series of concerns up to 1812 (elections, the role of a National Assembly, parliamentary procedure, the nature of the 1808 events) and, predictably, other preoccupations after 1812 (mainly questions raised by the Constitution). The presentation and discussion of the articles here will have to be chronological rather than thematic since, more often than not, Blanco's ideas are connected with topical events. Once more, to follow every twist and turn of dozens of articles over several years would be unreasonable and fruitless. I have selected those pieces that offer some evidence of the editor's political thought and its moral assumptions.

In the "Prospectus" of the first number Blanco declared that the chief aim of his periodical was to oppose the injustice of Napoleon and spread "en la opinión pública las máximas que hacen aborrecible todo género de tiranía."[19] The arguments against Napoleon would be provided by the

---

[18] John Hamilton Thom, ed., *The Life of the Rev. Joseph Blanco White, written by himself; with portions of his correspondence.* 2 vols. (London: 1845) 1: 273. Blanco White also edited what could be considered a light magazine called *Variedades* (London, 1824-25) which contained miscellaneous writing. Unlike *El Español*, it published a lot of illustrations and virtually only literary and fashion articles. The target area was "Spanish America," not among the subjects of the present discussion for reason of space.

[19] "… among the public opinion the maxims that would show the hatefulness of all kinds of tyranny" (*El Español* 30 April 1810: 2). The volumes are not numbered consis-

very principles that determined the French to start their Revolution. Blanco promised to wage a "guerra de opinión" in order to stop the military advances of the French.[20] Twelve years earlier this had also been Mallet's purpose. But in 1798 Bonaparte could appear as an invincible liberator spreading revolutionary ideas and Mallet intended to dispel this image among those who admired or feared the general. The appeal to those who held and expressed thoughts on the matter was made by Mallet from the point of view of a moderate monarchist invoking the value of tradition and Continental peace agreements. By 1810 Napoleon was an absolute ruler bent on military expansion and Blanco's own campaign proceeded from a more radical perspective. While the war was going on in Spain, he saw himself as waging a war by other than military means; his was a frontal attack against tyranny by spreading the "máximas" which directly opposed it. In the light of this contrast, what the two exile editors meant by "opinion" differed only slightly: both hoped to influence an educated readership, but while Mallet tried to change mistaken perceptions, Blanco attempted to undermine tyranny by the sheer force of argument.

In this introductory piece there is an indirect explanation of Blanco's flight from Spain. In his political articles published in the periodical he had co-edited at home, he had been forced by an "ignorant and suspicious" government to be over-cautious until he had to stop writing altogether (30 April 1810: 2). From the only free nation in Europe, as he called Britain, Blanco hoped "sino instruir, al menos excitar á sus paysanos al estudio y conocimiento de los principios en que está cifrada la esperanza de una libertad futura." The "Prospectus" concludes with details about the monthly appearance of the magazine and the contents:

---

tently, and beginning with January 1813 the separate issues are only dated, not numbered. The references here are to the date and page.

[20] On the point that this conflict was just as much a propaganda war see Jean-René Aymer, "Un épisode de la guerre d'Indépendence (1808-1814): le moine Concha entre la Résistance et l'afrancesamiento'" in *Recherches sur le monde Hispanique au dix-neuvième siècle* (Lille: Éditions Universitaires, 1973) 20: "[Concha] a saisi que la Guerre d'Indépendence est une guerre d'opinion, une guerre civile: c'est cet aspect qui retient son attention. Tout comme les chefs insurgés et les autorités imperiales, il croit aux vertus de la propagande écrite."

there would be sections on politics, literature and the foreign press but the literary section may occasionally be left out.

In "General Reflections on the Spanish Revolution" the concern is still with the nature of the 1808 events.[21] Blanco doubted that what happened then could be called a revolution. For him such a phenomenon presupposed people's awareness of their unhappiness, concern with their rights (or lack thereof), and a common set of opinions (30 April 1810: 7). This was not the case in Spain, despite the need for change. Blanco distinguished between radical changes triggered off by external events and by internal ones. A genuine revolution occurs as a result of internal causes, according to him, not as a consequence of a foreign invasion.

Blanco suggested here two rather incompatible solutions in order to save Spain: either a true revolution or an outstanding leader (30 April 1810: 24-25). These solutions seem to belong to different political approaches. Their juxtaposition may betray his confusion or simply his indifference to methods as long as the country was "saved." Despite his approval of the British political system, he still tended to think in terms of a country where one person could make a massive difference. Some sympathy shown towards the French Revolution in a note, nevertheless, indicated the alternative he preferred. Yet any revolution would be impossible because of the "Juntas Provinciales," these local councils being the chief targets of his criticism at this time. In his opinion they were put together by self-seeking local notables who blocked the way for talented and patriotic representatives of the people. The setting-up of the Junta of Seville, a case personally known to the journalist, served here as decisive evidence. One of Blanco's main reproaches was that the members of this Junta had not consulted the people's intentions (30 April 1810: 17). "Junta Central" was not spared either in his discussion. The standard contemporary nostalgic reference to the old Cortes was used here as well. Soon, other Spanish exiles would refer to the ancient, supposedly fair constitution whose return would remedy numerous evils. In this article the return of the ancient assembly would be the only way to op-

---

[21] "Reflexiónes generales: sobre la Revolución española" (30 April 1810: 5-27). The initials B.W. appear in a parenthesis below the title, and a note explains that the articles thus signed are written by the editor, the others are signed by the contributor or marked "artículo comunicado."

pose the rise and the arbitrary power of royal favourites (30 April 1810: 10).

Judging by these early articles, Blanco's way of opening his journalistic campaign clarified a little his position and, therefore, his point of view. On the face of it, he had left Spain because of the French military advance towards Cádiz. Moreover, when he stated the aims of his publication he placed first his opposition to the French invasion. Yet, his very first article dealt with the perception of the 1808 coup, and the dangers presented by the local councils as well as the central one. His harsh criticism and the subsequent attempt of the Cortes to discredit *El Español* indicate that Blanco's relationship with the authorities was not of the best. His flight was not only prompted by the dangers of a foreign invasion but probably also by the internal political difficulties. Indeed, some of the developments at home seemed quite worrying. When he mentioned the actions of the "Junta Central" Blanco referred to the "tribunales de policía que formaron los centrales para su defensa."[22] These courts established by the central authorities looked sufficiently intimidating to make people afraid of them and to utter their objections surreptitiously (30 April 1810: 24).

Blanco explored contemporary controversial concepts in further articles where the "representatives of the king" and the quality of "independence" were examined from a Spanish American point of view (30 Aug. 1810: 369-77). The assertion that interim governments represent the monarch in his enforced absence gave Blanco the opportunity to discuss the origin and nature of representation. True to the ideals enshrined in the early documents of the French Revolution, his assumption was that ultimately power resides in the people. Consequently, the representativeness of a national council was granted by the people who in the king's absence "repossess their rights" ("el pueblo reasume sus derechos" [30 Aug. 1810: 372]). These rights include sovereignty, and the people, or peoples (various groups in Spanish America), would be entitled to claim it. It follows that the "americanos" have a legitimate right to

---

[22] "… courts constituting the instruments of its defense" (30 April 1810: 24).

their independence.[23] Further, when the people regain their rights, in this case their sovereignty, the rule of the monarchy ceases to extend over the colonies despite the oath of fidelity sworn on a previous occasion. The "liberales" in exile would develop the idea of representation somewhat differently when a restored despotic monarchy silenced any debate in the country.

Blanco's criticism of the Junta Central, and then of the Cortes, was not delivered in a spirit of relentless hostility; he also intended to help their members by offering them the latest ideas on the way such assemblies work. His intention of translating one of Bentham's texts on this point was mentioned in an early article (30 Sept. 1810: 430-37). In a discussion with Étienne Dumont, the Genevan who edited and translated Bentham's works into French, Blanco learned of an unpublished manuscript on which he intended to make a series of comments. But, first, the reader got Dumont's account of the manuscript that contained sketchy passages expanded by the Swiss editor.

The main subject of *Tactique des assemblées politiques* is parliamentary procedure. The internal rules of the British Parliament were held up by Dumont (in Blanco's report) as an example and as the decisive way of maintaining and increasing the country's national liberty (434). The absence of such regulations, as the contrast with the French General Estates showed, led to weakness and, possibly, to the disintegration of the representative body. Rehearsing a familiar argument, Dumont underlined the view that the British system was pragmatic and not theoretical, having acquired its strength and coherence gradually, as a result of experience (433).

When Blanco takes over this line of the argument, he quotes Bentham approvingly on the composition of an assembly, hinting at what he himself considers to be the relevant human qualities under these circumstances. The formation and guidance of such an assembly is an art. The contribution of the moral force of each individual gathered together shapes "un resultado completo del saber y la opinión de todos."[24] By

---

[23] Blanco White's attitude towards the colonies made him popular overseas, and he was praised by Bolívar, see Blanco's entry in *Diccionario de Historia de España*.

[24] "... a comprehensive outcome of everybody's knowledge and opinions" (30 Sept. 1810: 431).

"everybody" Blanco probably means all the deputies, not every citizen, in which case fairness of representation is crucial. Blanco draws a comparison between such an assembly and an army where the disciplined physical force of the soldiers amounts to more than the sum of the individuals. The importance of a result based on all opinions becomes even more significant later when Blanco worries about the divisive effect of the incipient political parties.

The interpretation of the 1808 upheaval offered by Blanco in the first issue is followed up by an almost anonymous "D.F.M. de la R."[25] This argument followed one of the traditions established during the previous century, namely that Spain started to decay in the sixteenth century. The author discerned a glimmer of hope only in March 1808. The initial support given to Joseph Bonaparte by some people ("afrancesados") could be explained by the honesty and innocence of the Spaniards who, according to this explanation, were ignorant of the events on the continent. The pro-French group had a distorted image of the situation because they received their news from the French periodicals, which gave the impression that the kind of justice they were told triumphed during the Revolution still obtained in France (30 Oct. 1810: 30-31). People were misled by Napoleon's propaganda. To a large extent, France's expansion was due to "la manera insidiosa con que ha corrompido la opinión de los pueblos" by creating dissensions, destroying their patriotism and making false promises about reforms and happiness.[26] El Español was carrying on here its "guerra de opinión" by pointing out Napoleon's successes in this very field. The matter was stated rather bluntly. By the end of the decade, with a good deal of the Continent under French control there was no need to worry any longer about dispelling the illusions of Napoleon's admirers. The fact that the conflict was not only carried on the battlefield is stressed in a subsequent article by "M. de la R." where he gives an example of the French propagandistic efforts: the invader even tampered

---

[25] 30 Oct. 1810: 27-40. The author is probably "Don Francisco Martínez de la Rosa" (1787-1862), professor of philosophy, novelist and prime minister. On de la Rosa contributing to El Español see the entry on the periodical in Diccionario temático, vol. 5 of Enciclopedia de Historia de España.

[26] "... the malicious way in which it has corrupted the beliefs of various nations" (30 Oct. 1810: 31).

with the language, changing the names of things "por que no queden ni aun vestigios de la antigua monarquía española."[27]

There is more than a hint that "D.F.M. de la R." had been among those taken in by the ideals skilfully deployed by the French propaganda: "Quál fué nuestra amargura, quál nuestra indignación, quando disipadas las dudas, escuchamos amenazar como conquistador al que abrimos los brazos como amigo ..."[28] Some of those dismayed by Napoleon's imposition of Joseph on the Spanish throne had in fact supported the French invasion. The degree of their disappointment only reflected the level of their expectations. These expectations concerned both the situation in France (in reality less just and proper than the faded Revolution would have warranted), and the role of France in bringing Spain closer to the advanced countries in Europe. One of the dominant recent topics in Spain—actual backwardness and necessary modernization—allowed some groups to see the solution in a foreign intervention. "M. de la R." performed here a kind of *mea culpa* as he fumed against the turn of events.

In the sequel to this article the author argued that the Central Council's claim that it was necessary to concentrate power in order to exercise it properly, and the subsequent creation of a Supreme Government raised and then dashed the hopes that a free exchange of ideas would become possible (30 Nov. 1810: 92-93). This was a lost opportunity. Allowing open debates would have helped the government's reforming work. Such exchanges had never been possible under the earlier tyrannical rule. The learned (or the intellectuals, "sabios") had a clear role here: to "spread sound ideas" ("disfundir las sanas ideas" [93]) in order to combat the deadly routine that hindered the authorities' initiatives. But the government did not seem to be keen on new legislation that would create favourable conditions for open debates. As in the case of the French constitutional monarchists, the model suggested by this exile periodical was that of "las leyes inglesas" (93). The only achievement of

[27] "... in order to erase any traces of the ancient Spanish monarchy" (30 Nov. 1810: 102).

[28] "Imagine our bitterness, our indignation, when, once our doubts were dispelled, we heard the friend whom we received with open arms threatening as a conqueror" (30 Oct. 1810: 32).

the French Revolution worth deriving inspiration from was the 1791 Constitution (101).

"M. de la R." agreed with the editor that one of the chief errors was not electing and calling a National Assembly after the early victories against the French in Galicia. This would have increased the people's participation in the governing the country and familiarized them with political matters (107). Summoning the Assembly would also have served a defensive purpose as "la valla mas fuerte contra los enemigos, el único apoyo de nuestra libertad política y civil."[29] These series of suggestions were made during a period when *El Español* still thought that political changes could be introduced as soon as the war was over. The tone is one of robust criticism but assuming the possibility of a dialogue. The vituperations of the earlier French émigré journalists, or the later massive condemnation of absolutism by the Spanish exiles is absent at this stage of Blanco's activity, hence his reluctance to consider himself a political émigré as such. His worries about the chances of an open debate, however, would soon be justified.

The Spanish Government's decreee on the freedom of the press reprinted by *El Español* in December 1810 (217-19) was remarkable above all by the creation of a "Junta Suprema de Censura" consisting of nine censors (219). In his commentary on the implications of this new measure, Blanco concentrated on the vagueness of the transgressions that a writer, an editor or a printer could be guilty of. The lack of precision as to what may constitute a crime could only be used by a commission so close to the Central Council to control and block uncomfortable opinions; the decisions would be bound to be arbitrary, what may seem only critical to some, may appear libellous to the censors (221). Blanco argued that the nine censors should be appointed (actually, elected) by the people, not by the Central Council. Since not every transgression could be spelled out, the advantage of having a number of persons chosen by the people would be that they could function as a jury whose verdict would reflect the reaction of the general public (223-24). Abolishing censorship altogether did not seem to have been an option for Blanco White.

---

[29] "… the strongest barrier against the enemy, the only support to our political and civil liberty" (30 Nov. 1810: 108).

The editor granted the readers the right to define the norm. It would have been a norm established by the "people" but, practically, by those who presumably had access to periodicals, books and possessed the education and leisure to discuss topical issues and indicate some sort of general consensus. The British tradition of trial by jury with all its assumptions of fairness seems to be extended by Blanco to the cultural sphere. He contrasted the influence of power, the proximity of which may corrupt and put pressure on the appointed censors, with the influence of the people, which would improve constantly the performance of an elected jury (225-26). Ideally, Blanco went on, judges should be changed every three years. The expectation of being familiar with complicated matters would thus be satisfactorily met. Finally, Blanco questioned the required presence of clergymen among the appointed censors; this was an unexpected objection from someone who was still an ordained Catholic priest, but it was not so surprising in view of his religious doubts.

The Impact

In November 1810 the Spanish Government banned the circulation of *El Español* in the colonies. The reason given in the decree was that the editor had been publishing subversive material (28 Feb. 1811: 341-42). Blanco reprinted the decree and explained his position. He rejected the accusation that while still in Spain he had been flattering the royal favourite Manuel Godoy, clarified the circumstances in which he fled the country, and invited anyone to examine the back numbers of the magazine and see that in fact he had not been critical of the Regency. It looks as if, instead of confronting the authorities, he was trying to defend himself by arguing that he had behaved well. A charitable explanation may be that the excessive attention he paid to accuracy may appear as a submissive attitude. He may have intended to make a fine distinction between criticizing a certain course of action, and not questioning the governing institutions as such. Blanco pointed out that his periodical was banned only overseas, not in Spain itself, and that the decree was published in *Gazeta de México* not in a Spanish periodical. The conclusion can only be that the Government was angered by his arguments in favour of independence for the Spanish colonies.

In the official announcement the authorities referred to Blanco as a "refugiado" in what was meant to be a disparaging manner. The editor, defensive and irritated, pointed out that he had left Madrid because of the French advance, and once in Cádiz, where the Central Council had found shelter, he was not willing to flatter anyone in order to get a job. Blanco made the curious point that he did not flee the laws which he had respected (28 Feb. 1811: 349), implying that it was rather certain individuals and the helplessness of the situation that determined him to leave the country. Blanco seemed to waver when it came to his status as a political refugee, although time and again he was clashing with the authorities. One tentative explanation may be provided by his ambivalent attitude towards Spain: despite the praise lavished on its many qualities in the articles about the French invasion, his tone in *Letters from Spain* where he described Spanish society is sometimes savagely satirical and even sneering.[30] Although he had numerous objections to its political system, it might be argued that he was fleeing a mentality (and a religion) just as much as an unpleasant government. It may also be assumed that he knew himself to be different from the other Spanish émigrés in so far as he did not intend to return and lacked their militancy and concern. The way he steeped himself in the English language and turned to Anglicanism suggests that he distanced himself culturally from his home country, in time dismissing its politics as well.

An attempt to discredit *El Español* by means of a forged letter from Spain resulted in a debate in the Cortes. From the extracts published in the periodical it appeared that in speech after speech the deputies showed their disapproval of the magazine and its editor for being subversive and unpatriotic (30 July 1811: 268-70). The assembly decided to submit one of the issues of the periodical to the censor to decide whether to allow its circulation in Spain. Blanco answered that after such fulminations in the Cortes the censor's decision could be easily predicted remembering also the recent reorganization of that office. Further, the editor rejected the accusations of lack of patriotism, intriguingly enough, and, ironically, connected the campaign against his paper with the recent

---

[30] Don Leucadio Doblado [J. Blanco White], *Letters from Spain* (London, 1825) passim.

decree on the freedom of the press. This exchange is significant mainly for the importance of this periodical in Spain. The ban on its circulation in the colonies seemed to have been only a first step. The further efforts of the Cortes to condemn a magazine edited in London suggest that *El Español* had a readership and influence of its own at home.

Scrutinizing the Constitution

After a couple of years in Britain Blanco began to have doubts about the Spanish people's readiness to accept radical changes. He commented on the unreasonable expectations of the *liberales* that the citizens should embrace the principle of "people's sovereignty" (30 Nov. 1811: 147-49). His point was that for centuries the Spaniards had grown accustomed to a very different idea of the place of sovereignty, and to expect them to grasp and accept the new concept would be just as dogmatic as the claims made by "los partidos religiosos más fanáticos" (148). Bearing in mind Blanco's views on the idea of publications being examined by a people's elected jury, it may be safely assumed that he was not against people acquiring sovereignty, in due course. The danger perceived by him was the ease with which "una proposición abstracta" (a category which for him contained both "el Misterio de la Concepción" and "la soberanía del pueblo") could be manipulated in order to create faithful followers (148). It is at this stage that a departure from his early opinions can be noticed. Only a few years earlier Blanco had criticized a possible return of royalist representatives to a wider assembly. The implication of his criticism at the time were that sovereignty should be relocated. Now, as the Cádiz assembly was working on this very issue his scepticism begins to emerge.

In March 1812 the Cortes published the new Constitution. The main model was the French one of 1791. Sovereignty was vested in the nation, legislation would be shaped by the assembly together with the king who had a semblance of a veto, but whom in the event the deputies could overrule. Some privileges were abolished and the rights of property were carefully re-codified. In contrast with the French text, a different note was sounded in the section on religion where it was stated that Roman Catholicism would be the only religion allowed in Spain.

Blanco had entertained hopes for a new constitution, but one inspired by the English example where precedent and experience were the basic criteria.[31] He did not explain how this could be done when drafting a new document, but this idea was repeated in a critical commentary where he expressed his worries that the document sounded so definitive (30 May 1812: 76 ff). Blanco would have welcomed a trial period of a few years followed by changes according to the citizens' suggestions. He was also troubled by the intolerant paragraph on the country's religion. But the most serious weakness of the text and a threat to its very existence was the way it defined the king's position. Blanco drew a comparison with Sweden where a similar attempt ended with the king suspending the Constitution.[32] In his writings Blanco White sounds like a royalist, albeit not a keen one, but what he fears is the unpredictable reaction of a re-stored monarch who would realize how his role had been defined in his absence. (Declaring Spain a republic does not seem to have been dis-cussed at Cádiz.) His fears were going to prove true.

The argument concerning these dangers was further developed in connection with the separation of powers codified by the new Constitu-tion. The intention was fine in theory, but it could not be achieved in practice, Blanco argued, and considered it as a "scholastic distinction" (30 June 1812: 120). The restraints placed on the executive power (the king) did not bode well and the much-employed contrast between this "división metafísica" and the English solution based on "sabiduría prác-tica" was invoked again (120). In the latter case the root of despotism was destroyed by reducing the power of the monarchy while allowing the king to share in the process of law making. In addition, the pragmatism of the journalist resented talk of principles of individual freedom as long as the practical safety of the individual vis-à-vis the authorities had still not been achieved. A basic objection to the Constitution, linked to the earlier point, was that it granted "unlimited power to the Cortes" (30

---

[31] *Letters from Spain* 30. Whether these letters published in the *Monthly Review* were drafted when dated (round 1800) or when published, the many verifiable autobio-graphical details suggest that Blanco's opinions on a new constitution precede 1812.

[32] 30 May 1812: 79. Blanco's observation on the Cortes' lack of foresight is still con-sidered relevant enough to be mentioned in a standard history of the period, see Carr (97). The Swedish king in question was Gustav III.

Nov. 1812: 484). All would have been well if the assembly had been a proper representative of the people, but Blanco was not convinced this was the case.

There is no question that Blanco idealized the English legal and political system when for instance, he talked about the popularity of the British judges who "han sido objetos de temor para los tiranos, y de casi adoración para el pueblo" as opposed to the antipathy such officials encountered in Spain.[33] Matters were less wonderful than that in Britain even if its legal system could be favourably compared with the Spanish one. The tendency to idealize things in the host country after long admiration from a distance and a traumatic flight is present in some, although far from all, émigrés. When it does happen it is of interest to see what elements are idealized. The Habeas Corpus Act praised by Blanco was briefly suspended in the late 1790s, and would be again a few years after this article was written. Yet, by invoking this law and the incorruptibility and esteem in which the judges were presumed to be held in Britain, Blanco indicates what aspects of the legal and political life he values and imagines as being constantly present in his place of exile.

Taking Stock

In an article called "Variaciónes Políticas del *Español*" from January 1813 Blanco White reflected on his own development and his writings since he had left Spain. He was aware that the reader might have noticed contradictions in his articles over the years. He pointed himself to the change that may have puzzled the readers: "¿Quien que se acuerde de mis elogios al decreto de la *Soberanía del Pueblo*, podra avenirlos con mi censura de la nueva constitución Española?"[34] Blanco further considered the particularities of writing on political matters in, and of, one's country in general. He claimed that he had no personal interest in the new insti-

---

[33] "… have been feared by tyrants and virtually worshipped by the people" (30 Nov. 1812: 482).

[34] "Could those who remember my praise of the decree of the *Sovereignty of the People* reconcile it with my condemnation of the new Spanish constitution?" (Jan. 1813: 4). On Blanco's change of outlook from a vague liberalism to a Burkean version of conservatism see also the entry on *El Español* in *Diccionario temático*. From this point on the editor dated the issues only by month and year.

tutions in Spain (5). Watching his country from a distance had led to a change in his ideas: "A haber yo permanecido en España, probablemente conservaria mis opiniónes primeras, porque no hubiera tenido ocasión de mirar las questiones por otro aspecto, ni con otra disposición de ánimo que la que daban de sí las circunstancias del pays. Lo que yo creo mi desengaño, se debe á la proporción que he tenido de observar á aquel reyno fuera de él mismo …"[35] His exile offered him the opportunity of comparing Spain with England. This seems to be Blanco White's final justification as an exile. Distance helped him to understand matters better even if that meant becoming disillusioned. Not carrying the same kind of guilt as other exiles because of not being really banished, Blanco found merit in his exile in so far as he was forced to re-assess his values.

As he confesses, his purpose at this stage is to reveal the true origin of his own illusions. Using a phrase from Burke, Blanco explains that these illusions were caused by the opinions codified as the "catechism of the Rights of Man" (Jan. 1813: 5-6). In a modest way, far from the epistemological feats of the day, Blanco was also concerned with how knowledge is acquired. In this case it was social and political convictions that offered material for study. Unlike the "ciencia práctica" where it is difficult to entertain illusions about non-existent progress in the laboratory, the "ciencia infusa" can deceive the enthusiastic would-be practitioner. An illustration of the latter is the first contact with a body of knowledge such as is contained by Rousseau's *Social Contract* (Jan. 1813: 7-8). Once the principle expounded early on is understood (for example, that of shared sovereignty) a young philosopher imagines that he has mastered "the entire system of the human societies" (Jan. 1813: 8). In passing, Blanco dismissed Rousseau's ideas and asserted that the difficulties started when the illusion, or the "empty speculation" was confronted with the world in which the reader lived (Jan. 1813: 9). This was not only a moment of difficulty, but also one of danger; the failure to comprehend the discrepancy between principle and its chance of being realized

---

[35] "Had I remained in Spain, I would probably have kept my initial opinions, because there would not have been any reason to regard the problems from a different point of view, or in a different state of mind than that created by the local circumstances. I think I saw things properly to the extent to which I had to watch that kingdom from a distance …" (Jan. 1813: 5).

brought along unexpected perils, because this was also a discrepancy between a claim to validity and concrete fallibility.

Blanco's remarks on the "cruel theories" which turn people against "the eternal and invariable order of nature itself" have the ring of Burke's objections against the French Revolution. The radical principles threaten the very "metaphysical preacher of the Rights of Man" when the masses take him at his word and proceed in search of equality lowering society far below the level envisaged by the philosopher (Jan. 1813: 10-11). The general point is not too far from Mallet du Pan's "politique expérimentale," a course of action resting on an empirical basis to be preferred, in his opinion, to the suffering caused by irresponsible theories.

This was therefore a considerable change from the earlier opinions held by Blanco on the need for comprehensive reform in a despotic and bigoted Spain. He admits in the same article that previously he had been keen on "doctrinas speculativas" (Jan. 1813: 12) that had to do with the Rights of Man. However, these early illusions were already being undermined by elements from the British tradition. In *Letters from Spain* he wrote about the necessity of introducing changes in his native country (30, 55-56). In these letters to an imaginary correspondent in England, the recently ordained Catholic priest Blanco y Crespo referred to the English political system as a model, but only because it was "sanctioned by the experience of time" (30).

The model of the time-honoured English constitution in the Spanish context was regarded by Blanco as a radical measure, but at an earlier stage he had contemplated revolutionary principles, mainly of French inspiration. In one of his letters he did not hesitate to assert that "[o]ur corrupters, our mortal enemies are religion and government" (31). By government he probably meant here despotic authority. Quite a few years had passed since he had held these ideas. His renewed contact with England, this time in his self-imposed exile, meant an obvious attenuation of his radicalism. Blanco claimed that he changed his mind because he realized that ruling according to radical principles would damage the texture of society (Jan. 1813: 12-13). He quoted and referred to Burke with great relish, even if Blanco's criticism of the 1812 Constitution did not issue from an exclusively conservative point of view.

The impossibility of a genuine people's sovereignty mentioned by Blanco at this later stage resembles the discussion from the late 1790s carried on, among others, by Madame de Staël and Benjamin Constant. By 1813 Blanco seemed to have become more of a monarchist than these thinkers. Nevertheless, royalism was associated by the editor of *El Español* with mild reformism and opposition to the Church (the memory of Carlos III was still fresh), while for a French-speaking person mentions of the monarchy had an almost exclusively absolutist resonance. It does not mean that Blanco had too many illusions about Fernando VII whom he correctly suspected of wanting to abolish the Constitution. But in his opinion there were serious obstacles to the assumption of sovereignty by the people, among them the ignorance of the population shared with a large number of deputies. Usually, in Paris this objection would be followed by proposals of educational reforms but Blanco does not seem to be able to overcome his scepticism.

Blanco did not believe that the members of the Cortes would surrender power to a newly elected assembly when the time came (June 1813: 414). He may have meant only those particular deputies of 1813 who had formed a government "arbitrario y despótico" (414-15) and who had been dismissive of large groups of people. Blanco did not quite trust that the system would work in Spain as it did in Britain. These were the very early days of party politics when factions advancing different opinions were considered to be damaging to the peace of the country. According to *El Español*, Spain was divided into two parties that profoundly disliked and feared each other: one keen to get into power, the other afraid to step down (416). The context of the article suggests that the country was fatally split rather than neatly crystallized round two political orientations. This hostility was caused by the laws passed by the Cortes. They seemed rather aimed "contra ciertas clases de ciudadanos, que de reglas saludables fundadas en el interés común del pueblo Español."[36] That was why, he explained, there were large groups of people in Spain who felt deprived or at least offended by such "precipitados decretos" (418).

---

[36] "… against certain classes of citizens, and not beneficial rules based on the common interest of the Spanish people" (June 1813: 418).

Blanco speculated on the present Cortes' attempt to justify its efforts to stay in power: the challenging novelty of the constitution may result in its being damaged by the next assembly, nobody could consolidate it so well as its creators, and so the present deputies would best serve the country by carrying on through "una usurpación temporal" (418). The reverse is valid for the incoming faction: they would rush through those laws that would suit them. The remedy for the arbitrary domination of a majority in the Cortes would be to balance it by the creation of a second chamber consisting of aristocrats and clergymen (the House of Lords with its bishops among its members was the obvious model).

The opposition between "liberales" and "serviles" (keen monarchists, against the 1812 Constitution) in the Cortes was beginning to become obvious. Blanco thought that a combination of the two would suit Spain better than just the rule of the former faction. Soon, though, the liberals would split further into "moderados" and "exaltados," a conflict reflected to some extent in the Spanish exile periodicals discussed below. The need for a second chamber was dwelt upon in the following issues (July 1813: 10; Aug. 1813: 83-84; Jan. and Feb. 1814: 87-88, 93-95). Blanco suggested a further measure that would ensure a proper national assembly: "elección directa del pueblo" (July 1813: 10). The authors of the Constitution made a further mistake, he argued, by deciding on the kind of electoral system enshrined in the text. Instead of an indirect system of electors, Blanco suggested direct voting, which he thought would give people back their rights. Clearly, his increasing sympathy for Burke's ideas did not mean that he was a consistent conservative.

Two decrees issued by the Cortes in August 1813 aroused Blanco's indignation and his comments showed his opinions on the main factions in Spain. One law stated that those who opposed the Constitution would be expelled from the country and have their fortune confiscated, the other that those who attempted to introduced other religions in Spain, in addition to Catholicism, would be sentenced to death (September 1813: 149). He was against both laws because they would punish the use of reason and holding certain opinions. He reiterated his earlier criticism of the demand to obey the Constitution as it was, which excluded any possible amendments (September 1813: 156).

Blanco understood the dangers of criticizing these laws inside Spain. His position was "muy distinta," and in this respect privileged. He would neglect his "sacred duty" if he kept quiet (September 1813: 158). His self-elected position of outsider raised him to the level of an arbiter, possibly a judge, certainly a detached observer, as he believed. His earlier criticism of the Cortes had been produced in the spirit of a still committed observer. It has been argued that the radicalism of the Cádiz deputies was a result of legislating in the middle of a war and of their reluctance to displease the people who bore the brunt of the fighting.[37] As a sceptical exile, Blanco did not have to worry about not being sufficiently grateful to the people involved in a liberation war, he could criticize any ideas or orientations in the Cortes. He had not withdrawn from the political discussion in Spain, but expressed his presence in a different way, by means of his periodical.

The final article showed even more clearly Blanco's position and the kind of opinions that he had been trying to put across. He claimed that more and more people, including some of his opponents, realized that there was a middle way between "la mal fraguada democracia de las Cortes y la arbitrariedad monárquica del tiempo de Carlos IV."[38] Despite the references to Burke towards the end of the periodical, the editor's ideals may have still appealed to a somewhat militant reformist.[39] As he anticipated factional discord, Blanco suggested once more a government based on the principles of "verdadera libertad religiosa y civil," needless to say, as in Britain (May/June 1814: 300-301).

Finally, the editor of El Español explained that he was going to stop publishing the magazine because, although he may still spread a few useful ideas, his criticism of royal despotism would endanger those who tried to follow his advice and oppose Fernando VII. His periodical, Blanco White concluded, would only serve as a weapon for those who

---

[37] Alberto Gil Novales, "Política y Sociedad," in Centralismo, ilustración y agonía del antiguo régimen: 1715-1833 (Barcelona: Labor, 1981) 278. Vol. 7 of Historia de España. Ed. Manuel Tuñón de Lara. 10 vols. (1977-1983).

[38] "... the badly devised democracy of the Cortes and the royal capriciousness of the times of Carlos IV" (May/June 1814: 295).

[39] On Voltaire providing the basis for "a militant reformism" see Anthony Arblaster, The Rise and Decline of Western Liberalism (Oxford: Blackwell, 1984) 195.

wanted confusion and civil war (307). In view of his subsequent development this sounds like a pretext. His overall interest in politics, regardless
of orientation, was waning. Religion and literature would occupy his attention during the following years. Apart from his personality that cannot be neglected in a discussion of Spanish exiles in London, his periodical was important for the critical opinions articulated here at a difficult
but hopeful time for Spain. By 1814 hopes had diminished and difficulties had increased, which was reflected in the fresh waves of Spanish
émigrés and their periodicals. The condition of exile is more clearly outlined in the two publications discussed below. Along with more combative arguments, there also emerged the rather familiar attempt at dismissing the guilt of banishment.

Chapter 5

"Liberales" and the Nation: *El Español Constitucional*

The unpleasantness of the Cádiz authorities mentioned by Blanco as a reason for his leaving Spain was mild compared with the persecution after the return of the king in 1814 which drove abroad numerous "liberales." These were mostly sympathizers or practitioners of constitutional politics. Not all escaped; some were arrested and executed as a result of Fernando VII's campaign. Before long, a few attempted from a distance to maintain their presence in the grim atmosphere at home, and influence matters by means of their own periodicals. The medical doctor, Pedro Pascasio Fernández Sardino, launched *El Español Constitucional* with the help of Manuel María Acevedo, spelling out in its title an orientation that Blanco had initially been hesitant about, and finally unable to adopt in his own magazine.

The Privilege of Virtue

After Fernando's repression of the constitutionalists the intellectual activity in Spain seemed to have come to a standstill until 1820 when the king was forced once more, again temporarily, to accept the Constitution. Between 1814 and 1820 most writers were in prison or in exile. Those who fled to France were regarded with suspicion by the Spanish nationalists: the "afrancesados" had compromised themselves by siding with Joseph Bonaparte and the French forces of occupation.[1] It was difficult to disentangle their adherence to the ideals of the "philosophes" from that manifested towards a fresh French dynasty and its army. The pro-French Spaniards had hoped that the values of the Enlightenment would be encouraged in Spain by the French, hence their willingness to collaborate with the invader. The problem was that they had in mind something like the spirit of Voltaire, while Napoleon thought in harsher terms. The irony was that by the time the "afrancesados" fled to France, they found themselves sheltered rather grudgingly by a newly restored monarchy, a shade less absolutist than the Spanish one but not too different. Almost ten years later French troops would again invade Spain in order to overthrow a liberal government and help Fernando regain complete power.

The Spanish liberals who fled to Britain seemed less tainted by dubious compromises and mistaken allegiances. On the whole, a periodical published by the Spanish refugees in London, unlike one in Paris, could have a better claim to articulate a point of view abroad and pass judgement on the repression at home. And for a few years after 1823, the next wave of absolutist repression, London virtually became the intellectual centre of the Spanish-speaking world.[2]

Among the refugees who arrived in London after 1814 was Fernández Sardino. He had already had conflicts with several Spanish generals in 1812 ending with his imprisonment because of the acerbic tone in his periodical *El Robespierre Español, amigo de las leyes*. A physician who had unsuccessfully tried his hand at play writing, he managed to attract a number of reasonably able writers to his London publication. *El Español Constitucional* appeared monthly from September 1818 until August 1820. After the "trienio liberal" (1820-1823 when the liberals returned to power), even larger groups of refugees, liberals and others, found themselves back in London and the magazine was re-issued by the same editor between March 1824 and June 1825.

[1] On the perception of the "afrancesados" as traitors see Abellán (4: 120-21).
[2] Lloréns (1968 243); see also Cruz Seoane (2: 110). This claim applies to the contemporary Latin American zone as well.

The texts were not exactly models of political theory although some can be profitably discussed. But whatever the quality of the contributions, the impact of the gesture, i.e. maintaining an alternative voice abroad, remained. Whether it was a litany of patriotic virtues or a lucid argument, this presence was ensured for a respectable length of time, considering the difficulties.

One of the aims stated in the "Introduction" was to present the main facts of the Spanish revolution.[3] The editor announced ambitiously that the recent events at home would be examined with the help of philosophy in order to establish their causes and find out the truth. Earlier, the French exiles had also thought it was important to establish their own version of what had happened and what had forced them into exile. Any justification, moral or otherwise, needed to be based on premises conveniently outlined for the purpose. However, the editor intended to go beyond a simple narration of events since he argued that a proper approach would imply analysis as well (Sept. 1818: 3).

Promises made in the opening editorials of exile magazines were seldom kept. Eventually, this periodical offered quite a lot of material not mentioned in the introduction, and not much of what the editor anticipated. Each number contained sections on politics, art and science. I concentrate on the political arguments, assuring the reader that hardly anything is missed by overlooking the other two sections. The cultural one usually offered lengthy nationalistic poems of negligible value, reviews and the occasional light feature. The science section simply reported the latest news, particularly in the field of medicine in which the editor had a professional interest.

The purpose of the historical analysis was to learn from the past. Towards the latter part of the eighteenth century history had been increasingly regarded in Spain as a practical instrument to benefit the nation (Abellán 3: 764-65). In this periodical history was also perceived pragmatically as a source of lessons for the future if only the facts could be clearly established. The editor patriotically stated that the Spanish revolution offered numerous edifying examples. However, no complete history of the revolution would be attempted here since this was not the job of a

---

[3] *El Español Constitucional* (Sept. 1818: 6).

periodical. The chief aspects would be approached objectively, relying on genuine documents (Sept. 1818: 7).

The Spanish resistance to the French invader is explained by the emergence of the liberal government at the time. The tone grows increasingly nationalistic as the editorial argues that it was this government which *"contribuyó mas que todos a la independencia de la Europa."*[4] The fact that Spain was never entirely conquered and controlled by the French, as was the case with most countries attacked by Napoleon, was repeatedly mentioned by the liberals.

The refugees discussed here were in exile because of political reasons. Therefore, the question of accepting a foreign military presence in one's country for the sake of having one's political cause favoured was a sensitive one and was touched upon by Fernández Sardino as well. While the French extreme royalists were willing in the 1790s to ally themselves temporarily with foreign powers backing their political opinions, the Spanish liberals did not contemplate such a manoeuvre. Yet, the earlier "Spanish Robespierre" does admit in a candid statement which makes him sound suspiciously like an "afrancesado" that, retrospectively there was no doubt that the fate of the constitutionalists would have been less unhappy under Joseph Bonaparte than under Fernando VII (Sept. 1818: 13). Nevertheless, a foreign domination resulting in the loss of political independence would have been unacceptable. Also, "la causa de nuestra Patria," and the Spaniards' "sagrada obligación" implied national independence despite a possible reactionary regime (14). The force of nationalism began thus to influence the arguments of the refugees even if it happened to be at the expense of their own political convictions.

The French ultra-royalists regarded the essence of "la nation" as being embodied by the king, and therefore would not have minded any reasonable compromise so that they could re-establish their own version of the proper order. The other main group of French émigrés, the constitutional monarchists (Malouet, Lally-Tollendal, Mounier), also favoured a foreign intervention, even if they did not allow the king an exalted role. Malouet and his companions represented an earlier form of

---

[4] *"... contributed more than any other government to Europe's independence"* (Sept. 1818: 9). Italics in the original.

liberalism—the 1791 constitution, parts of which they drafted, inspired the authors of the 1812 constitution—yet twenty years later the Spanish liberals would put national independence above their political creed. The liberal government had ensured both "independencia política" and "libertad civil," the editor argues, distinguishing between the aspirations of the state and those of private groups, or of the individual (Sept. 1818: 14).

The "Introduction" is punctuated by references to morality and the reader is left in no doubt who is in the right. The editor and his comrades possess the "privilege of virtue" ("privilegio de la virtud" [15]). The return of absolutism damaged religion, morality and progress. By bringing back the Inquisition the king insulted "a la vez a la Moral Evangélica y a la ilustración del siglo" ("at the same time the morality of the Gospels and the enlightenment of the century" [14]). The "crueles males" (15) are lamented but there was always one consolation: it was not the refugees who were responsible for this cruel evil. As will become clear in this chapter and will be enlarged upon in the last one, these are not the arguments used by the "liberales" to counter the guilt attached to them by the decision of banishment. Such direct references to morality have a predictable content and could equally have been used at home. The explanation that redeems the disgrace of exile, in so far as it was experienced in this way, emerges in contexts where morality as such is not the main subject.

There are a few topics that recur throughout the journal: the formation of the constitution as well as its nature and uses, the role of parties and factions, as well as legitimacy. The moral implications of the various political elements are also touched upon. It may be more profitable to discuss these issues thematically than follow the main articles chronologically.

Constitution and Legitimacy

The questions of legitimacy and of the significance of the constitution are connected and are given space early on in the magazine. They were discussed by one of the better-known contributors to *El Español Constitucional*, Álvaro Flórez Estrada, in his pamphlet "Representación hecha al

131

rei Fernando VII" several instalments of which were published in Fernández Sardino's periodical.[5]

Estrada's line of thought on the right of the people to act after the king's flight is similar to Blanco White's. Estrada backs his argument with references to the royalist Barclay and the less orthodox Locke, and draws the conclusion that in the king's absence "la Nación Española quedó en absoluta libertad de constituirse tal como tubiese por conveniente."[6] The nation recreates itself politically and the act of redefining itself is performed by means of a constitution. Having stated that sovereignty returned legitimately to the nation that was free to decide its own political framework through its representatives in the Cortes, Estrada offers Louis XVIII as an example to Fernando. The French king's merit on his return to the throne was to have given a "buen Constitución" to the French people and to have been loyal to it (Sept. 1818: 35-36). The implication here is that the king would have to adjust his position to the changes carried out in his absence in order to preserve some sort of claim to legitimacy. Louis XVIII's "Charter" was indeed a compromise and not a complete return to the past.

In this article written ten years after Carlos IV's abdication of 1808 and its retraction, Estrada employs the phrase "consentimiento de la Nación" ("consent of the nation" [Sept. 1818: 33]). It is not clear in what way the people could have expressed their consent to the abdication, but the idea is that they do have a stake in the fortunes of the kingdom and such decisions cannot be taken without them. Fernando's succession was not valid, particularly as Carlos IV changed his mind and wanted to return to the throne. Contemplating the absolutist regime from a distance, Estrada attempts to make two points: the people's consent is needed in the mechanism of royal succession, and implicitly some share of sovereignty is located in the people even under a monarchy; but, more relevant here, the author tries to undermine Fernando's legitimacy.

The location of sovereignty elaborated on by Estrada has through its legislative force a decisive role in defining what is a political crime, an

[5] Álvaro Flórez Estrada (1769-1853), economist and politician, fled after the 1823 Restoration to France where he wrote on economics.
[6] "… the Spanish nation was left totally free to constitute itself as it saw fit" (Sept. 1818: 32).

issue that particularly concerned the exiles. One of the crimes, which the absolutist monarchy implicitly attributes to its adversaries, is their claim that "soberanía residia en la nación" ("sovereignty resides in the nation" [35]). The sense of "nation" here was the same as that of the French 1791 Constitution, the overwhelming majority of the people, and not that used by the French ultra-royalists. From the Spanish constitutionalists' point of view, this principle is meant to describe a matter of fact, a reason for which it drafted one of the first articles of the 1812 document. According to the king, such a statement instantly occasions two more crimes: summoning a national assembly and diminishing the authority of the monarchy. Estrada dismisses the king's right to pass judgement on these matters, stating that "los reyes son hechos para los Pueblos, y no estos para aquéllos" ("the kings are made by the people, and not the other way round" [50]). The conclusion of Estrada's first section of his appeal is that "una Sociedad sin *Representación Nacional*, y sin que estén dividos los *poderes legislativo y executivo*, no puede dexar de ser una Sociedad de esclavos …"[7] Estrada tries to make Fernando change his mind by resorting to rational argument, rather than invective which is not always the case in the émigrés' texts.

Rumours about an amnesty granted to political refugees occasioned an article in December 1818 on the exiles' moral position. Unlike Estrada's general point on the definition of a political crime being founded on arbitrary legislation, here the argument is more direct: quite simply, to support actively a constitutional system is a good thing. A royal pardon presupposes a crime, and the crime is defined as the constitutionalists' political activities, which the "liberales" do not regard as crimes but as commendable actions (Dec. 1818: 300-301). A hard life in exile is to be preferred to taking advantage of an amnesty and returning to live under a despotic regime, tacitly having to admit that one has broken the law. The point is briefly made as a response to the definition of an outlaw formulated by the authorities in Madrid. The issue is starkly outlined without any elaborate analysis. This is an attempt to make a

---

[7] "… a Society without a *National Representation* and without separating the *legislative and executive powers* cannot cease being a society of slaves …" (Sept. 1818: 51). Italics in the original.

virtue of necessity. Exile is not only to be preferred to the benefits of an amnesty with its implications of pardoning an offence, but soon enough it would be argued that exile is a misnomer for the position of the "liberales" abroad.

A further indication of moral values attached to political orientations occurs in a brief mention of the émigrés' chief goal, "happiness of one's Fatherland" (Dec. 1818: 30). This happiness requires the reforms proposed by the liberals. Ostensibly, Fernando has the same purpose, but resorts to quite a different set of measures to fulfil it, for instance, the preservation of the true faith through the re-establishment of the Inquisition. It all amounts to what needs to be done in the country, and opinions differ. Besides, some of these opinions, i.e. those of the constitutionalists', can be labelled as crimes. By displaying concisely the divergent goals of the two main conflicting sides, the émigrés attempt to make an ethical point. The suggestion is that the incompatibility between absolutism and constitutionalism has a moral analogy; and having presented the question of right and wrong in this light the exiles show the unreasonableness of the accusations against themselves. This line of thought would lead in due course to the decisive point about the inability of the Spanish people to assert itself under a despotic rule, leaving those who can challenge absolutism to take over the role of representatives of the nation.

Not only the moral and legal implications of a proper constitution preoccupy the editors of *El Español Constitucional*, but also the form of the Cortes. The issue of a bicameral assembly was raised by the editor in February 1819 (406-416). Fernández Sardino is against bicameralism, an arrangement supported by Blanco White a few years earlier in his own periodical. This polemical article is not an answer to Blanco, but combats a suggestion that circulated mainly outside Spain (there is hardly any evidence that Fernando VII contemplated the idea). The British Parliament, always a point of reference, did have an upper chamber, but although it worked reasonably well, it would not do so in Spain. The objections presented here are of a pragmatic nature: the upper clergy's lack of competence in political and economic matters, and the difficulties of sorting out the aristocratic hierarchy in Spain where the claims to nobility were numerous and hard to reconcile. In addition, there would be the difficulties of attending the sessions due to bad communications. Finally, the editor has a moral objection as well: most of the higher clergy and the aristocrats (who would make up the upper chamber) had been compromised by their association with the French invaders.

Flórez Estrada also makes this particular point in his criticism of the decree of 4 May 1814, which banned the Constitution (March 1819: 472). Among his lengthy, accusing questions addressed to Fernando in the sequel of his pamphlet, Estrada brings up an issue relevant to the liberals' perception of their work on the 1812 text. Towards the end of the eighteenth century there were calls for a return to a supposedly untainted, ancient constitution. Estrada believes, together with like-minded liberals, that "las Cortes de Cádiz no han hecho otra cosa que restablecer algunas de nuestra antigua Constitución, que en mejores días formaban el paladion de nuestra libertad …"[8] Again, the argument of an ancient constitution which should be recovered was frequently used at the time. And despite the deputies' talk of reforms, change or novelty, some liberals were convinced that the Cortes achieved what many "ilustrados" had been asking for, namely a return to the principles that had first emerged in a distant, unspoiled age. It may well be that this was not only an illusion about what 1812 signified, but also a perpetuation of a useful ideal needed in opposition. The opposition was now in exile, which becomes once more a space ensuring the survival of such aspirations. On occasion, the local tradition of political thought influenced the émigrés' convictions: Burke, for a while, in Mallet's case, Bentham and Burke in Blanco's; but the opposite could also occur, Spain's (or France's) history is ransacked and various arguments are revived as part of the claim that the true national spirit can be preserved only in exile.

In search of a definition, it is argued that if a constitution is a pact between individuals expressing the rules and principles that ought to be observed by all, then it should be the product of a sovereign community.[9] A constitution is the expression of the "voluntad general," and its observance is ensured by the "medio de la libertad de imprenta," ("in-

---

[8] "… what the assembly of Cádiz did was precisely re-establishing to some extent our ancient constitution which in happier times was the guarantee of our freedom …" (March 1819: 475).

[9] Sept. 1819: 356; the subsequent quotes are on the same page.

strument of the free press"). Terms such as "pacto" repeatedly linked to "voluntad general" are opposed to "usurpación " and "fuerza." The idea of consent is implied throughout the argument and, so, the authority of a government derives from its being created by the people.

The document as such confirms a pact that may exist as a valid agreement even before it is legally codified. A constitution can be "de palabra ó por escrito" ("oral or written"). Its force is manifested as long as it fulfils one of its chief aims, the limitation of royal power ("restricciónes á los reyes"). An instance of such oral pacts is mentioned in a later article (Oct. 1819: 404); the "pactos de asociación" formed for the purpose of defense in pre-medieval times represent in fact "un bosquejo de constitución" ("a sketch of a constitution").

The idea of contract, seldom invoked in this periodical, does emerge at times, as in an article sent from Paris (Aug. 1819: 255). Its meaning here is that of an agreement between equals, and not between the subjects and their ruler. The contributor from Paris deals with the nature of citizenship, i.e. enjoying the rights and the protection of a particular national community and owing allegiance to it. Ideally, "the law, or the general will of Society" ("la ley, ó la voluntad general de la Sociedad" [255]) ought to ensure favourable conditions for the citizen to develop into a mature and free person. Society is defined here as a group of active individuals who can modify the laws, a fact which enables them to enjoy the rights granted by reason, the main one being freedom (255). The subsequent step in this argument is that Fernando's absolutism deprives the Spaniards of the proper quality of citizenship and denies them their rights. Pursuing the issue along these lines, the writer links citizenship with legitimacy and concludes that a despot is not a proper ruler. The suggestion is that the members of a nation (again, the great majority) cannot possess the advantages of proper citizenship without a legitimate ruler, be it a person or a representative assembly. When the quality of citizenship and legitimacy are missing a nation cannot be constituted as such.

National Character and Despotism

The interconnection between morality and politics is discussed in an article on the "public spirit" ("espíritu público") of a nation defined as its virtue (Dec. 1819: 562). The decisive connection is made in the statement about this spirit being conditioned by the kind of constitution a nation possesses (562). There are vague echoes from Montesquieu, but the article does not follow exactly the philosopher's pairing of moral qualities and political systems. The link is straightforward: the spirit (or virtue) is influenced by the type of constitution adopted. The most satisfactory form is a constitutional monarchy. Its merit is that it promotes the principle of honour. A citizen has a right to have his opinion heard, and in so far as he is indirectly part of the mechanism of legislation, by electing representatives to a national assembly, he cultivates his virtue and the quality of the collective spirit is enhanced. Moreover, despotism breeds apathy in a nation. Apathy saps "las fuerzas morales" of the citizen (563). The contrast set up here is between "the spirit of apathy" and "the spirit of freedom" ("espíritu de apatía, espíritu de libertad" ibid.). Unsurprisingly, it is under a liberal government that the qualities promoting "public happiness" can flourish.

"Espíritu público" and "carácter nacional" (Dec. 1819: 561, 564) seem to be used synonymously. They change in accordance with the kind of constitution a people receives. The degree of freedom allowed by a constitution results in various modifications of the national character (564). The implication is that a proper constitution has an educational value, anticipating J.S. Mills's emphasis on educating the citizens in order to enable them to vote. The conclusion of this particular article signed "E.S." is that the difficulties encountered by the reforms necessary to improve the national character are due to the lack of political education which is the fault of the despotic governments. This thought of "E.S." appears to have ended in a vicious circle. But the implication in this article of December 1819 is that the impasse could be solved by a radical change in Spain and the imposition of a liberal government.

A subsequent article in the same issue returns to the people's character being shaped by a particular kind of government (571 ff). This time it is not the "spirit" but "las costumbres," "las ideas civiles y la moral pública" that are conditioned by the political framework. The use of the phrase "moral pública" shows that the exiles see the issues in terms of an ethics of the community when they discuss the educational virtues of a constitution. An ethics of the individual may indeed emerge in their own particular cases when they opt for one course of action rather than another. The two levels meet, for instance, in the "carácter español" whose chief moral components are "honradez" and "constancia" (Dec. 1819: 572), as the individuals merge into a nation.

The explanation given here is that decay set in and corruption increased because of the arbitrary power of the kings and their ministers and due to the excessive riches arriving from the colonies. The argument is not exactly consistent, since the causal sequence becomes more difficult to establish when the interdependence between "ideas políticas" (shaping a constitution) and "sentimiento morales" is examined (571). The reciprocity between the political and the moral means that when one deteriorates the other is also affected. But "[l]a difficultad está en conocer, cuando aparece un Pueblo cuyas ideas políticas están tan corrompidas como sus sentimientos morales, en buscar cual corrupción fué la primera, y dió causa á la otra."[10] This is the case in general. As for Spain, the tone remains constantly nationalistic. The hope of moral, and implicitly political, recovery lies in the Spanish national virtues, preserved collectively by the mass and individually by the citizen. Whatever happened in politics, "la moral pública, esto es, los sentimientos de virtud se conservaban en nuestros corazónes" ("the public morality, namely the virtuous feelings were preserved in our hearts ..." [572]). As ever, the favourite example is Britain where the commendable human qualities have resulted from an "excellent" constitution (574).

The much-discussed issue of the most suitable development of a constitution recurs in an article of January 1820. The irony is that the liberal editor praises the sort of constitution advocated by Burke, rather than the French revolutionary one of 1791, the source of inspiration for the Cádiz deputies. Fernández Sardino contrasts favourably a constitution as

---

[10] "When we come across a people whose political ideas are as corrupted as its moral sentiments, it is difficult to know how to find out which was corrupted first and caused the other one" (Dec. 1819: 571).

a slowly maturing set of statements on the political structure of the country with one produced at a given moment by a small group of people (Jan. 1820: 40). In the early days the customs *were* the laws because of their immediate relevance to the people's living conditions (40). This is a familiar argument that leads the editor to the conclusion that the individual passions opposed to the "imperio absoluto" of a constitution have to be resolved in favour of the "bien común" (41). The opinions of this exile periodical are far from representing a crystallized liberal ideology. This becomes even more obvious in the significance attached to the community when it comes to a particular difficulty when drafting a constitution: the fundamental indivisibility of sovereignty ("La soberanía es una é indivisible por su esencia ..." [44]). The aim is that sovereignty should be embodied by the entire nation (the eclecticism of the editor has carried us far from Burke by now). The complications arise when it comes to the question of representation.

The idea of the indivisibility of sovereignty had been forcefully argued for as early as the sixteenth century. For Bodin indivisible sovereignty meant sovereignty not shared. Bodin's purpose was to justify royal absolutism. At the time, the reasons were quite plain: the secular leader, the king, had got the upper hand in the conflict with other contenders for power (the Church, powerful aristocratic rivals) and the monarchy needed theoretical backing in order to show that its victory was the proper way forward. As territories and populations acquired an increasingly strong identity the meaning was shifting. During the French Revolution the term was applied to the republic (the much repeated refrain "une et indivisible"), to the nation, and, by extension, to the assembly representing it. The indivisible sovereignty becomes to a certain extent a legal fiction, as it is no longer associated concretely with one individual's power of making laws (Bodin's definition), but with power exercised in a complex manner by a representative group on behalf of all citizens. The degree of abstraction of the attribute increases along with the strain of accepting the emerging convention that the nation does in fact exercise sovereignty collectively. Unity was valued more and more as the accretion of particular issues was pierced by the challenge of general and decisive questions.[11] And even when the parts—the various political and administrative bodies—function separately, they have to relate themselves constantly to one entity, the people, and to its goal, the common good. This entity has to be sought beyond a particular group: a member of a national assembly has to keep in mind his role as a spokesman for a limited number of voters with their local interests, while he has also to remain aware of a general, possibly ideal kind of sovereignty whose effects are thought of as an unimpaired whole.

The relevance of all this to the article in *El Español Constitucional* has to do with the representatives' authority being overshadowed by a contradiction: while the exercise of authority should not be hindered at every step, it has to be supervised and modified as necessary by the citizens at large (Jan. 1820: 45). The solution offered in this article is the separation of powers which is expected to lead to freedom, while their being exercised by one person means tyranny (46-47). The other extreme is anarchy: "la tiranía de todos" where the individuals are afraid of one another (47). In a subsequent discussion by a different contributor but on the same issue, the king is allowed a role in initiating legislation but "el cuerpo legislativo" should have an active role as well (Feb. 1820: 85-86). The king should have his right of veto since, it is claimed that he is informed about "the public needs and the present state of the Nation" ("las necesidades publicas y del estado presente de la Nación" [86]). In a note the editor does raise an objection to the suggestion that the judges should be appointed by the king; he wants the judges to be elected by the citizens, a point similar to that made by Blanco White.

The Part and the Whole

Besides its interest in constitutional matters, *El Español Constitucional* refers frequently to the question of party and faction. While in Britain political life had acquired a certain complexity which led to the Whigs and

---

[11] See below, Koselleck on several local freedoms in France becoming an all-encompassing liberty, p. 204. However, a complication, which Koselleck does not tackle and for which there is no room in the present discussion is that the kind of limited freedom he refers to had quite often the meaning of privilege, in which case his argument becomes problematic.

Tories being increasingly referred to as "parties" by the 1770s, and in France there was much talk of "factions" on political grounds in the 1790s, the terms were used rather loosely in Spain: "el partido fernandino" were those who gathered round the heir to the throne against the royal favourite Godoy after the turn of the century. The pejorative connotation of court intrigue had not disappeared. As the term took on the meaning of a group of adherents to a set of ideals or a certain policy, it was still possible to play on the unsettling sense of a troublesome sect that disturbed the general consensus. It is in this sense that the periodical employs the word in its endeavour to dismiss the condition of exile. This implies a re-definition of the people at home in terms of the political creed of liberalism and a strong emphasis on the quality of representing them. These bold assertions follow a pattern resembling the argument of the French ultra-royalists, although the assumptions about the idea of nation are quite different.

The sense of exclusion experienced by the émigrés determined them to turn the tables on the absolutist king and insist on *their* being part of the nation, arguing that those who separated themselves from the people, and implicitly from the common good, are the supporters of the despotic king. One of the insults directed at those who were on Fernando's side was that they were members of a "partido" or "facción," the words appear to have been used synonymously (Aug. 1819: 258). The political duel was not yet a matter of competing ideologies, but a conflict in which it was important to define who was completely outside the national sphere and the potential political arena. Hence, even if freedom of expression was one of the rights that the constitutionalists were fighting for, at this stage they could regard any group that opted for a rival tendency as a destructive faction.

In a note to an army general's appeal to Fernando VII Sardino gives his definition of a liberal and clarifies his views on the significance of a political party. For him the definition of liberals is "amantes de la racional libertad, sectarios de la Ley, amigos del orden y de la felicidad del Pueblo" ("lovers of rational freedom, supporters of the law, friends of order and of the happiness of the People" [Nov. 1819: 483, n.]). It is worth emphasizing here the elements of reason and freedom. The components of the definition with their recognizable source in the Enlightenment ideals, however simplified, are mentioned throughout the periodical. Even if fleetingly present throughout the magazine, they indicate the tradition of thought within which Fernández Sardino and his companions placed themselves.

The liberals by definition cannot be only a part of the people because ”*Los Liberales*, pues, son la Nación;—y los *serviles* no son más que una facción ...” (”*The Liberals* are indeed the Nation;—while *the servile ones* [the king's adepts] are just a faction ...” [483, n.]). The difference between the all-encompassing nature of the liberals' outlook and the marginal presence of the ”serviles” is underlined in later articles where party and faction are used as synonyms. The view of liberalism defined here pre-dates its crystallization as a political ideology promoted by a party, however further back the budding concepts can otherwise be traced. The assumption here is that the liberals and the nation overlap; the development of the whole community cannot but follow reason in order to achieve freedom and eventually reach happiness. Anyone who opposes this can only belong to a faction, a restricted group that has broken away from the main body of opinion. (The French ”fraction” used pejoratively during the 1790s is even more telling.)

At the time of this article (November 1819) the great majority of the population was forced to remain silent, and the opinions presumably shared by most citizens could only be articulated by those who were banished. Reason and freedom, the chief values of liberalism as it was understood here, could only be exercised outside Spain, and the obvious implication is that those who were able to do it *were* the nation. The rest, i.e. the absolutist authorities and the ”serviles,” have separated themselves and are not part of the nation, whoever may temporarily possess power. This categorical reversal of the roles of the exiles recalls the French ultra-royalists' claim only very generally. The traditions from which these arguments are derived, as well as the reasons for which the French and the Spanish émigrés resort to them differ widely; the ultra-royalists regard the people at home as a separate community, while the Spanish liberals see themselves as part of a community silenced by oppression. Nevertheless, the attempt to vindicate their position in exile is common to both groups. I would suggest that the sense of exclusion and the need for justification drives them to over-emphasize their identity with a particular historical tradition or a recent political creed. The exiles turn their displacement, meant as a punishment or at least as an embarrassment, into an opportunity that reveals their particular virtue, and on these grounds they claim that they are in the right, a moral stance deserved in their view by being the proper embodiment of their nation. Those who forced them abroad are a "fraction" of the people, a "party," not the community as a whole whom they actually claim that they represent.[12]

A consensus similar to the belief of Fernández Sardino that most Spaniards were liberals is assumed by a contributor in November 1819. The argument concerns a ruling group's legitimacy and rehearses the familiar issues: when the ruler's whim replaces the general will, authority is wrongfully assumed and an act of usurpation occurs, consequently such rulers no longer possess legitimacy (512). The correction of this state of things would require a revolution, but the author assumes the same unanimity of opinion that Fernández Sardino did. The necessary forceful changes can hardly be called a revolution when the great majority wants to re-establish a legitimate leadership and therefore acts against a small group. This course of action is compared with a physical body correcting its own malfunctions. The return of a physical or political body to its proper activity where most of the constituting entities work in agreement, does not amount to a revolution in the sense of a conflict because there is hardly anyone or anything that would oppose these adjustments (512). However, this was an optimistic view. Back in Spain, the distribution of political support was somewhat different from the exiles' estimation.

The metaphors vary, but in an attempt to gain precision the author of this article resorts to a more elaborate comparison between the government and a mechanism: "El gobierno es en lo moral lo que en lo físico es un relox. Es preciso arreglarle cuando se adelanta ó atrasa, y el reloxero debe ser el Pueblo, que debe compasarlo con la voluntad general."[13] The relevant point here is the link between morality and politics as seen from

---

[12] For a more complete analysis of this point, see the last chapter.

[13] "The Government is in the moral sphere what a watch is in the natural world. It is necessary to adjust it when it is slow or when it gains, and the watchmaker should be the People who should do it in tune with the general will" (Nov. 1819: 513).

exile. The existence of a dubious government implies a flaw in the realm of morality, as is the case in the Spain of 1819. The people, silenced by despotism, is unable to put matters right, and, as the only active and vocal part of the nation, it is incumbent on the exiles to act, which they do in the realm of opinion. Once more, the issue is translated into moral terms in order to vindicate the émigrés' position.

The preoccupation with parties or factions is carried on in a further article where they are contrasted with "la voz popular" (Feb. 1820: 109). The isolated groupings do not reflect any other point of view than their own, this contributor argues. And he makes a further distinction between "la voz popular" and "la opinión pública." The latter is endowed with a rational nature that the former lacks. "La voz popular" is seen as fickle, ephemeral, and easily split by factions. People change from one day to the next, "ya favorables, ya contrarias á los partidarios" ("now for, now against members of factions" [110]). This contributor ventures an emphatic definition of the formation of public opinion which is *"la voz general de todo un Pueblo convencido de una verdad, que ha examinado por medio de la discusión."*[14] The formation of public opinion is constantly seen in opposition to the taint of party interest. The distinction appears to be between the biased opinions inflicted on the citizens, absorbed and turned by them into "la voz popular," and the emergence of the people's own opinions after discussions. This process is reliable because "no se puede suponer en la masa general de los ciudadanos ningún interés de partido ..." ("one cannot presume the existence of any party interest among the general mass of citizens ..." [112]).

In the March sequel to this article a distinction is made between the "partido filosófico" and "espíritu filosófico" in France in the 1790s (162). A party has its own interest at heart and worries less about "la virtud, la verdad y la justicia" (164). A debate conducted in a philosophical (or intellectual) spirit would probably avoid the more obvious biases. The assumption is that the common good can be aimed at and worked for only by a political grouping that represents the "entire" community.

---

[14] *"... the general voice of a whole People persuaded of one truth, having examined it in a debate"* (Feb. 1820: 110). Italics in the original.

However, community is understood here in a restricted sense, the author of the article means only property owners and educated individuals (164).

These issues were discussed in February and March 1820 when Spain appeared to have shaken off the absolutist regime by a collective endeavour whose triumph was threatened by the emerging tensions between factions. Another topical subject was raised by Jeremy Bentham in a letter to the editor of the *Morning Chronicle* (18 April 1820). The philosopher criticized the decree banishing those Spaniards who did not support the constitution reinstated by Fernando. Bentham, always ready to offer legal advice to foreign governments, suggested an attenuation of the decree so that it only required of those suspected of hostility a "simple approbation of the Constitution in the most general terms" instead of an oath of loyalty.[15] Bentham was making his point on grounds of toleration, listening to his "petition of mercy" would be a sign of wisdom. He also considered that it would be a pragmatic approach ("It surely is not in the power of opinions to change at the word of command ..."), and a sensible one as, otherwise, Spain would lose much-needed citizens.

In his brief reply Fernández Sardino disagreed with Bentham, resting his argument on the idea of the constitution as a contract; those unwilling to enter it cannot be expected to be part of the community (May 1820: 369). It was only a tiny group, according to the editor, so the country would not lose too much. On the contrary, their presence would be a constant danger to the security of the nation.

Thus, after six years in exile the editor of *El Español Constitucional* was keen to defend a decree banishing others. His explicit arguments have to do with mutual trust and national security, adding that the death penalty would be worse than exile (370). But there is the assumption that the proper place of such opponents of the liberal authorities is in fact abroad. Again, even if he professes a liberal creed, he cannot conceive of open opposition under a constitutional government. The authorities in

---

[15] The copy of the text in the British Library has the catalogue entry "Proof-sheet of a letter by Jeremy Bentham to the Morning Chronicle, dated 14 April 1820, on the Spanish Decree of the 30 March 1820, imposing an oath of adherence to the constitution." Fernández Sardino mentions the date of the newspaper issue in which, presumably, the letter was printed.

Madrid would prove more tolerant during the "trienio liberal" and allow them to stay. Fernández Sardino had fled an absolutist Spain where open opposition would have been out of the question, and he expected the same treatment to be applied to the opponents of the new liberal leadership. There is a suggestion here that opposition means lack of loyalty. So the political outlook of at least this early liberal refugee had not yet become a fully-fledged political ideology that would allow the presence of dissenting voices.

A Liberal Interlude

In January 1820 a few officers declared their allegiance to the constitution of 1812 (Carr 124 ff). The rebels succeeded due to the passivity of the rest of the army and the government's weakness. The imprisoned liberal leaders were freed to form the new government. Fernando VII was forced once more to accept the constitution of 1812. During the first few months of the new regime a split emerged between the moderate and the radical liberals. Most of the former had until recently been either in exile or in gaol. They were for a bicameral assembly and were willing to preserve the monarchy, appeased by Fernando's acceptance of the constitution, the first European king since Louis XVI (under far greater duress) to have accepted a constitution not imposed by him (Britain being the constant exception).[16] This may explain Fernando's anomalous presence on the throne in 1820 after the return to power of the very people recently imprisoned by him. The militant "exaltados" who stood for "the anarchical stage of the primitive revolution" (Carr 132) saw the updating of the constitution as a dilution of its principles. In the meantime, the constitution had acquired "un aire europeo" (Gil Novales 7: 296), as it became the banner under which the revolutionaries of Naples, Sicily, Portugal and Piedmont were beginning to march. However, after prolonged disturbances caused partly by the militants' suspicions of the king, Fernando dismissed this cabinet and appointed a more malleable one in March 1821.

---

[16] For the "immense resonance" of Fernando's gesture, see Gil Novales in *Historia de España* (7: 292).

Further discontents and conflicts between permutations of various factions, the king, the ministers, the army, and what some historians call "the mob" (Carr passim) ended with the invasion of the French army. Fifteen years earlier Napoleon's troops had met with fierce opposition: this time the "Sons of St. Louis" (as these forces styled themselves) advanced virtually unmolested. It was becoming obvious that the 1820 revolution had in fact been made by the army, not the people, and now the military leaders were concerned with maintaining their high positions. As for the appeal of the constitution, a liberal officer summed up the situation by saying that "the constitution of 1812 was made entirely for the people but they hated it" (qtd. in Carr, 141). Natural disasters, economic difficulties and the disconcerting switch from despotism to an embryonic democracy accompanied by anti-clericalism in a solidly Catholic country did not contribute to the popularity of the constitution, or of its authors and supporters.

In a rare explanation of his aims, Fernández Sardino wrote in April 1820 when he could have returned home why he stayed on in London: he could better serve his country by editing a periodical in Britain than by returning to Spain (319-20). He added that not being a military man he would be of little use in Spain, a curiously sceptical view of the prospects of internal harmony in his country. In August 1820 he stopped publishing his magazine. When absolutism returned three years later he made a fresh effort and resumed publication for almost another two years in the knowledge that, once more, he was working to good purpose.

The aim of the second series, the editor announced quite predictably, was to explain the failure of the constitution ("Prospecto," March 1824: i). The magazine would particularly criticize the claim that the 1812 constitution was too democratic for Spain, and that it should have been toned down so that it resembled the French Charter granted by Louis XVIII on his return in 1814. The gist of the editor's analysis in the first issue of the new series was that Louis's behaviour had done more damage in France than the Jacobins. This time the conclusion was that "la libertad y felicidad de las naciones es incompatible con la existencia de los

Reyes, aunque sean constitucionales."[17] After Fernando's second failure to keep his pledge to the constitution the disappointment was unmistakable. Former constitutional monarchists were turning into republicans. This became the subject of a controversy with *Ocios de Españoles Emigrados*, another Spanish exile periodical that began to appear in London after 1823. This is the subject of the next chapter.

---

[17] "… the freedom and happiness of Nations are incompatible with the existence of Kings, even if they are constitutional" (March 1824: 32).

Chapter 6

Constitution and Monarchy: *Ocios de Españoles Emigrados*

There was time enough during the three years of liberal rule in Madrid for dissensions to emerge between the liberals themselves. The hesitant attitude towards Fernando VII who remained on the throne throughout this period, and the pressures from abroad ended with the invasion of the French troops who restored the absolutist rule that the king had imposed between 1814 and 1820. Britain received new groups of "liberales" who fled Spain along with many of the old ones.

Preparing for Controversy

This time the recent political experience assimilated in Spain or contemplated from London provided material for arguments on various lines of thought. The "Spanish Robespierre" who had stayed in London went on supporting a more radical version of liberalism in *El Español Constitucional*, while the émigrés who had participated in the work of government in Madrid during the "trienio liberal" or shared the problems on the spot tended to adopt a more moderate attitude. Among the new periodicals started in London, one of the more substantial ones was *Ocios de*

Españoles Emigrados edited by the "moderados." A monthly from April 1824 to October 1827 (it became a quarterly in 1827), it was edited by the brothers Jaime and Joaquín Lorenzo Villanueva and José Canga Argüelles (Lloréns, *Liberales y románticos* 255).

Joaquín Lorenzo Villanueva (1757-1837) was a clergyman and one of the liberal deputies at Cádiz. After Fernando VII's return he was arrested and confined to a monastery for six years. He became politically active again during the three years of liberal rule, was appointed ambassador to Rome but the Pope rejected him, whereupon Villanueva broke with the Catholic Church. He fled to England after 1823 where he translated Protestant works and the New Testament (the latter a highly unorthodox occupation for a Spanish clergyman). However, he died in Ireland reconciled to the Catholic Church. Much less is known of his brother Jaime who wrote an erudite work on literary and ecclesiastical history. Argüelles (1770-1843) was a more prominent figure: politician and economist, he took part in the revolt against Napoleon, was a deputy in the Cortes of 1812 at Cádiz. As a finance minister he went on consistently supporting liberal ideas. He was exiled by Fernando VII but, quite intriguingly, was entrusted with "un delicato puesto administrativo" in Valencia in 1816. Once more a finance minister after 1820, he fled to London in 1823 where he published works on economics. He returned to Spain six years later where he concentrated on writing literary criticism.[1] As usual in the case of émigré periodicals, it is difficult to establish their circulation or impact at home. Fragmentary evidence indicates that *Ocios* was of some consequence in Spain: the issue for October 1825 announces that the journal was banned at home for being "alarmante y subversivo."[2]

The editors' modest claims include making Spain and its culture known in England. This implies the optimistic assumption that a sufficient number of Englishmen could read Spanish to make this a worthwhile enterprise. The periodical would contain articles on literature, economics and politics. Discussions on statistics, the public debt, industrial

---

[1] See *Diccionario de Historia de España* (1986). After Jaime Villanueva's death in November 1824 a certain Pablo Mendíbil joined the editorial team.

[2] *Ocios de Españoles Emigrados* (Oct. 1825: 289).

and commercial improvement would proceed "no por medio de indaga-ciónes filosóficas, de que hay tanta copia en el dia sino históricamente y por medio de observación y anecdotas contraidas a la Península ..."[3] The intention to deal above all with facts is reinforced in the promise that the political contributions will concentrate on "sucesos políticos pasados y presentes ..." ("past and present political events ..." [April 1824: 5]), and not on "teorías." This programme indicates the intentions of the editors, but it may also say something about the kind of readership they had in mind. Assuming that they wanted the publication to be read by as many Spanish readers as possible, the emphasis on facts and obser-vation at the expense of abstract speculation may suggest a disinclination towards the latter among the Spanish exiles.

The Mirage of the Ancient Constitution

Constitutional matters preoccupy the editors of *Ocios* just as much as those of the other Spanish periodicals in London. Karl-Ludwig Haller's book on the Spanish constitution occasioned a number of articles during 1824. Haller was at this time in Paris working mainly as a journalist and making himself known as a strong partisan of the Restoration. A strong believer in authority, his zeal in supporting the royal legitimist principles had driven him to abandon Protestantism to the horror of his family in Berne where he had been practising law. The editors defended the con-stitution against Haller's criticism, arguing that in principle it renewed the social contract through the king's oath of allegiance, although sadly bro-ken again (June 1824: 211-12), and that the text was compatible with Christianity (217). It is obvious in such arguments how the "moderados" were willing to overlook the monarch's misdemeanours. It was in con-nection with the position of the king that this periodical clashed with the "exaltado" *Español Constitucional*. Haller's criticism proceeded from a con-servative point of view, while Fernández Sardino's issued from a radical republican one. The editors of *Ocios* tried to maintain what they consid-ered to be a proper balance by defending the text of 1812. They invoked

---

[3] "... not by means of philosophical investigations which abound nowadays, but historically and by means of observation as well as anecdotes from the Peninsula ..." (April 1824: 4-5).

the ancient constitution, by now a trite reference in contemporary discussions, and in this context they did make a concession; the text established at Cádiz was not impeccable: one of the advantages of the old constitution is claimed to be its religious tolerance as opposed to the much debated article 12 of the 1812 document which prescribes Catholicism as the only religion in Spain (Aug. 1824: 72 ff).

The disagreements between the "exaltados" and the "moderados" were becoming so great that it was increasingly difficult to regard both of them as liberals. "Miso-Basileo" (possibly the main editor) expressed his republican opinions in *El Español Constitucional*. Before developing his anti-monarchist argument, the author prepares the ground by returning to what he still expects to be a common platform of the "liberales": Spain exists only through its exiles ("La España no existe sino en miembros diseminados, tímidos y proscriptos ..." [Aug. 1824: 502]). The nature of this justification is emphasized here more than on previous occasions: if nations were represented by moral qualities and not numbers of individuals "estos hombres justos deberían donde quiera gozar la consideración de cuerpo represantativo nacional ..." ("these just people should enjoy everywhere the respect due to national representatives ..." [502]). When subsequently "Miso-Basileo" dismisses absolutist and constitutional kings as equally evil, he does it from a position, which has appropriated both the moral and the national attributes. Banished by the king, the émigrés transfer the guilt to the monarchy by identifying the nation with moral attributes whose expression is blocked at home.

A series of comments on the ancient constitution published by *Ocios* are "indirect" replies to *El Español Constitucional* (Lloréns, *Liberales y románticos* 246). The statements on the significance of the Spanish exiles are taken for granted; the "moderados" are above all concerned with the anti-royalist attitude. The intention of the "primitiva constitución española" had not been to establish a despotic regime (Sept. 1824: 155). Kings were removed when they proved particularly unsatisfactory, a sign that the limitations imposed on the supreme power worked (among the examples given by *Ocios* are Alfonso X "El Sabio" and Enrique IV, under the circumstances somewhat unfortunately remembered as "El Impotente" or "El Liberal" [155]). These instances from the thirteenth and fifteenth centuries along with later ones are meant to support the argument that a moderate monarchy is possible within a proper constitutional framework. It is the traitors round the throne who are responsible for the present state of things in Spain, argues the author of the article. He who is called a tyrant now "en el régimen constitucional era aclamado Padre de la Patria ..." (161).

Fernández Sardino and Acevedo's periodical further clarified the chief points of the matter. A republic is understood as a system characterized by equality before the law irrespective of the citizens' fortunes, and by equality of opportunity based on merit (*El Español Constitucional* Oct. 1824: 680-81). Then this contributor returns to the question of monarchy. A king would always damage a constitution, so a monarchy, even if constitutional, is undesirable (684); more than that, a constitutional monarchy is simply a contradiction in terms ("... constitución y rey se excluyen mutuamente" [685]). Consequently, the solution is a republic. Besides, it is impossible that the king's interests should coincide with the interests of the nation; the routine exception is made: the relationship between king and constitution in Britain is different because the latter is based on precedent and tested by practice (686). Both periodicals assume that a constitution is an indispensable condition for a proper political system in Spain. This tacit agreement is extended to the role of émigrés and their debates that recreate a temporary Spain, as it were, and modify the meaning of exile.

Legitimacy was a sensitive and important question in the post-Napoleonic era. The various restored monarchs needed to demonstrate their right to their thrones. Already a quarter of a century earlier the French royalists had accused Bonaparte of being a usurper, and with Peltier's help, among others, they protested even more ferociously when he made himself an emperor. As dynastic claims were regulated by the great powers after 1815, the issue of legitimacy also gained currency outside the discussions about proper royal descent. The term could be used to buttress even the validity of texts such as that drafted by the Cortes at Cádiz. The constitution as a summary of people's rights and duties is spelled out in a discussion on how its legitimacy was reinforced by the recognition of several European states including England, Russia, Prussia and Sweden (Nov. 1824: 318). The Spaniards themselves welcomed the constitution because they found in it "el compendio de los derechos y deberes del hombre en sociedad, reconocidos por la razón, apoyados por la justicia, y santificados *por la antiguas leyes* …"[4] In this discussion the sources of legitimacy are to be found both in the approval of contemporaries (particularly when they are powerful states), and in any links that could be found between the new and the old, half-mythical set of laws (Nov. 1824: 321, 326).

The dispute between the various versions of legitimacy is most obvious in a later article where the much-reviled Congress of Verona is mentioned. (It was this gathering that decided in 1822 on the French military intervention in Spain to replace the liberal government by a royal one.) The participants at this Congress stated that the great powers formed a happy Christian family who could not be divided (Sept. 1825: 285). *Ocios* points out the particular way in which these powers invoke their favourite principle as the base for a continental legal framework: "[Las grandes potencias] han proclamado el principio de la legitimidad por base del derecho público europeo. ¿Pero como entienden este principio y el derecho que de él pretenden deducir? Invocándolo é interpretándolo siempre á favor de los gabinetes y de la dinastías; jamás á favor de los pueblos."[5] The aim of these powers is European political and military balance (an element discussed by Mallet du Pan when he criticized Napoleon's invasion of Switzerland). But *Ocios* replies that, indeed, there cannot be a proper balance without moral principles and respect for the rights of nations (Sept. 1825: 287).

The 1812 document is also defended in a couple of articles reviewing, or rather dismissing, a *History of the Spanish Revolution 1820-1823 by a Witness*. The work was anonymous, but it appears to have been written by a clergyman called Miñao who sided with the absolutist authorities after 1823 (Lloréns, *Liberals y románticos* 260). In response to the way the argu-

---

[4] "… the summary of man's rights and duties in society, recognized by reason supported by justice, and sanctified *by the ancient laws* …" (Nov. 1824: 318). Italics in the original.

[5] "[The great powers] have proclaimed the principle of legitimacy as the foundation of the European public rights. But how do they understand this principle and the rights which they claim to infer from it? By invoking and interpreting it constantly in favour of the governments and royal dynasties; never in favour of the people" (Sept. 1825: 285).

ment of the ancient constitution seems to have been deployed in this instant history, the editors qualify their resort to the evidence of the ancient laws; such laws do limit royal authority but there is a risk that some people praise them in order to defend despotism (July 1825: 54). The periodical emphasizes that in the light of the ancient constitution, the legitimacy of the present monarch is questionable and he is guilty before the nation. This is one example of an argument used by both sides because of its vagueness. On the whole, the old constitution was most frequently referred to in liberal texts as an important means of limiting absolute power. But the reviewer is aware here of how the other side may employ this reference and warns against its misuse.

The ancient laws need to be revived in order to recover the ancient rights, if a constitution for a hypothetical state is to be devised (Aug. 1826: 128-30). The question of who should shape the constitution ought to have an obvious answer if one accepts that sovereignty resides in the people, even if there are difficulties when it comes to the manner people understand and exercise sovereignty. On the other hand, kings have often been reluctant to grant a constitution unless forced to do it. *Ocios* would again like to see an exception here in the way Britain has solved the problem (130-33).

The question of the substance and the form of a constitution is raised in a comparison between Spain and Britain (Oct. 1827: 539). Having referred throughout innumerable discussions to an ancient constitution whose quality it would be desirable to recover, the editors state here that in fact neither country possessed such a document in the old times. Nevertheless, even without a formally drafted code, natural rights were observed due to a series of decisions, laws, and agreements. The Castilians and the Aragonese did enjoy their freedom in the early days (no precise date is given), but not as a result of any fundamental text (540). In the continuous disputes with the "exaltados," this may well have been an ironical reference to the contrast between the existence of the 1812 Constitution as a text and the lack of rights in reality. This Constitution had never been put into practice but enjoyed a considerable prestige in Europe among revolutionary groups. The revolutionaries of 1820 in Naples and elsewhere in Italy were invoking the principles enshrined in this document. The series of imaginary letters including this article en-

titled "The English Constitution" emphasized the value of the old regulations, a term occasionally used instead of constitution. The conclusion
seems to be that the essential thing is to enjoy natural rights, not to have
a set of principles codified on paper, a commendable document that
could easily be dismissed by a despot. This sounds like a further criticism
of the attitude of the "exaltados" who held firm to the 1812 text regarding any updating as an attempt to adulterate its ideals.

In the regular review of political developments in the same issue the
editors notice a certain instability in Europe, a probable reference to the
persistence of despotism and increasing tensions: the authors mention
Rousseau's statement that one cannot deceive the people for long (no
reference is given). The review turns into an analysis, which anticipates
the triumph of liberalism. The question is whether this victory will be
achieved by means of violence or "por la fuerza de las cosas," a phrase
that echoes Mallet du Pan's "la force des choses." The phrase seems to
have been something of a common place in political writing during the
eighteenth century; it can be encountered in Montesquieu and Voltaire
and it was rather often employed by Rousseau. It was a forceful sound-
ing and sufficiently vague phrase to be invoked on both sides of an argument. By the time Joseph de Maistre used it, the sense was of the
weight of tradition on present circumstances rather than an inevitable
outburst against despotism, as the liberals meant it. However, the reviewer concludes, if it came to a revolution, a free Spain would force the
main European leaders to recognize "more liberal principles" in their
own countries (Oct. 1827: 570). During the decades when new philosophical systems were structured round the stages of historical development (Hegel's, Saint-Simon's, Comte's), the idea of "la fuerza de las cosas" seems to have resurfaced in the guise of the inevitability of historical
progress. Whether the emphasis was on logic or faith, it was assumed
that at the end of the sequence the desired state of things would be
reached, in this case a liberal system in the version envisaged by the
Spanish exiles of the 1820s.

Crusade against the "Curia"

The constitution was not only endangered by internal despotism, but was under attack from outside as well. The Holy Alliance was accused of intending to damage it (May 1824: 123), a criticism that was woven into another theme recurrent in this periodical: the papacy as a danger to Spain but also to other European states. The Pope had looked with suspicion on the Russian Tsar's initiative and saw the Alliance with its religious claims as something of a rival in Europe, hence his refusal to cooperate when approached. The Spanish émigrés in London were not the only ones who realized that, despite their lack of overt cooperation, the Holy Alliance and the Pope had interests in common. They perceived the danger with particular acuteness having just been removed from power. In a Europe characterized by a return to absolutism under international auspices as it were, the three years of liberal government in Spain had been a exception. The decision to put an end to the liberal rule had been made collectively at the Verona Congress in 1822, the liberals had experienced the force of cooperation between despotic governments. This outlook may have influenced the actions of the Spanish émigrés: if the absolutist regime in Spain benefited from the international circumstances, it was more difficult to urge their fellow-countrymen at home or abroad to revolt. It was perhaps more fruitful to alert people to the fact that some groups in various nations had common interests, and to point to the attempts of several royals courts and governments to coordinate their policies in order to prevent any militant moves on the Continent.

The wider international context in which these exiles considered the development of Spain was worrying enough, but the possible reach of papacy inside Spain caused a particular brand of anti-clericalism. The large numbers of clergymen and their influence in Spain raised questions concerning the Pope's attempts at interference, particularly after the re-establishment of the Jesuit Order. The old conflict between monarchs and papacy had lost most of its topicality by the early nineteenth century. Yet by having a say in administrative clerical matters and, at least in Spain, complete domination in doctrinal questions, the papacy caused resentment among both reformists and revolutionaries. The argument against the papal claims to appoint and remove kings (Nov. 1824: 300-301) moves on to the attempt of some clergymen to thwart the abolition of the Inquisition in 1812, resulting in the government's request that the papal envoy should leave Spain (303). This was the decision of a liberal administration, and so was the decision of the Cortes in 1820 to pass laws on church matters. The article argues that this was the proper course of action "para que tiene y ha tenido siempre autoridad, especialmente en España, la potestad civil" ("authority has always belonged to the secular administration, particularly in Spain" [303]). Whether this claim can be fully backed by evidence is another question. The relevant point is how the author of this article chooses the terms of his discussion. There is a difference between the liberals' attitude towards the Spanish Catholic Church and that towards Rome: mentioning the Pope's dismissal of the laws passed by the Cortes, the author quotes approvingly the bishop of "Guadix" who stated that bishops hold everything "de jure divino" and not by Rome's permission. Some of these liberals had been educated in the 1780s and 1790s when it was known that the Church contained a sizeable number of clerics willing to contemplate reforms; Blanco himself had been an unorthodox clergyman, increasingly so in Britain. The liberals writing in *Ocios* could make these distinctions that qualified their anti-clericalism.

Natural rights are brought into the discussion as a bulwark against the papal abuse of power (Nov. 1824: 305, 306). An explanation of the emergence of despotism resorts to a theory of the sources of royal legitimacy, a constantly sensitive issue at the time. Kings used to depend on popes for their crown and not on their own people, the writer explains. When they stopped being dependent on Rome, the monarchs' conviction that their position did not depend on their subjects "fue cresciendo hasta el punto de no reconocer en ellos derechos, sino obligaciones" ("increased to the point of not seeing rights, but obligations" [305]). This account of how people's rights came to be neglected assumes that it had been the people all along who lent authority to the king, both during, but also before, legitimacy was apparently granted by the Pope. Further on, the article argues that the legitimacy granted by Rome made the kings forget their earlier "pact" with those who agreed to become subjects (306). The implication is that the effort undertaken to recover the proper role of the people requires disentangling the claims and counter-claims to the right of granting power. Rome's interference has distorted the relationship between the ruler and the ruled, and liberals intend to bring about a situation where the individual may decide on how to be represented.

The accusation that Rome makes monarchs forget their subjects' rights is made in a discussion where national sovereignty is opposed to universal sovereignty, the latter understood as papal domination (Dec. 1824: 386-87). In this article where the adversary is constantly identified as "curia romana," the author urges those states that want to get rid of despotism to shake off first the ecclesiastical one (393). And abandoning the idea of gaining the cooperation of the more reasonable clergymen at home, at the risk of contradicting himself, the writer concludes trenchantly that all states, whatever their government, ought to get rid of Church domination, papal but also domestic.

A further dimension is introduced by a discussion of the Inquisition and the Jesuits as instruments of the "curia romana" (Feb. 1825: 137 ff). Here "ultramontanismo," loyalty to Rome and not to the national Church, is opposed to "amor de la patria" (Jan. 1826: 138). It is not entirely clear whether the loyalty of the entire Spanish Church is in question, or only that of certain clerical institutions or groups, such as the Jesuits.[6] The fact is that the issue of loyalty does recur, and the context in which it is placed hints at the nationalistic tone of this Spanish émigré circle, the assumption being that such a periodical was the reflection of more than just one person's opinions. The earlier suggestion of the editors of *Español Constitucional* that peoples should cooperate across borders is a result of the international cooperation among absolutist leaders such as the one suggested by the Holy Alliance. This high-level cooperation brings along its own understanding and definition of legitimacy, closer to that of the "ancien régime" than to that based on natural rights. As various unreformed monarchs returned to power after Napoleon's fall "los pueblos se vieron de nuevo esclavizados con las doctrinas de la

---

[6]On the Spanish clergy being more loyal to Rome than to Spain, see also Sept. 1825: 232-33.

santa alianza, de la legitimidad, del orden de las sociedades europeas, del statu quo …"[7]

There was concern about educational matters as well. The Jesuits who had dominated the teaching profession to such an extent before their expulsion in 1767 were allowed, indeed encouraged, to return in large numbers. Back in action, they were resorting to theocratical ideas in order to combat the teachings recently introduced by means of the Lancastrian system. The issue was not only a matter of syllabus; it had wider political and national implications, according to the journal. *Ocios* saw here yet another chance for the "curia" to spread its doctrines in order to discredit liberal values.

Further Undermining of the Clergy

A series of articles summarize the lectures on legislation given by a certain Joseph Rey of Grenoble (Feb. 1826: 174-81; May 1826: 415-21; June 1826: 519-30). Rey seems to have been an ex-Jacobin involved in the activities of the secret societies in France. This is not material produced by an exile, but is selected and presented approvingly by *Ocios*. To a reasonable extent it can be considered to represent the editors' position on the issues discussed in these lectures.

Rey bases his arguments on Destutt de Tracy's thoughts on ideology (Feb. 1826: 176-75), but what is worth emphasizing here is Rey's argument about the impact of theology on morality. The influence of the theological ideas in the moral sphere has been one of the main obstacles in the way of its development (Feb. 1826: 176). This development, according to Rey, has been thwarted by the distortion of reason and of the "naturaleza" of the moral ideas. The editorial line against the papacy continues here by finding ammunition against the adverse effects of theology in Rey's lectures that *Ocios* presents at some length. In step with

---

[7] "… the nations realized that they were again enslaved by the doctrines of the Holy Alliance, of legitimacy, of the order of the European states, of the status quo …" (Feb. 1825: 139).

the topical theory of utilitarianism, the periodical sums up Joseph Rey's outlook on morality as defined by the effect of actions.[8]

The clergy emerge once more as the villains in a later discussion on whether the aristocrats or the priests are most guilty of the internal troubles in Spain. The former have been mainly an inert obstacle, but the latter, particularly the higher clergy, have fought against the liberals from the very beginning feeling threatened by reforms (July 1826: 36-37). The clergy should be aware of the spirit of the age ("El clero no debe perder de vista el punto á do se inclinan las opiniones del siglo" [39-40]). The editors are once more willing to exempt some prelates, making a distinction between "la parte fanática del clero secular y regular" (Jan. 1827: 34), and a more reasonable group. This distinction is made as a result of various claims that a majority of the Spaniards want a despotic system, something that *Ocios* dismisses. The editors conclude that there are a few groups in the country, who do want an absolutist government, for instance all those who depend on the monarchy: among them, courtiers, the higher clergy (although not all fanatics), and some fanatic clergymen (not all highly placed). But on the whole, the periodical argues, the clergy turned out to be one of the chief groups hostile to the constitution as they claim that "[c]atholicism is incompatible with moderate monarchies" (Jan. 1827: 33). "Moderate" is to be taken here as referring to monarchies whose powers are limited; the implication is also that Catholicism, in the version promoted by the extreme Spanish clergy, must go on at any cost.

Apart from such groups, the conclusion is that a majority of the nation, "la masa general de la nación" (Jan. 1827: 38), is against an arbitrary government. The explanation of the failure of the people to bring about a constitutional government lies in the nefarious influence of France and its military force, while Portugal, for instance, benefits from British help and influence (39). The clergy would not even be desirable in a national assembly because of their being isolated from the population due to their celibacy, and because of their loyalty to Rome (315-16).

---

[8] Feb. 1826: 179. See also May 1826: 416-17 on the foundations of economics being conditioned by pleasure and pain.

The presence of the Church in the society of the 1820s is once more set against the spirit of the age, sometimes called "espíritu de exámen" (July 1827: 319), or "espíritu analítico" (322). These variations show what the editors considered to be the characteristics of this contemporary mood: a critical, questioning, inquiring approach. Further more, a periodical like *Ocios* most probably saw itself as part of the intellectual make-up of the age weakening the prestige of the Church.

Any anti-clerical criticism may have had a further intent and effect than combating the impact of Rome and of the local priesthood. The Spanish king was the only one who by papal dispensation was allowed to call himself "Catholic King." The French monarch, for instance, could only boast the attribute "très Chrétien." It is conceivable that by reinforcing the obstructive role of the "curia romana" and of a good deal of the Spanish Catholic Church regarding civic rights and development in general, *Ocios* was indirectly attempting to diminish the prestige of the monarchy. The power and significance of the monarchy, at least of the recalcitrant Fernando VII, could thus be limited not only by formal, legalistic, constitutional means (assuming the king observed them), but also by undermining the attributes supporting the royal image.

The Count of Provence had not been crowned as Louis XVIII in the traditional ceremony at Reims due to the agitation of 1814 and 1815, as well as his frail health. The coronation of the Count of Artois as Charles X was the first one for nearly six decades. But there were additional worries that the papacy was trying to reassert itself. These worries were expressed in the same article with its telling title "Combinación teocrática en Europa contra los libertades públicas, el poder y la independencia de las naciones civilizadas" (July 1827: 318-40). The periodical found signs of such a tendency in the ceremonies at Reims. The overall impression given by this ritual, and the insistent presence of various prelates at the king's side conveyed the point that France was receiving its monarch from the Church and not from the people (330-31). The editors of *Ocios* may have known of Charles X's attitude during his own exile as the Count of Artois; it was likely that his strongly reactionary views of 1790s were unchanged, and that anyone who was against "las libertades públicas," such as segments of the higher clergy, was to be encouraged.

Ethical values or the issue of morality as such are to be encountered explicitly only a few times. Morality is linked to Christianity in a remark on the "máximas de la moral pura" which were established by Christ (June 1824: 217). Their aim was the preservation of social order and of "los derechos del hombre" (217). This comes at the end of a reply to Haller's work on the Cádiz Constitution and is meant to show how this text possesses the virtue of reconciling justice, religion and the wish for order in society. Any direct mention of moral issues tends to fall into predictable patterns. A more oblique approach is called for: it is necessary to wade through quantities of texts in order to discern eventually the relevant assumptions.

The explicit references to morality and exiles are not particularly fruitful either. A few occur in connection with the reason for the flight of the "liberales" and their reception in Britain. Thousands of learned, sensible men ("sabios") fled after 1823 in order to avoid perjury or worse. Like most justifications in exile, this one tends to turn into a criticism of those who stayed at home by attributing to them an unethical behaviour, which could have been avoided in exile. The discussion does not proceed further than that. Contenting itself with this brief remark, *Ocios* shows caution regarding the further divisive effect such a line of thought might have.

Another reference to morality is made after an article on the Spanish émigrés in England. Again, this is a brief, restrained note; this time probably intended not to offend local sensitivities (Dec. 1824: 465-67). These remarks are occasioned by an appeal in aid of the Spanish refugees initiated by the Lord Mayor. Arrived in London, the exiles see "la moral reducida á sus verdaderos elementos" (466), that is, they witness Protestant clergymen, but also laymen, helping people of the much-reviled Catholic faith. The gesture of the Anglican Church and the Spaniards' surprise have to be seen against the contemporary debate on Catholic Emancipation. People all over Britain were taking sides on whether Catholics should be granted full rights (access to certain jobs, to university education) that the government intended to do. However, the authorities in London were bombarded by anti-Catholic petitions from all over the country. Consequently, the Spanish exiles were so much more willing to see moral merit in the support received from whatever quarter.[9] But the *British Monitor* published several objections, quoted by *Ocios*. The *Monitor* had called the Spaniards "schemers" and the Spanish periodical pointed out that the generous asylum granted by the British people (on the whole) shows that they considered that the Spanish exiles fought for "la verdadera legitimidad" and for the freedom of Europe. Again, true legitimacy was tacitly contrasted with the official legitimacy invoked by the restored aristocratic regimes.

Generally, as in the previous cases, the ethical values of the exiles have to be extrapolated from their writings on reforms, on militant action and from any other political reflections. Without being moralists as such, they were politically motivated and keen to appear as being in the right. All the editors and contributors to the Spanish exile periodicals discussed here had left their country for the same reason, their adherence to incipient liberal values encountered the reaction of absolutism and the indifference of the uneducated citizens. In so far as liberalism was for these exiles the exercise of reason and freedom (taking their political creed very generally), they could argue, as *El Español Constitucional* did explicitly, that most people would opt for these values. The implications derived from this argument for the moral stance of the "liberales" in exile indicate the way in which they would dismiss the guilt of being banished. These implications are discussed in more detail in the final chapter where they are considered in an extended context together with the other exiles' claims. Without arguing in the same manner, Giuseppe Mazzini resorts to similar categories in the texts published in his own periodical published in London. He arrived in Britain a decade after *Ocios* ceased appearing. The social tensions noticeable more and more after the post-1814 Restoration were about to turn into full-scale confrontations by the 1840s. New entities could be appealed to and used in arguments. The

---

[9] On distant villages petitioning against Catholic emancipation see Linda Colley, *Britons: Forging the Nation 1707-1837* (New Haven: Yale UP, 1992) 330. On the women's prominence in this anti-Catholic campaign see 333.

right of nations to unity and independence and the position of the workers as a coherent social group would recur in Mazzini's periodical.

Chapter 7

In Search of People's Divinity: Mazzini's *Apostolato popolare*

As in Spain, the area and people that made up the Italian states could look back on what was considered a period of greatness, possibly several, and compare the present with the past. The political and cultural decline after the peak of the Roman power or after the Renaissance was palpable. It is not surprising that the intellectual revival starting in the 1690s and continuing throughout the eighteenth century had antiquarian erudition as one of its chief characteristics.[1] There was also a fresh interest in the work of scientists and philosophers produced outside the Peninsula. Local erudite endeavours were undertaken in a more critical spirit than before. The intellectuals were becoming involved politically in the effort to limit ecclesiastical power, particularly censorship. This struggle made them increasingly aware of the significance of a secular state. There was no shortage of state formations in the area, but the level of debates was uneven. Due to papal claims over Naples, for some time the local lawyers had been accustomed to oppose the scholastic arguments of the

---

[1] Stuart Woolf, *A History of Italy, 1700-1860: the Social Constraints of Political Change* (London: Methuen, 1979) 75-76.

Jesuits in terms of historical precedent but also of natural law. Jansenism was making inroads among the more daring clergymen, and there was an overall French cultural influence, more in French-speaking Piedmont, less in the southern states. The last decades of the eighteenth century saw an increase of the importance of the philosophy of history that was replacing antiquarian erudition (Woolf 122).

From Nostalgia to "Carboneria"

By the turn of the century the Peninsula was fragmented into states mostly under various degrees of foreign domination. Piedmont could boast some sort of sovereignty but the strong presence of French culture, and soon the presence of French troops, made its autonomy rather questionable. Lombardy was under Austrian rule, while the Kingdom of Naples and Sicily was under Spanish domination. The Papal States centred on Rome, and the few republics, tiny or no longer strong (Lucca, Genoa, Venice) did not suffice to form a proper "Italian" counterweight. Joseph II's attempts to put into practice a number of reforms ended with his death before the end of the century. Naples and Sicily did not benefit much from Carlos III's rule who a few decades earlier had departed to become king of Spain and to prove an enlightened despot in the other southern peninsula.

The society formed in Milan in the 1760s by a group of nobles interested in concrete social and legal reforms, among whom there was Beccaria, carried on its discussions quite openly. They published their thoughts influenced by Locke and the French Encyclopedists in the periodical *Il Caffè* (1764-66). Further progressive thought, and later a good deal of militant action, would issue from the new secret societies, which were beginning to emerge in the latter part of the century. Younger Masons were adopting egalitarian views brought over by members of the Bavarian sects. Disappointment in the results of some of these sects led to the establishment of the more revolutionary and conspiratorial "Carboneria" whose activity took place mostly in the south. The French invasions of the 1790s also brought the much-repeated phrase "the Republic one and indivisible."[2] With parts of Italy occupied by Napoleon, the defence of Italy became more than just an academic exercise. The essay-competition announced by the French-dominated administration at Milan in 1796 on the best type of government for Italy presupposed the existence of such a national entity lacking only a proper political structure. At the time it suited the French to encourage Italian unity. Later things changed. However, the new idea received a fresh impulse. Terms like "patria," used to describe one's home province, were increasingly meant as the area of all the Italian states. Because of the French identification with ancient Rome, the Italian nationalists tried to find a link with the Etruscans or the medieval communes.

The poet Ugo Foscolo, who ended up in exile in London after the revolts of the 1820s, stated that "all Italians are exiles in Italy." He was much admired by Mazzini who later on would make an effort during his own London exile to edit Foscolo's manuscripts. Giuseppe Mazzini (1805-1872) was born in Genoa where he took a degree in law and began to publish literary criticism. His interest in Herder, but also in Vico, Condorcet and Rousseau, can be seen in his notebooks.[3] His militant activities led to his expulsion from Genoa, first to Marseille, from which the French authorities expelled him in their turn. Switzerland and soon Britain would provide shelter until the end of his life, although he would spend brief periods in Italy, most memorably as a tolerant triumvir of a briefly republican Rome in 1849.

The organizations set up by Mazzini followed the pattern of the secret associations in Italy. He would continue this form of militant activity all his life, but would also publish a constant stream of texts, some of them in his chief periodical published in London. The idea was to use journalism as a weapon in order to reach his ideal of a united and independent Italy. His objectives also included the achievement of democracy and equality in the new state. Before 1830 Mazzini had been influ-

---

[2] For this and some of the following points, see Adrian Lyttleton, "The national question in Italy," in Mikulas Teich and Roy Porter, eds. *The National Question in Europe in Historical Context* (Cambridge: Cambridge UP, 1993) 63-81.

[3] Dennis Mack Smith, *Mazzini* (New Haven: Yale UP, 1994) 3 ff. For Mazzini's interest in Herder, see also Harry Hearder, *Italy in the Age of the Risorgimento: 1790-1870* (London: Longman, 1983) 159-60.

enced by Victor Cousin's theory of progress (seeing European civilization as a period of transition), and by Guizot whose favourable opinions on Italy appealed to him.[4] Disappointed by their conservatism after the July Revolution in France, Mazzini took an increasing interest in Saint-Simon's ideas and started emphasizing the importance of collectivism (Lyttleton 82). Yet his view of collectivism had an inclusive quality. Earlier he had sympathized with the objectives of the extreme Jacobin, Buonarotti, Babeuf's friend and collaborator. Due to a certain amount of rivalry and misunderstanding regarding the loyalties of other Italian exiles (Buonarotti had Paris as his base), Mazzini broke with him, and separated the idea of nationalism from communism and class struggle. The national community envisaged by Mazzini would incorporate all classes harmoniously (Lyttleton 81).

Apostolato popolare

Mazzini's writings have received far more attention than any of the exiles discussed above, although not in the kind of context outlined here. The present study deals with several émigrés of whom Mazzini is only one, however prominent. I ought to point out again that I only consider in detail his texts printed in the *Apostolato popolare* which means that I stop before 1848, as promised in the sub-title, although his activity continued well beyond that year. Why only this periodical, and why hardly anything after 1848? Having come to Mazzini, it may be useful to emphasize again the limits of the present study and the reason for choosing these particular sources. For practical reasons, in a comparative study of this nature resting on a selective choice of sources assumed to be representative, I have confined myself only to exile periodicals published in London. The short pieces printed regularly in such periodicals reveal a particular aspect of the émigrés' thinking, as their various points are repeatedly asserted, expanded into fiery appeals, or developed into bitter indictments. Longer works or private letters do not carry the same impact or urgency and therefore lose their force as examples of reflection marked by extreme circumstances. Finally, there is agreement that after 1848 Mazzini's

---

[4] Romano Bracalini, *Mazzini: Il sogno dell'Italia onesta* (Milano: Mondadori, 1992) 44.

influence was on the wane in Italy and on the continent. This is not the place to demonstrate that a new social, political and intellectual phase could be discerned in Europe after 1848. Mazzini did go on producing political texts containing ethical values but they emerged in a different context that is not part of the present work.

Mazzini arrived in London in 1837 dejected after the setbacks in his revolutionary activity. By 1839 his interest in political matters returned and among his new projects was the publication of a periodical. The intention appears more clearly if this initiative is placed in the context of Mazzini's militant activities. After the enthusiasm of the early 1830s resulting in failure in Genoa and then in Marseille, his first place of exile, not much was heard for a while of Mazzini's organization "Giovine Italia." But by 1840 he was trying to revive the association. He explained to Giuseppe Lambertini in a letter of 30 August 1840 that, in the name of unity, factionalism must be avoided; considering that the aim is to create one nation there can only be "un sola Associazione nazionale; una fede, dunque una sola chiesa. Dobbiam esser religiosi, non settarii, esser insomma come i primi Cristiani."[5]

Calling his new periodical *Apostolato popolare* points to Mazzini's sense of mission. And since in the first editorial the chief objective is announced as spelling out the duties of the Italians, being part of the relaunching of "Giovine Italia," the moral basis on which Mazzini places his thought and action is quite emphatic already at this stage.

Apostolato popolare appeared irregularly from November 1840 to February 1843. Occasionally it came out in successive months, but sometimes half a year could pass between issues. It was clearly meant as a periodical, but judging by its erratic rhythm and the fact that it carried instalments of Mazzini's long essay on duties, it may also be seen as an outlet for his own writings and not only as a regular journal commenting on current developments, like most of the other émigré journals discussed above. In a later notice the editor states clearly that his journal

---

[5] "… a single national Association; a single faith, therefore only one church. We should be religious, not factional, all in all we should be like the first Christians" *Scritti editi ed inediti*, 94 vols. (Imola: Galeati, 1906-1943) 19: ix. See also G.H. Berkeley, *The Making of Italy: 1815-1846* (1932; Cambridge: Cambridge UP, 1968) 241-42.

does not intend to review books.[6] Each number consisted of only eight pages, unlike the fifty or sixty in the case of the French or Spanish periodicals. Private funds, donations, and subscriptions seem to have provided the necessary backing, however meagre; the size and the quality of the paper show the precarious financial situation of the Italians in London.

There is little evidence of the impact of *Apostolato popolare* in Italy. Some proof that it was distributed and read in the United States is provided by a notice in the journal itself on Italians in New York ordering and paying for five hundred copies of the magazine (1 January 1842: 31). Some copies were burned in France, and others reached various Italian cities and Northern Africa where a few saint-simonians may have been following the surviving influence of the master (Mack Smith 38).

There were altogether twelve issues of the periodical containing a modest amount of material. Mazzini returns to his main ideas time and again throughout the almost four years of the journal's existence. Since the main themes keep recurring, I have decided to follow the contents chronologically; under the circumstances this is practically equivalent to a thematic approach. The material is not presented exhaustively below, but the chief points are outlined in more detail and discussed.

Workers and Italians

According to an editorial in the first issue, the initial impulse to start the periodical had been an awareness of the situation of the Italian workers, which could only be gained outside the Italian-speaking areas. Whether this awareness was reached by travelling workers or exiles such as Mazzini, the fact remains that it was the broader view that revealed problems almost impossible to grasp at home. In the first issue the editor explains that the magazine had come about as a response to the realization of the difference between the condition of the Italian workers and those of other nations. The key elements that the journal would concentrate on

---

[6] *Apostolato popolare* 1 January 1842: 28.

are set out at this early stage as the editor points out that this difference is "più morale que materiale."[7]

From the discussion of the workers' hardships it appears that morality, as used here by Mazzini, has to do with correcting economic and social injustice. And this can be achieved by an organization rooted in national solidarity, itself a result of national unity. The Italian worker's fragmented existence is contrasted with the lot of the French, English or Belgian worker. The Italian is confined to a limited area leaving him "ristretto nel pensiero alla piccola sfera in cui vive" ("confined in thought to the tiny sphere in which he lives" [Della Peruta, ed. 1: 470]) and making him feel doomed to constant weakness. The solution is education. Workers in other states are aware of this and have some access to books, periodicals, courses, but in the Italian states a worker lacks any means of education and only receives "ciecamente alcune idee, quasi sempre false perché gli vengono da uomini interessati a mantenerlo nell'erore …"[8]

This text is not exactly an analysis of the workers' condition, but mostly an appeal to them not to accept the position of their masters as the normal state of things. There is an implicit urge to action, increasingly explicit in subsequent articles. Mazzini also spells out the need, indeed the obligation, to reflect and to work out the reasons of the present situation: "non pensare al rimedio è in voi una vera colpa" ("you are in fact guilty if you don't think of a solution" [473]). This appeal switches constantly between the two kinds of limitation that hinder the workers' development. They are urged not to think of themselves as "romagnoli, genovesi, piemontesi, napoletani" (473), but as Italians; also, they are confined within a soulless activity since "la vostra, operai italiani, è non vita d'uomini, ma esistenza di macchine" ("Italian workers, your life is not the life of human beings, but the existence of machines" [474]). Rising above provincial loyalties and becoming aware of belonging to a na-

---

[7] "Agli Italiani, e specialmente agli operai italiani," Franco Della Peruta, ed. *Scrittori politici dell'ottocento* (Milano-Napoli: Ricciardi, 1969) 1: 468, reprinted from *Apostolato popolare*, 10 Nov. 1840. Some texts published in the periodical have later been reprinted elsewhere and, although I have examined the original versions, for practical reasons, I use the later editions.

[8] "… blindly some ideas, almost always false because they come from people interested in keeping him in ignorance" (Della Peruta, ed. 1: 471).

tion is directly connected with breaking the monotonous toil that seems to deprive their work of meaning. An increased national conscience would lead to an increased sense of belonging to the same community, and hence to new possibilities of education and change.

Judging by the terms occasionally used by Mazzini it becomes obvious that he does not always see the stratification of society in economic terms as for him the dominant social groups are "le classi educate" (474). Whatever advantages they had initially, it is not the possession of capital or hereditary privileges that he chooses to characterize them by.

This appeal sounds in places like a series of reproaches. Social and economic oppression are the result of passivity. The absence of the necessary force possible through a national effort is a consequence of narrow local loyalties. Indifference is seen by Mazzini as incriminating: "Voi non potete, senza colpa, essere indifferenti ai mali di milioni dei vostri concittadini …" ("You cannot be indifferent to the misfortune of millions of your fellow-citizens without being guilty …" [478]). Having mentioned the difficulties (oppression, exploitation) and one solution that is still a distant goal (education), Mazzini mentions another, more immediate solution: revolutionary action. This would be the concrete means to have access to education and moral improvement (475). And here emerges another one of Mazzini's chief aims in this periodical; making a revolution in Italy is both possible and easy "e noi ve lo proveremo nei numeri successivi di questa pubblicazione" ("which we'll prove to you in the subsequent issues of this periodical" [475]). This requires preparation, education (such as is possible at the moment), and organizing people within one association which Mazzini explains that he is trying to achieve by means of his "Giovine Italia" with its slogan printed on the cover of each number of *Apostolato*: "Libertà: Eguaglianza: Umanità—Indipendenza: Unità." Further on, the editor states that his particular work is explaining the truth of the claims made above, but also the duties towards one's country, towards God, and towards one's compatriots (476). These sets of duties almost coincide with the chapters of Mazzini's long essay and shows that the periodical was to a large extent a means to print and spread what became *The Duties of Man*.

The conclusion reminds the readers that, although they are part of a great European group of workers, they need to be led by their own fellow-countrymen. If the unification and independence of Italy is achieved with the help of foreign leaders among whose followers various erroneous doctrines prevail, there is a risk that they would bring along "sistemi di comunione dei beni, d'owenismo, di leggi agrarie, d'abolizione di proprietà, funesti, assurdi, contrari al progresso o alle virtù della specia umana."[9] It is plain that Mazzini dismissed recent utopian theories, although he was still believed to be influenced by Saint-Simon. Neither did he incline towards the kind of militant action that he witnessed in Britain in connection with the Chartist movement launched in earnest a year after his arrival in London. His remedies would be peaceful: "Noi predicheremo nell'amore di tutte le classi, nell'abborrimento d'ogni riazione e d'ogni ingiustizia" ("We shall preach in the spirit of friendship towards all classes, of abhorrence of all kinds of reaction and injustice" [479]). The idea of unity seems to dominate completely Mazzini's thought making him envisage a corporatist society with its own utopian traits.

Having tested the waters with the first issue, Mazzini admits in the second number that the publication "comparirà d'ora in poi, se non regolarmente, certo a non lunghi intervalli di tempo" ("will appear now and then, if not regularly, certainly not at long intervals of time" [25 July 1841: 9]). In an age of manifestoes, declarations and proclamations it is not unusual to find that the main two articles of this number are called "Agli Italiani" and "Agli operai italiani" (the title of the editorial in the first issue combined the two categories). The revival of "Giovine Italia" is linked here with the education of the people. Mazzini sees a change of opinion among the workers who seem to understand that they would not dominate a future society, a change of mind that he ascribes to his writings and the principles of his association: "Il numero degli operai convinti que la Nazione Italiana non può fondarsi da una classe sola, ma abbisogna degli sforzi del Popolo tuttoquanto, e que i principii profesati dalla GIOVINE ITALIA sono i soli che possano dirigere utilmente l'educazione del Popolo, è cresciuto."[10]

---

[9] "... systems of common ownership, of Owenism, of agrarian laws, of the abolition of [private] property which are sinister, absurd, against progress or any human virtue" (Della Peruta, ed., 1: 479).

[10] "An increasing number of workers have become persuaded that the Italian Nation cannot be established on a single class, but it needs the efforts of the entire People,

This editorial appeal changes tone and turns into a warning to the privileged classes. They are urged to heed the poor classes' requests for rights, otherwise the "errors of *communism*" would be fuelled by inequality as in France, or that massive, threatening demonstrations may take place like the one Mazzini believes is about to be organized in England (25 July 1841: 10, italics in the original). The drift of the article is plain: the poor need education and a proper place in society, if not, the upper class is cautioned that they are in danger. But he does not make these points by stating them as such: they are embedded in appeals, dire predictions, and apocalyptic statements. This piece is indeed an appeal, but in comparison with similar ones in other exile journals meant to state a problem, suggest a solution and voice a call to action, this one is strikingly rhetorical. The title itself, "Agli Italiani," may seem more visionary than practical addressing itself to a group still uneasy as an ethnic community. (For instance, quite a few Sicilians thought that "Italia" was the distorted name of someone called in fact La Talia who was the mistress of the king of Piedmont.) When Mazzini asked the workers in the introductory editorial not to think of themselves as "romagnoli, genovesi, piemontesi, napoletani," but as Italians, it was precisely because the general term was alien to them.

Social Harmony Through Education

Two ideas often associated with Mazzini, the importance of education and the cooperation between the social classes, appear already at this early stage of his periodical. They are joined together by the reference to the nation. Mazzini writes about the possibility of showing in Italy "il primo spettacolo d'una rigenerazione fondata sulla concordia e sull'armonia dei lavori fra tutti gli elementi che formano la Nazione."[11] He urges the privileged citizens, to whom he addresses himself at this point, to help "nel disegno di cacciare fin d'ora i primi germi d'un Edu-

---

and that only the principles of GIOVINE ITALIA can guide the education of the People" (25 July 1841: 9).

[11] "... the first demonstration of a regeneration based on the understanding and harmony of all kinds of work amid the elements that make up the Nation" (25 July 1841: 11).

cazione Nazional [sic] nel nostro popolo" ("in the plan of promptly planting the first seeds of national education in our people" [25 July 1841: 11]). A closer look at these passages may show why at a time when revolutionaries would increasingly see social processes in terms of class conflict, and offer solutions based on its irreconcilability, Mazzini perceived developments in terms of harmony between classes, even if aware of the chasm and tensions between them, and despite the fact that often his texts have a radical tone about them.

The explanation may lie in the particular significance ascribed by him to education. Mazzini appears to consider education as a national enterprise whose effects would be felt accordingly, one of which could be attuning people to each other, making them aware of each other's interests, and thus reconciling the various social groups. When praising the importance of education, Mazzini does not have in mind only the education of the workers, or any other underprivileged section of the population. The key to his social harmony presupposes an overall pedagogical effort comprising everybody. Occasionally, Mazzini may seem to favour national unity over social justice. But I would argue that in texts such as his appeal of July 1841 it appears clearly how the two are equally important. However, his solution requires that the first stages should concentrate on education within a national framework.

One of the aims of the periodical is mentioned in passing when discussing the duty of the Italian workers to organize themselves according to nationality. Mazzini renews his attack against the tempting doctrines that compete with his ideas for the support of the workers. He has noticed that workers gather in associations whose slogans are "comunione di beni, abolizione de la proprietà; dottrine tiranniche, assurde, nemiche al progresso dell'Umanità, che noi dovremo confutare in alcuno de' numero succesivi dell'*Apostolato*."[12] In his opinion, this misguided attraction towards what seems a recognizable form of communism risks paralyzing the activity of many "veri amici del popolo" and wasting energy on "progetti impossibili" (25 July 1841: 11). Curiously enough, not much is

---

12 "... common ownership, abolishing [private] property; tyrannical, absurd doctrines, hostile to the progress of Humanity which we are going to refute in the following numbers of the periodical" (25 July 1841: 11).

said in the later issues of the dangers of being lured by the seducing call of communism, but in the latter part of the *Duties of Man*, not published in the periodical, Mazzini attacks at length the new trend, sensing the increasing peril, once more calling it by its name, and this time granting it a capital C. (It ought to be said, that Mazzini also dismisses the rest of the contemporary budding ideologies in his long essay.)

Unlike the other exiles commenting on politics in their periodicals, Mazzini was writing at a time when the concept of social class was acquiring an increasing importance. He could not overlook the effects of the social and economic developments as shown by his appeals to workers not to accept the masters' domination. His insistence on harmonizing potential social conflicts indicates that he grasped the possible consequences of the antagonism between various classes. There was a certain difficulty about the level at which Mazzini pitched his appeals to the, presumably Italian, workers. From his vantage point in Britain, Mazzini was aware of the plight of the large working-class in the most industrialized nation at the time; yet, he was addressing people in Italy where most of them toiled in the fields rather than in factories. Some of his warnings may have arrived too early in a far less industrialized Italian Peninsula in comparison with Britain, a problem which distance was bound to create for any exile still willing to give advice to people at home.

Mazzini goes on contrasting "Umanità" and "Patria." Working for the latter, one works for the former. There is a tension in his arguments between internationalism and nationalism. Only a few years later Mazzini would start new international organizations (e.g. "Young Europe") based on his understanding of the mission of humanity as a whole. Yet, at least in the early 1840s, there appears to be a hierarchy of ideals in his understanding of the ways of reaching social harmony. He sees his duty as pointing out the right sequence in which these values should be worked for and achieved.

The Italian workers ought to establish their own identity before joining foreign associations; still addressing the Italian workers, but clearly meaning all the inhabitants of that territory, Mazzini claims that "voi non avete esistenza riconosciuta, perché non avete Patria, e non appartenete a una Nazione" ("your existence is not recognized, because you have no country and don't belong to a Nation" [25 July 1841: 12]). The more exalted passages point out that this is more than a question of identity: belonging to a well-defined nation with its own political presence acquires an ontological resonance. However, the editor's basic point is that such workers' associations can only exist and function properly if equally backed by a national sense of identity. When each foreign worker brings along the force of his belonging to a well-established nation, the worker coming from a fragmented Italian-speaking area would be at a disadvantage.

The national ideal is never articulated separately from those who shape it: "Fondiamo l'Italia del Popolo" Mazzini urges his readers (12). His strong republicanism would often make him disagree with the monarchists, even if they also wanted a united Italy. The question of priority mentioned above does not arise since unity implies social justice, creating a people's Italy presupposes the acquisition of basic rights as well: "Acquistiamoci diritti d'*uomini* e di cittadini" ("Let's acquire the rights of *human beings* and of citizens" [12]).

The desire to define one's national entity does not exclude solidarity and even active defence of the freedom of other peoples: "Dovunque vi troviate, in seno a qualunque popolo le circonstanze vi caccino, combattete per la libertà di quel popolo, se il momento lo esige. Ma combattete come Italiani ..."[13] The somewhat paradoxical point is reiterated here that internationalism and a common ideal ought nevertheless to be approached in a spirit of clear national awareness.

The theme of concern about the social question is continued and developed in a review of Giuseppe Ricciardi's imaginary *Storia d'Italia dal 1850 al 1900* (1842). Ricciardi had fled to Paris and his book was about how insurrection would be undertaken in Italy in the near future. The editor reproaches the author that he neglects the aspect of social justice in connection with such a visionary uprising. Freedom would be a chimera for most people "Senza un riordinamento sociale fondato su basi d'una equità ch'oggi non esiste ..." ("Without a social restructuring based on a fairness which today does not exist" [25 Sept. 1842: 58]). An-

---

[13] "Wherever you find yourselves, in the middle of whatever people the circumstances drive you, fight for the freedom of that people if the moment requires it. But fight as Italians ..." (25 July 1841: 12).

other criticism is that Ricciardi forgets "l'inviolabilità e l'eternità del sentimento religioso" (59). One of the first steps taken by a revolutionary government would be to abolish the papacy, which seems to the reviewer rash and wrong. Mazzini, if he is the author of the review, was not known for his sympathy towards the papacy, but his deeply religious outlook may explain why he argues that an old faith cannot be dismissed without being replaced by a new one.

Apostle in Exile

Further remarks on Ricciardi's book reveal Mazzini's image of exile and of his mission as a refugee. Few émigrés have grasped "la misione e la santità dell'esilio: pochi intendono come Dio li chiamava, cacciandoli nelle terre straniere, a incarnare in sè l'Unità futura Italiana, a farsi apostoli, tra le genti e in faccia ai loro concittadini, dell'asociazione fraterna destinata a spegnere le gare intestine, cagione perpetua del comune servaggio."[14] This may also be seen as the editor's programme in a nutshell regarding his periodical. More revealing when referring to other contributors' remarks on exiles (such as Ricciardi who seems to venture a few observations on the subject), Mazzini shows to what extent he saw a restricted group of exiles as a chosen elite preserving the ideal of, and defining, a future united Italy by their very existence. As the real embodiment of their goal and future achievement, the exiles have the duty of constantly articulating their aim by means of information and education.

Once more, the sphere of exile is not seen as a negligible area where a few ineffectual and marginalized people plot unrealistic changes. An émigré like Mazzini conceives of exile as a space where proper values and ideals have a chance of surviving and developing. It could be Marseille or London; the main thing is the existence of a world outside the home country, a temporary but essential configuration facilitating the

---

[14] "… the mission and the holiness of exile: few have understood how, by chasing them into foreign lands, God called them to embody the future Italian unity, to become apostles among people and in the sight of their compatriots, the mission of the fraternal association meant to appease the internal conflicts, the constant threat to collective service" (25 Sept. 1842: 59).

development of an idea, or of a political programme. Some of the political ferment is transferred away from a country locked into paralyzing tensions to an external space. Yet, it is not another Italy that is created in exile, but a temporary realm where the evolution of certain ideas, the debate, can proceed, and various concrete initiatives can be taken. Subsequently, this ferment and possibly its results shift back, while the exile stage as a stepping-stone remains even more significant in retrospect.

Mazzini defended his intention of gathering in one national association all the forces that may lead to the unity and independence of Italy (15 April 1842: 40-44). In this article he dwells on a few concepts recurring in his texts. This is not exactly a crystal-clear piece of reasoning, but here he resorts a little more to analysis and somewhat less to rhetoric.

First he asserts that for him all revolutions are basically social; the political order is only the form of these changes. This point becomes clearer as Mazzini makes a distinction between a political and social revolution. Having mentioned that for him there are no classes distinguished by occupation and that he uses "operaio" (worker) as he would use lawyer, merchant or surgeon, Mazzini points out that "[l]e sole differenze che noi ammettiamo tra i membri d'uno Stato sono le differenze d'educazione morale" ("the only differences that we admit between the members of a State are the differences of moral education" [Della Peruta, ed. 1: 488]). As mentioned above, he does see the difference between the class that owns the means of production ("possessori esclusivamente degli elementi d'ogni lavoro, terre, credito, o capitali" [488]) and that, which owns only its labour. For him the chief consequence is that the former benefits from education while the latter does not. The aspiration is for both to have access to the same kind of education, and consequently to rest on the same moral foundation.

When it comes to revolution ("revoluzione" and "insurrezione" are used interchangeably) the former may contemplate a political revolution in order to get rid of foreign domination and internal despotism, which are obstacles in the path of individual development (the argument of the Spanish liberals). The workers, living in misery, "hanno principalmente bisogno d'un ordinamento sociale" ("mainly need a [proper] social order" [489]). What Mazzini appears to mean here is that the underprivileged classes would need a proper social and economic order which requires one kind of radical change, while the propertied groups need a framework which would guarantee their individual rights necessitating a change of a different kind. At times Mazzini seems to argue that the former sort of change, that which would satisfy the dispossessed people, constitutes a real revolution. His argument gains in precision when he next states that so far insurrections (or revolutions) have been only political, but the next one must be both political and social (489). This is why when he argues that "l'ordinamento politico è la *forma* e non altro dei mutamenti" ("the political order is only the *form* of the changes" [490]), while the substance of a profound change is of a social nature, Mazzini means that achieving independence, unity, and a wider franchise, may not improve the life of the poor. According to Mazzini, the revolution—social and political—should come about as a result of the workers understanding their situation, of coordinating their forces, and of being able to express their demands, but also as a result of the propertied class being willing to sympathize with, and accept, them. This is where education would prove essential. Otherwise, Mazzini warns, revolutions may turn into civil wars and would only substitute one sort of tyranny for another (489-90).

Being privileged means for him not only having particular economic, and possibly political, advantages but also being educated. It is education that would regulate his curious version of such an upheaval, socially harmonious and radical at the same time. This is one of the rare occasions when Mazzini seems to concentrate on the social and economic problems rather than on the need for national unity and independence. Finally, in the same text it becomes obvious how the two sets of questions are joined: the workers have not derived much benefit from previous revolutions, their programmes have been drafted by others, but now the time has come to articulate their own demands, since they are "il nucleo della nazione futura" (493).

The question of revolution recurs in the open letter to the Italian youth published in two numbers (31 December 1842: 73-75, and 3 February 1843: 81-83). After warning against passivity and the sin of "hateful individualism," Mazzini writes that the revolutionary movements of 1821 were only "il grido di monarchia costituzionale, grido escito da scuole straniere oggimai decrepite" ("the call of the constitutional monarchy, a call launched by foreign teachings nowadays decrepit" [Della Peruta, ed. 1: 499, 500]). We are a long way from the values of the Spanish liberals. The royal revolutions ("revoluzione regie"), as Mazzini calls them, were useful enough for diminishing the power of the feudal lords, but now they are not a solution; kings are insincere and the people lack enthusiasm after the weakening, in some cases the elimination, of the aristocracy during the previous fifty years (500). A proper revolution needs a programme and a clear set of principles and this may be found in the recurring phrase "Nel vostro intelletto sta la norma dei vostri doveri" ("The guide of your duties is your mind" [501]). Mazzini suggests this as a point of reference in a world and a country (Italy) where the political and ecclesiastical "dictatorship" try to hinder thought (501).

In August of the previous year he had published the fourth instalment of his essay on the duties of man, and regarding intellect as the source of duty offers a synthesis of his argument: "L'uomo è pensiero ed azione" ("The human being is thought and action" [501]). This may suggest that Mazzini believes strongly in reason as such, but this is not entirely the case: thought comes down from God, and people have to articulate it and turn it into action (501). That is why the "national philosophy" of the Italian youth ought to be based on Pythagoras' philosophy "prima in Europa ad armonizzare in unità religiosa tutte quante le manifestazioni dell'umana vita, prima a cercare nell'ordinamento sociale un simbolo al concetto puro …"[15] In conclusion Mazzini addresses more reproaches to those who avoid practical commitment to action and withdraw within the world of literature and philosophy. He has harsh things to say about this "codarda teorica" ("theoretical cowardice" [504]) as his appeal turns into a veritable indictment.

Several numbers of *Apostolato popolare* contain instalments of the long essay published later by Mazzini under the title *The Duties of Man*.[16] Even

---

[15] "… the first one in Europe to harmonise within a religious unity the various manifestations of the human life, the first one to search in the social order for a symbol of the pure concept …" (ibid.).

[16] 15 Sept. 1841: 17-21; 1 Jan. 1842: 25-28; 15 April 1842: 37-39; 15 Aug. 1842: 45-48. The page numbers following the quotes in Italian refer to *Doveri dell'uomo* (Pallazzo di Montecitorio: Camera dei deputati, 1972); the translations are from Ella Noyes' ren-

if only about half of this work was published in the periodical it makes sense to discuss it separately, glancing only briefly at the latter part.

It appears that the more messianic sections of the essay were printed in the journal while the more analytical ones, were written later. This indicates the development of Mazzini's thought, but it may also suggest that he published the more rhetorical parts in his periodical because they were bound to have a more immediate impact on his readership. There is another difference between the texts published here and the rest: the latter, possibly drafted two decades later, become more concrete and analytical, particularly in the detailed criticism of communism, showing that they belong to another historical period. It was during the 1860s that Mazzini also attacked the First International, turning both against Bakunin and Marx. The ideologies emerging in the early 1840s had developed by the late 1860s and that is why the two halves of Mazzini's essay on duties seem to, and indeed do, address different issues. Besides, the unification and independence of most of Italy had occurred by 1860, and so one of the chief aims had been achieved, even if the fiercely republican Mazzini could not bring himself to return to a monarchical Italy. However, the latter part of the text is not written by an exile, but by a person revered by many in his home country where Mazzini travelled rather frequently from his home in London. Therefore, it seems reasonable at this point to look at the first half of *The Duties of Man* as part of the periodical.

Mazzini sees himself in a spiritual tradition, as a messenger and a teacher spreading the word in order to enlighten humanity: "ma seguitemi … se mi trovate apostolo della verità" (17).[17] The text is tuned accordingly, appealing less to reason or to factual judgement, and more to emotion. He explains that he starts from duties and not rights because although the revolutionary initiatives of the last fifty years were undertaken in the name of rights, people's life has not improved much even if productivity has increased and "l'idea dei diritti inerenti alla natura umana è oggimai generalmente accettata" ("the idea of rights inherent in

---

dering, *The Duties of Man* (London: Dent, 1966). Page numbers without quotes refer to Noyes' translation.

[17] "Follow me … if you find me an apostle of truth" (7).

human nature is today generally accepted" [9]). The value of rights may not be questioned, but people often find it difficult to exercise them, and where they can be used they have a fragmentary effect because attached to individuals. Mazzini's example here is the French revolution of 1830 when, at first, some of the leaders took advantage of the upheaval but later forgot all about the humble revolutionaries.

Utilitarianism with happiness as the main aim is dismissed in favour of a new principle of education "che guidi gli uomini al meglio, che insegni loro la costanza nel sagrificio, che li vincoli ai loro fratelli senza farli dipendenti dall'idea d'un solo o dalla forza di tutti. E questo principio è il DOVERE" (24).[18] The workers' present hard life does not allow them to get educated properly; therefore there is a need for a radical change in their material circumstances (16-17, 20). Moreover, people need a common belief so that the majority does not oppress the rest. This belief should be based on a morality which resides "[n]ella *conoscenza* della nostra legge di vita, della LEGGE DI DIO …"[19] This knowledge is reached by reflecting whether one's aspiration are confirmed by one's fellow human beings, and when they do "there is God" (35).

Apart from the religious resonance, the moral one is of particular interest here. Mazzini constantly returns to the importance of the connection between thought and action. His total commitment to the cause of Italy's unity and independence indicates how he regarded "the law of life" in his own case. The insight in his own "legge di vita" amounts to realizing his purpose in life. Since his mission, properly comprehended according to his premises, can only be part of a higher divine law, any subsequent action ought to be morally sound. The condition of exile, which overshadows his entire campaign, acquires a clearly outlined, ethical dimension. This moral vindication of the action that resulted in banishment contains an appeal to a final instance that resembles only superficially that of the French extreme royalists. In both cases the divine will

---

[18] "… which shall guide men to better things, teach them constancy in self-sacrifice and link them with their fellow men without making them dependent on the ideas of a single man or on the strength of all. And this principle is Duty" (15). Capitals in the original text.

[19] "… in the *knowledge* of your law of life, of the law of God …" (32). Italics and capitals in the original (but no capitals in Noyes' translation).

or inspiration is invoked as the ultimate proof of being the in the right. But whereas the divine right of kings requires only faith in, and obedience to, a tradition, Mazzini's use of "God's law" contains a necessary element of understanding which results in knowledge and leads in a very different direction from the French royalists' moral justification. Mazzini's morality ratified by the divine law concerns the needs of a suffering people and oppressed nation, not the unquestionable perpetuation of a monarchy.

Finally, the terms of the argument are restated as Mazzini points out that conscience is influenced by education and needs the guidance of "Intellect" and "Humanity." The latter term seems to be used now in the sense of history, now in the sense of community (37-38). The part published in the 1840s concludes with the necessity of a single law governing that single entity which is humanity: "... questa legge è *Progresso*, progresso qui sulla terra dove dobiamo verificare quanto più possiamo del disegno di Dio ed educarci a migliori destini" (60).[20] This is how duty is built into an overall system, and the need for fulfilling this duty defines Mazzini's idea of morality. Since these values must be adopted by everybody, Mazzini urges finally: "[s]iate apostoli di questa fede, apostoli della fratellanza delle Nazioni e della unità ... del genere umano" (63-64).[21]

Mazzini combines some of the religious tone still surviving after the post-1815 restoration in a number of countries (he mentions approvingly Lamennais's writings) and an increasing concern with social questions during a rough phase of industrialization. He must have become aware of the workers' problems after his arrival in England, while he remembered vividly the poverty of the Italian peasant. However, his main con-

---

[20] "... this is the Law of Progress, progress upon earth, where we have to accomplish God's design as much as in us lies, and to educate ourselves for better destinies" (47).
[21] "Be apostles of this faith, apostles of the brotherhood of nations, and of the unity of the human race ..." (50).

cern, the reason for which he had to leave Genoa, was national unity and independence, also a significant contemporary line of thought and action. His awareness of new social difficulties appears to have compelled him to reconcile values and solutions addressing different issues.

Chapter 8

The Transformation of Exile

So far I have presented and discussed the various groups of émigrés separately. This was necessary in order to familiarize the reader with the refugees' arguments before I proceeded to an analysis of their significance. In this final section I intend to analyse two particular ways in which the exiles' arguments shape a particular strand of thought by their use of certain topical concepts and their attempts to dismiss the stigma of their expulsion or flight. These are not claims regarding the world of exile in general, but the result of observing and interpreting the manner in which the émigrés discussed in the present work articulated their opinions. In the course of the following discussion I refer to the texts without dwelling too much on details as I assume by now some familiarity with them.

Testing Concepts and Transferring Guilt

There are two issues I concentrate on. The first point concerns the French émigrés' choice of concepts indicating or confirming the strength and clarity of particular topical ideas in the 1790s. The second has to do with the exiles' way of rejecting the guilt of banishment by means of recurring claims about being the true representatives of their nation.

These claims counteract the stigma of exclusion by attaching moral values to the exiles' position. Among the political arguments in the émigrés' periodicals, these are the two issues that stand out as having had to be developed in exile, and that may have not followed the same course at home.

The firmness of some of the chief contemporary concepts (i.e. agreement or disagreement on them) can be gauged by the way the French refugees attempted to employ them in their own cause. Even if such a debate may have arisen within France as well, the use of these concepts in exile is charged with additional intentions, e.g. proving one's moral rightness, as they are modified according to the royalists' needs. The analysis of the use of concepts is confined here only to the French exiles simply because the abundant intellectual activity proceeding at the same time in Paris facilitates a contrast between the way these concepts are employed at home and in exile. The dearth of debates in Spain and the timorous and controlled ones in Italy against a background of censorship and persecution in both countries make this task virtually impossible in their cases.

A more comprehensive issue discussed below is the insistence of the exiles on being the real representatives of their nations. This claim is present more or less explicitly in at least some of the texts discussed here. This is a claim where the ethical dimension comes in quite noticeably, as it represents a clear effort at re-defining one's position by seizing the high moral ground.

Some contemporary aspects of the emerging notion of nationalism did contain moral dimensions (the commendable love of *la patrie* much dwelt upon in revolutionary Paris), while some explanations were conveyed as a matter of fact (Herder's theory that each language, hence each culture and group of people embraced by it, possess an intrinsic characteristic). What can be noticed in these periodicals is that the émigrés infuse a sense of morality where apparently there is none, and emphasize it in an idiosyncratic manner where it does exist. One of the main issues of this final analysis is the manner in which the exiles reverse the roles of the accused and the accuser as part of vindicating their point of view.

Had it been at all possible, some political matters discussed in these periodicals could have been debated at home, for instance the divine right of kings, constitutional monarchy, or the importance of education for social harmony. These issues have their own moral implications but do not necessarily contain a dimension developed by the émigrés as part of their defence. Therefore I dwell less on these problems, and concentrate more on the way the refugees shift the moral opprobrium, which is their contribution to the strand of intellectual history stressed here.

The Nature of the Context

A few preliminary considerations are in order. They concern the circumstances in which the émigrés developed their thoughts and the nature of their texts. At the outset it is worth clarifying the place of these periodicals in the activity of their editors. How much did they resemble other work done by their editors? To what extent were they a continuation of a professional occupation?

In Mallet du Pan's case there was a smooth transition from his earlier work as a political commentator for *Mercure de France* in Paris to editing *Mercure Britannique* in London, passing through an intermediary phase of providing more or less confidential political analyses for various European courts and governments. Peltier was even more in his element. Having published his satirical magazines in Paris, once in London he went on bringing out periodicals filled with invectives, their satirical edge somewhat blunted, but issuing in a steady stream from the pen of an experienced hack. As far as is known, the prelates who brought out *Mercure de France* had no practice in this field. It can safely be assumed that in France they had produced and perhaps published their share of sermons, but editing a periodical in London must have entailed an effort that indicates the intensity of their commitment. Blanco White and Fernández Sardino had tried their hand at journalism in Spain, yet the former was a writer worried by religious doubts, less and less keen on political militantism, while the latter was a medical doctor who had only attempted a few plays and produced some articles. Blanco started with a good deal of commitment which petered out, but Sardino's eagerness for the cause drove him to carry on editing his magazines after years of interruption. In London he went on practising medicine, so the magazine must have been an additional burden. Villanueva and his fellow-editors brought out various learned productions. Although in a sense part of their work, *Ocios* was different from their other writings. As for Mazzini, his *Apostolato popolare* was of a piece with his other texts, indeed parts of the periodical *were* his other texts re-issued in the form of a book, or spread as pamphlets, obviously a driven militant and not a man to use a line only once if he could help it. His commitment to the cause is obvious from the large space he gave to his reflections at the expense of more routine news and reports. Unlike *Apostolato popolare*, the French and Spanish magazines did contain, to various degrees, news, press reviews, and lighter fare, in addition to ardent political pieces.

Another preliminary point concerns the way in which various émigrés perceived their exile. As the place and significance of the individual was changing throughout the eighteenth century and, more markedly, as a result of the French Revolution, being excluded from one's community would be perceived differently at different times. The absolutist norms still overshadowing most French aristocrats would turn their banishment or flight into failure because of the revolutionaries' successful defiance of the hierarchy, in addition to the sheer frustration of being removed from power or just forced to leave one's country. Hence the defensive claims of the royalists that the higher aristocracy constituted France itself and that its members carried the nation with them wherever they found themselves. At the other extreme, a refugee such as Mazzini would turn his exile into an assertion of individual freedom. Mazzini's sense of being excluded was not necessarily experienced as a failure, and not only because of his different social background. He did not relate himself to the past, but to an independent, united Italy that was not yet a reality but the aim defining his outlook and work in emigration. The Spaniards would also regard their exile as a successful defiance since they saw themselves as the only ones among their fellow-countrymen able to articulate the opinions of a political opposition.

These various cases show the difficulty, indeed the futility, of generalizing on such matters. They are mentioned here in order to indicate the divergent starting-points that determined the émigrés' choice of justifications and that conditioned the particular strand of intellectual history pursued here. An émigré would regard his moral position as part of the dominating conventions that determined his perception of himself.

These conditioning factors, derived both from their background and the contemporary conflicting norms, suggest the chief "positions" and "idioms" that the refugees would have to take into account when they strove to fit a new value into their framework.

These two extremes, the weight of tradition and the energizing ideal, add a further factor, namely a particular tension, to the forces that shaped the refugees' thought. They found themselves suspended between a selectively remembered past and the image of a future political system of their countries—whether a modified or a restored one—held with particular determination. Thus their arguments tried to bridge the gap between a cultural inheritance marred by mythical embellishment and biased emphasis, and a future based on an imperfect grasp of the mood at home. Occasionally, this fact gave some of their arguments a strident, unrealistic, hollow sound.

Further, there is a difference between the refugees' justifications and explanations of what happened in the past and those concerning their visions. Even if it is possible for the same set of values to rule in either case, there is a freedom of argumentation when it comes to states of things not yet tried out which is unavailable to discussions dealing with past occurrences. Consequences on the one hand and intentions on the other receive varying amounts of attention depending on the political outlook and the immediate background of a refugee. A discussion of known, inevitably flawed consequences, is bound to be more defensive than a programmatic argument containing commendable intentions. The moral subtext varies also according to whether imperfections have to be justified or ideals have to be persuasively explained. In turn, this suggests how the émigrés tend to use the concepts and values they resort to. This is also an indication of the caution needed when discussing together émigrés as different as the French royalists and Italian nationalists. Moreover, their readiness to exploit any suitable material was also due to the fact that these exiles were not rigorous moral philosophers exploring the issues according to a system, but more or less temporary political journalists arguing for their cause (mainly in terms of political values with moral assumptions).

When discussing aspects of political morality in exile one must bear in mind the concrete circumstances of isolation from the main debate.

Even if most of these periodicals were circulating at home, monitored
and occasionally banned by the authorities, the émigrés did not really
have an interlocutor. At least in the cases discussed here they hurled their
arguments at hostile listeners, the authorities at home, which did not care
to engage in a proper dialogue. Far from the mechanisms of power, the
exiles were also far from their intellectual community, where such a
group existed at all. Their opinions were unable to influence openly and
directly the mood in which decisions were taken, and so the exiles were
not concerned with immediate political responsibility. It may be argued
that these circumstances affected the way in which they articulated their
opinions. It is reasonable to assume that the absence of practical considerations shifted their arguments to a more general level, possibly abstract
but usually vague. Distance and excessive commitment may have
clouded some of the issues and allowed their political imagination to
gloss over difficulties whether the topic was the social contract, a proper
constitution or removing the monarchy in an independent and united
country.

Since the goals were chiefly political and the chances to turn them
into realities were quite remote at the initial moment of banishment, the
refugees developed an idiosyncratic manner of evaluating matters at
home and of arguing in general. In the process, there emerged a peculiar
political morality of an "exilic" nature. There was a tendency to resort to
"legal fictions" such as an initial social contract or an ancient constitution. There was no firm belief that these entities really existed but they
were nevertheless used in order to establish present valid claims. Burke
provides an example of the use of such a concept when he claims that
"The idea of a people is the idea of a corporation. It is wholly artificial;
and made like all other legal fictions by common agreement …"[1] Departing from empirical evidence, but unwilling to resort to the much decried
"metaphysics" and "theories," Burke nevertheless found a non-empirical
way to prove his point by employing the device of legal fiction. Thus he
suggested a method used later on by some émigrés in their own arguments. The more forceful statements in these periodicals have a legal

---

[1] Quoted in Charles Parkin, *The Moral Basis of Burke's Political Thought* (Cambridge:
Cambridge UP, 1956) 14.

ring about them and it would not have been unusual for these authors to select a suitable legal tool. The occasional writer even extended the concept of legal fiction to other entities less legally recognizable than Burke's corporation. For example, the journalists from *Mercure de France* amplified the ultra-royalists' claims and, without using the juridical terms as such, elaborated an explanation of the monarchy embodying France that expected to be accorded the same validity as any other juridical convention. The argument could not be carried on an empirical basis—it was difficult to insist that the French nation really found itself in exile—and so the émigrés' realm of legal fiction became in this case the counterpart of the revolutionaries' Reason. The aspect usually overlooked in such uses of legal fiction is Burke's point about consensus. Claims based on this concept gain validity if they are the result of some sort of "common agreement." The Spanish refugees, arguing their case more than a decade later, did not have to match any stringently rational adversaries at home. Yet they resorted to an entity in the shape of a legal fiction as well, the ancient constitution.

In addition, the Spanish émigrés put their trust in legislation invoking Bentham's ideas. Still, their periodicals discussed here stretch over a long enough period (seventeen years) in order to occasion changes of opinion. Blanco White discovered gradually the value of tradition in Burke's sense of the word, while the later refugees, disappointed after Fernando's second betrayal, inclined more and more towards militant action. Mazzini advocated constantly a two-stage solution: militant action to get rid of the foreign occupier, followed by education in order to ensure a proper united Italy and also as the key to improving the lot of all citizens. It was such solutions that would have allowed the return of the exiles. Therefore they are endowed with moral attributes and constitute desirable goals. They are valuable both for the respective countries and for the refugees themselves, and it all had to do with the triumph of their cause.

The French ultra-royalists had a more forlorn outlook since their solution appeared less constructive, or at least had a more passive, a more unsurprising ring to it: a return to a system based on the divine right of kings along with clerical and aristocratic privileges in the name of stability. (When the restoration did occur it was quite far from the early wishes of the ultras.)

Once the exiles' goal was achieved that meant that they were safe. It also meant they had been right all along. Those who did claim that they embodied their nation at various times in various ways had to put up with an uneasy tension. Considered on their own terms, they may have been the real nation, or its representative part, but they could not contribute anything directly since the home country was out of reach and its system, on the surface, depressingly well entrenched.

After these initial remarks, I turn now to the first main issue which I intend to outline as one of the émigrés' chief contributions to shaping a particular strand of intellectual history: the way some of their arguments indicate the looseness ("unsettled status") of certain concepts by the specific manner in which they were employed.

The Deployment of Concepts

The main line of enquiry here is the extent to which the exiles resorted to concepts that became somewhat diffuse while acquiring a new meaning or fading out. The assumption is that, because of the need to justify their position, the émigrés fell back on notions whose prevailing sense was in doubt, and therefore could be used in a more partisan fashion.

Some of the chief contemporary ideas remain in the background in this section of the discussion. At this stage it seems worthwhile to look at concepts that have to do with the criteria and the process of constituting and legitimizing the structure of a community, and with granting, receiving and preserving possibilities of action within that community. Furthermore, it seems relevant to look at how some of these concepts were used both at home and in exile. They are important during the initial phase of an event seen by some as a new sequence of development (social, political, cultural), and by others as a questionable challenge to an existing structure. The discussions kept returning to contract, consensus, nature, natural law, representation, and sovereignty. These are also some of the notions used by the exiles for their own purposes.

A Hypothesis

The uncertainty of the meaning of certain concepts was increased by the rapid and radical changes during the last decades of the eighteenth century. A word, apparently accepted in one sense, would turn out to denote a variety of complex, developing situations. At the same time, "quite traditional forms of social action could suddenly take on different meanings in a redefined political situation."[2] In other words, a variety of new terms emerged in the course of re-naming the same concrete phenomena. Such lack of synchronization would tend to result in the blurring of the meaning of frequently used notions. The urgent need to seize the initiative in defining, naming, or "fixing" the interpretation of an event, a need present in the arguments of both the revolutionaries and the émigrés, compelled the latter (lacking a power base) to resort energetically to whatever ideas and arguments seemed most flexible. The perusal of some contemporary texts shows occasional tugs-of-war in the attempt to appropriate a term or impose a particular account of events.

In the sphere of ethics itself the latter half of the eighteenth century was a time when the social and political developments affected a series of basic assumptions, again, causing uneven modifications among phenomena, words and ideas. The background of eighteenth-century thought was characterized by the hypothesis that there were two governing faculties in human beings (conscience and self-love) as opposed to only one (reason) in Greco-Roman thought.[3] The emergence of psychological elements as part of the sensationist theories and the transition from a communal to an individual way of perceiving oneself in society, according to other historians, contributed further to the unsettling of hitherto fairly well established concepts.[4] The natural law, whether of divine or secular origin, that had provided a widely accepted foundation for ethics, as for so much else, during the previous one and half centu-

---

[2] Baker 5. For concepts such as "nature" and "law" being used in different senses, see also Lester G. Crocker, *Man and World in Eighteenth Century France* (Baltimore: Johns Hopkins Press, 1959) 100.

[3] Henry Sidgwick, *Outlines of the History of Ethics*, 6th ed. (1886; London: Routledge, 1946) 198.

[4] On the rise of individualism, the arrival of psychology and their ethical relevance, see Alasdair MacIntyre, *A Short History of Ethics* (London: Routledge, 1967) 167 ff.

ries, was turning into a doctrine of natural rights towards the end of the eighteenth century, and was modified in its turn by the increasingly dominant principles of utilitarianism and social control.[5] In addition an intention-based ethical system was about to offer a rival option. It was a transitional phase with natural law fading out, and the values of utilitarianism and Kantian ethics becoming noticeable, though not necessarily to the French émigrés.

There were very concrete reasons for most of these conceptual shifts. The succession of social and political changes meant that the moral standpoints multiplied accordingly.[6] The old concepts and ways of arguing had for a while to do extra work while being used in this fluid situation. The contour of some ideas would inevitably become imprecise in the process of serving more than one cause.

The issues raised by the French Revolution—equality, the proper location of sovereignty, the significance of the social contract, the need for a written constitution based on new premises—directed the debates both in France and abroad towards these topical areas and concepts, irrespective of the more sedate discussions on other ethical developments elsewhere. The burning questions for the revolutionaries and the émigrés also included legitimacy, the place of various individuals and the relationships between them in a political and social system, representation, and aspects of consensus. It is among the current concepts employed by the exiles that I intend to identify some which were convenient to use because "unstable in meaning."[7] My suggestion that some of the French exiles seized on those concepts whose sense was shifting may indicate, or confirm, which ideas were temporarily in a state of transition,

---

[5] Lester G. Crocker, *Nature and Culture: Ethical Thought in the French Enlightenment* (Baltimore: The Johns Hopkins Press, 1963) 12, 15.

[6] For this multiplication of moral standpoints being "rooted" in political changes, see Alasdair MacIntyre, *Three Rival Versions of Moral Enquiry* (Notre Dame: Indiana University of Notre Dame Press, 1990) 137.

[7] MacIntyre's phrase (1967: 10). This is not the kind of conceptual change meant by Koselleck when he talks about Janus-like concepts where one aspect (looking towards the past) needs commenting and explaining, while the other one is more easily comprehended (Introduction [xv] to *Geschichtliche Grundbegriffe*). The meaning of a concept chosen by the exiles is possibly questionable or dated, but its understanding is not necessarily obscured by that.

therefore possibly vague, and consequently likely to provide ammunition for both camps in a dispute.

Shifts of Sovereignty

The justifications of absolutism that emerged in the sixteenth century had been preceded by a longer tradition arguing the case for resisting monarchy. This was the tradition of civil law, often aspiring to match natural law in order to oppose absolute kings. Echoing the Stoics and Cicero, Marsilius of Padua argued that in order to achieve good government sovereignty must belong to the people who elected the king. The monarch would then rule within the framework of the law. The force of secular law derived from the people's consent, according to William of Ockham, and the monarchy was to be limited by these legal boundaries. The idea that the ruler's authority was received from the people was claimed with renewed strength by the monarchomachs (the writers who defended the right to oppose the king) during the sixteenth century. This line of thought encountered opposition from the claims of Jean Bodin that the position of the monarch was sanctioned by divine right. It was a recent argument needed by the increasingly powerful national kings.[8]

The royal apologists had to contend with opinions such as the Huguenot juristconsult François Hotman's who argued in his *Francogallia* (1573) that there was no historical base for an absolute monarchy. The theologian Theodore Beza stated at about the same time that people had natural rights protected by a contract with a ruler, and if the latter violated the pact the people ought to resist, a point made even more forcefully by Hotman, both anticipating Locke. Even Bodin wrote that the sovereign was limited by the natural law and that a tyrant can be removed by the people.[9] Bodin and Hobbes would be referred to by the

---

[8] MacIntyre (1967: 277) underlines the paradox that in morality and politics the innovators revived old theories (the contract and natural rights theorists revived "features of medieval doctrines" in the seventeenth century), while their conservative opponents invented new ones (the doctrine of the divine right of kings being a sixteenth- and seventeenth-century invention).

[9] On Jean Bodin affording "to be liberal at the fringes of his theory" after forcefully establishing his doctrine on absolutism, see Quentin Skinner, *Foundations of Modern Political Thought*, 2 vols. (1978. Cambridge: Cambridge UP, 1996) 2: 286.

French émigrés in search of respectable backing for their justification of absolutism.

Whether of divine inspiration or based on human reason, natural law had been invoked by political theorists as an ideal which positive law would try to approach. This principle presupposed a series of actions such as agreeing on a pact with a particular aim in sight: the self-preservation of the individual (Hobbes), or of the community, once the first goal was achieved (Locke). The assumption in the Levellers' understanding of the law of nature was the existence of individual rights (including the right of property) meant to be protected by the institutions set up by the community, while the Diggers saw the principle as consisting in the preservation of the community by means of collective property and activity. Yet, on the whole, one particular interpretation prevailed by means of Locke's writings: Thomas of Aquinas's argument against tyranny surfaced in Locke's copious quotes from Hooker's *Of the Lawes of Ecclesiasticall Politie*.[10]

The idea of contract, hypothetical or not, offered a choice of meanings early on as it was used to justify the legitimacy claims of the state or a personal ruler. Leaving aside the contract of a religious nature, there was the *pacte d'association* (an agreement between equal members of a community) and *pacte de gouvernement* (an agreement between the people and a ruler). The latter presupposed people's consent to the transfer of power to the monarch, and also his continuing observance of the well-being of the community. This kind of claim acquired importance in the seventeenth century and was in contrast with the way legitimacy was justified in the Middle Ages through a number of relationships of obligation and duty.[11] Confusion over this term would be noticed later in the way Hobbes handled this hypothesis; he assumed the existence of a community sufficiently organized and self-aware to reach such a covenant, but a covenant that would be agreed upon for the very purpose of establishing such a community. The self-contradiction was not apparent in the seventeenth century while this version of the contract became one

---

[10] Sabine (523); see also the editor's "Conclusion" to J.H. Burns, ed., *The Cambridge History of Political Thought: 1450-1700* (Cambridge: Cambridge UP, 1991) 655.

[11] See MacIntyre (1967: 155-56) for this and the subsequent point.

of the chief arguments in support of the existing ruler's legitimacy. But when Rousseau gave currency to another version the possibility of the notion being used subjectively became more and more real.

The circumstances that occasioned the use of such concepts had to do with the kind of shift of authority that had occurred in France in 1789. Unlike earlier transfers of power, in various degrees, from one kind of ruler to another (pope and emperor), or from one ruler to a restricted group (from King John to a few feudal lords, an event sanctioned by the Magna Carta), or from a ruler to a more or less representative parliament (from Charles I to the Puritan leaders), this one implied a radical shift from an absolutist monarch to an entire people as part of a massive social adjustment. Along with the attempt at a collective exercise of authority on this scale, questions of representation and consent acquired a sudden importance and urgency. New procedures had to be invented and, above all, convincingly explained in order to ensure the functioning of the new system. The inhabitants of the territory were also in urgent need of an uncompromised and defining identity shaped by equal status as members of a "nation." There was an on-going process of self-clarification and differentiation by means of oaths, apparel, choice of symbols, language, which confirmed the quality of belonging or determined the exclusion of a person. The conquests were recent, the mood was tense, and it was just as much a matter of security as of doctrinal commitment to identify those who could be relied on. It was a dynamic process, the tactics and some of the priorities were occasionally revised, the ideals were diluted by some, purified by others, and today's friends and allies could and did become tomorrow's enemies, discovering each other afresh as victims and executioners.

Since matters were not yet clear-cut, and the confident tranquillity to sort out the pros and cons was not available, it was important (and expedient) to be perceived as a good citizen. The public virtues desirable at the time defined the chief moral quality of a person, but in a feverish manner, absent in Aristotle's world where, in different circumstances, such ethical features had been dwelt upon. The émigrés had been excluded—or had excluded themselves—from this option. Instead, they were falling back on their own convictions, working out the reasons and aims of their allegiance with the help of any suitable idea, inevitably less like registered and reliable citizens and more like baffled and resentful individuals.

It was not difficult for the exiles to turn to "unsettled concepts" by the late 1790s. The succession of attempts from 1787 (the first calls, including La Fayette's, for summoning a true national assembly) to 1795 (the formation of the Directory) to establish French society on a fair basis, along with the clashes between various factions provided the émigrés with what looked like sufficient proof that there was a lack of consensus on the chief principles and ways of putting them into practice. The main achievements of the Revolution (the abolition of privileges, the extension of franchise, the administrative and economic reforms, among them the nationalization of Church property) had been energetic and fairly uncontroversial, hardly requiring lengthy debates on the finer theoretical points. Other issues betrayed a certain hesitation on the meaning of particular concepts, and that was apparent in the disputes on the role of the monarchy and of representation in the new constitution, or on the question of sovereignty (Baker 244 ff).

The persecution and executions of "aristocrats" and other "counter-revolutionaries" could be deplored but not really used in arguments by the theoretically inclined émigrés. The elimination of leading or more humble revolutionaries by their own comrades in successive waves was another matter; it could be taken to betray more than just a scramble for power, possibly a sign of disharmony in the conceptual sphere as well. The visible disagreements in Paris, leading steadily towards a military dictatorship and expansion, gave the impression at a distance that some of the main ideas and principles had failed to maintain the consistency of their initial commitment. The conviction was being formed abroad that there was no monopoly on the concepts frequently invoked in Paris, as there seemed to be no agreement on their meaning. The field was therefore open to other users who could employ the disputed notions according to need.

The Range of Concepts

The pre-revolutionary political "discourse" had been shaped by the concepts of reason, will and justice, used both by the opponents and the defenders of monarchical authority (Baker 25 ff). Now the émigrés reproached the revolutionaries with wanting to make a new start by an arbitrary act of will. The militant rulers in Paris were accused of emphasizing will and reason while neglecting justice. The excesses of reason were conveyed as caricatures of theoretical efforts to be imposed on the unwilling masses, while those of will as voluntaristic measures, again, supposedly uncongenial to the daily life of the people.[12] As the exiles pointed to the display of new departures (a new calendar, a new supreme being, new names in key areas of the social life), they underlined their capricious and reversible character. By making a virtue of the sanction of tradition, the émigrés perceived this alleged inconsistency of the new system as reason enough to assume a conceptual inconsistency as well, and thus appropriate the terms that seemed most available. And some of these terms were connected with the early difficulties of the radical reforms.

At the initial stage of the Revolution new groups of citizens were enfranchised, and even if this implied a share in power, it did not mean that they could all exercise it directly in practice. The point of the vote was delegating power on the basis of trust. Even if this resembles Locke's pact where a group of rulers are temporarily appointed (and, therefore, power was not surrendered by the large majority), there is in fact, at the very least, a tacit exchange of pledges between the voter and the representative. There was already a choice between two senses of contract. As the émigrés were returning in the 1790s to an earlier meaning of the concept, a third sense was emerging, along with the extension of franchise. I would call this a "contract of representation."[13] During the early constitutional debates of August 1789 when the general will and the idea of representation provoked a certain amount of discord in the National

---

[12] See, for instance, *Mercure Britannique* (1: 21-22).

[13] See Emmanuel Sieyès, *Qu'est-ce que le Tiers état?* (1789; Genève, 1970) 179 for contemporary radical ways of regarding representation (for example, Sieyès writes about *"un gouvernement exercé par procuration"*). François Furet is one of the most recent historians to have pointed to the difference between the ideal of the unity of power and the fact of representation, but he does not place it in a context of an exchange of pledges, see Stephen Kaplan, *Farewell, Revolution* (Ithaca, NY: Cornell UP, 1995) 71 where there is a discussion of Furet's article "Terror" in Furet's and Mona Ozouf's *Dictionnaire critique de la Révolution française*.

Assembly, the idea of *mandat impératif* (binding mandate) was invoked as an explanation of how the deputies would be prevented from acting on their own, in isolation from the voters' wishes (Baker 226-27). However, this was a notion that implied the restraining of a deputy rather than ensuring that the voter may participate directly in the administration of power. This problem arose in August 1789 precisely because, once trust had been expressed on both sides, the representative had in fact power while the voter did not. The appearance of this new form of pact in the constellation of relationships and procedures necessitated by the Revolution contributed to the further dilution of the concept.

The cause of the ultra-royalists was served by using the word in the sense of subordination by consensus, while a majority of the revolutionaries implied by its use that power was wielded by the people. During the Directory (1795-1799) the exiles began pointing out that the ruling assemblies in Paris seemed to accept the fact that they were exercising power on behalf of, but not necessarily with the cooperation of, the people.

Even if not always spelled out, the ideal of the normal, natural state of things was never far from the arguments for radical action or against it. The exiles would criticize the development in France by referring to the experience of the past as vindicating a particular social and political situation. The very actions condemned by the émigrés were explained by the revolutionaries with the help of reason, the only way to detect the growing distortions and put them right. Reason and tradition were contrasted here, but both were tacitly claimed to express what should be expected in the course of normal development.

In France Robespierre coupled "nature" with "reason" in one of his main speeches.[14] The two were obviously not synonyms here, Robespierre used them as complementary fundamental forces or criteria in support of his remark about the normal place of the foreign forces, but above all of the foreign peoples, as the allies of France. Yet in the recent

---

[14] *Le Comité de Salut Public à la convention Nationale. Rapports faits en son nom par Robespierre* (Paris, 1794) v: "Nous venons remettre sous vos yeux la situation de la république à l'égard des diverses puissances de la terre, et sur-tout des peuples que la nature et la raison attachent à notre cause, mais que l'intrigue et la perfidie cherchent à ranger au nombre de nos ennemis."

tradition of radical thought "nature" had been understood in a less commendable sense. For Saige, one of the most militant pre-revolutionary writers "nature" meant an undesirable state of things (Baker 141). The division between the royalists and Robespierre follows that between Burke's and Rousseau's use of the word: the former claiming that the present state of things is natural because of its very existence, the latter that what ideally ought to exist is in fact natural. Except that Saige does not fit in with this distinction, complicating matters and not helping towards a consistent use of the term by those sharing his convictions.

The émigrés oscillated between deriving their moral justifications from the tradition of natural law of divine inspiration, and the more recent, secular one shaped by the Spanish jurists, and also by Suárez and Grotius. The choice depended on whether the divine right of monarchy was the chief item, or whether the argument took on a legalistic tone underlining, for example, aspects of property. Cicero had written of natural ("true") law as "right reason."[15] According to the older tradition, natural law and reason cannot be separated, but here it is divine reason that is meant (Crocker [1963] 5). When Robespierre used the phrase "nature et raison" in his speech he vaguely remained within a tradition of natural law which, nevertheless, by the latter half of the eighteenth century "could be either anti-historical or excessively historical, according as one chose to interpret it" and depending which aspect one emphasized, the rational one being one option (Crocker [1963] 70).

Mercure de France persisted in using nature (with its implicit force of law) as part of the divine order linking it to the fixed point whence the ancestors commenced the tradition that vindicated the present order.[16] However familiar Robespierre's use of the word may seem, he was certainly far from implying that it was the divine nature that "imposes on all physical and moral beings the law of safeguarding one's survival."[17]

---

[15] *De Re Publica*, trans. Clinton Walker Keyes (London: Heinemann, 1948) III, xxii: 211.

[16] See *Mercure de France* (30 July 1800: 420), where the "trône de l'Auteur de la nature" is mentioned.

[17] "La nature impose à tout être physique et moral la loi de pourvoir à sa conservation" in Robespierre's speech "Sur les principes de la morale dans l'administration intérieure de la république" (16).

Emmanuel Sieyès resorted to "droit naturel" in order to explain the birth of the nation and contrasted it with "droit positif" which caused the emergence of government.[18] Not only is this law the cause of generating the nation, but it is also the supreme judiciary level; again, it is very doubtful whether Sieyès meant it in a divine sense. It is also worth remembering that for the extreme royalists the nation was made up of a restricted number of persons who had been embodying and carrying throughout the centuries the defining features of the French identity.

The idea of contract was understood in different ways by the émigrés and the revolutionaries. The extreme royalists appealed to the version of the contract between the people and the ruler, as part of their argument about the divine right of kings; Mallet referred to it indirectly by invoking "droits primitifs" lost by his compatriots subjected to the pernicious effect of contrived "theoretical" solutions, while only a few years earlier Robespierre mentioned a new "pacte social" after the first anti-Girondin uprising in May 1793.[19] Clearly, the revolutionary government saw such a new agreement, concrete or metaphorical, as having become possible only after the exclusion of the rival factions. The meaning in Robespierre's speech seems also to be rather close to re-establishing the right priorities. This was quite different from what the *Mercure de France* writers meant when they referred to the contract as *pacte de gouvernement* as a covenant made between the citizen and a set of traditions on which society is based (20 Sept. 1800: 398). The qualification here was that these traditions were embodied by the monarchy. Such a contract was compulsory and implied respecting the "conventions" by means of which the citizens had acquired their rights. And so, while the revolutionaries in Paris invoked the importance of a new contract that would justify the formation of a community on the basis of equality, the émigrés in Britain

---

[18] "La nation se forme par le seul droit naturel. Le gouvernement, au contraire, ne peut appartenir qu'au droit positif" (Sieyès 181). Also: "Avant-elle et au-dessus d'elle il n'y a que le droit naturel" (180).

[19] "... le 31 mai, le peuple s'éveille, et les traîtres ne sont plus. La Convention se montre aussi juste que le peuple, aussi grande que sa mission. Un nouveau pact sociale est proclamé ..." "Sur la situation politique de la République française" (x). The Girondins would be purged from the Convention in June, tried and executed in October. (The pagination occasionally resorts to Roman numerals.)

appealed to the kind of contract that was assumed to have guaranteed and sealed the transfer of power from the members of the community to one ruler. (The exiles chose to ignore Hobbes's point that a successful revolt was also a valid one.) It appears that the concept had become sufficiently loose in order to be used in support of different claims, remaining available for rhetorical and speculative purposes.

The exiles thought in terms of a France made up of corporations, guilds, orders. Individuals tended to be defined by their membership in any of these bodies. Their rights, relationships, perhaps solidarity tended to exist within a particular association, possibly without being aware of other interests. These bodies were concerned mainly with themselves and each perceived itself as only one part of society. The traditional claim was that only the monarch related himself to the whole, only he gathered in his person all particular, fragmentary aspects, thus embodying and representing the nation. The facts and some of the claims changed after 1789. The corporations were abolished and the nation was re-defined as consisting of all the individuals in the population. The condition of equality linked the members of the former associations based on occupation across the former borders of regulations, interests and traditions.

These developments had a corresponding impact on the way the emerging norms and values were described and understood. Separate entities cohered as the "singularization and simplification which were directed socially and politically against the society of orders" resulted in modifications where "Freedom took the place of freedoms, Justice that of rights and servitudes, Progress that of progressions ... and from the diversity of revolutions, 'The Revolution' emerged."[20] Here was an opportunity to opt for various meanings of a term before a new sense crystallized. When Mallet ridiculed talk of "the rights of Man" as being a meaningless abstraction which overlooked the concrete rights of particular people, he chose to ignore the shift from the isolated person entitled to limited sets of rights prescribed by his social position to a citizen of a

---

[20] Reinhart Koselleck, *Futures Past*, trans. Keith Tribe (Cambridge, MA: MIT Press, 1982) 31 (the translation here is slightly modified); *Vergangene Zukunft* (1979. Frankfurt am Main: Suhrkamp, 1992) 54.

whole nation, entitled to all the rights that such a community decided it should possess.

This is a case where concepts changed in accord with social transformations. But the reverse could also occur: new concepts could anticipate and require social and political changes.[21] The point was also made by Sieyès in his most influential pamphlet when he defended the validity of theoretical contributions in the general debate on improving the system.[22] I would suggest further that such a utopian strategy where concepts are advanced first and the facts are expected to be modified accordingly would be used by writers intent on discrediting particular developments: the dimension of expectation is overlooked, the concept is considered as contemporary with sets of facts to which actually it is not related, the discrepancy is emphasized, and the ensemble is ridiculed and dismissed.

A factor that may well have contributed to the ambiguity of various concepts and ways of arguing was the way philosophy was supplementing, or even replacing history, in the attempt to fix and re-define basic forms of exercising power.[23] The tension was between the radicals who invoked theoretical principles to place matters on new foundations, and a wide range of moderate to reactionary authors and politicians who wanted to preserve or use earlier ways of understanding human beings and organizing society. Continuity, assuming various degrees of fidelity to the past, rested on arguments decisively strengthened by historical evidence, while the radical changes were backed by reasoned explana-

---

[21] See Koselleck (1992: 113) for the conflict of political and social definitions of positions to be occupied in future.

[22] Sieyès justifies theory by underlining that it contains sets of truths and ideas corresponding to empirical factors, but then emphasizing its advantage of preceding empirical events: "Qu'est-ce que la théorie, s'il vous plaît, si ce n'est cette suite correspondante de vérités que vous ne savez point appercevoir avant leur *réalisations*, et qu'il faut bien cependant que quelqu'un ait apperçues, à moins que tout le monde n'ait opéré sans savoir ce qu'on faisoit" (216). When Koselleck mentions the "concepts of the future" which have increasingly been created since the French Revolution, Sieyès' insight is not acknowledged.

[23] See Baker (275) for the task of fixing the constitution by means of philosophy supplementing history. However, I apply Baker's point to a different kind of material. See also 278-79 for Grégoire's disparaging remarks about history being invoked because it offers arguments of all kinds, while philosophy is better because more rigorous.

tions of the need for a new system. This came across particularly strongly in Mallet's diatribes against what he considered as damaging principles and theories uncongenial to human nature and pernicious to the requirements of practice.

Unlike the ultra-royalists, Mallet du Pan was aware of the various points of view from which an historical matter could be regarded (*Mercure Britannique* 1: 56, 544). That may have made him more aware of the terms he was using, and less compelled to put together an argument at any cost in order to prove his ideas, or to justify the return to an earlier order. Not that he was any less vehement in his condemnation of the radical changes in France, mainly those after 1791. It must be remembered that he represented a group of refugees that had been active during the early stages of the Revolution, some being among the authors of the 1791 Constitution. Otherwise, as a Swiss, a well-known political commentator in Paris in the 1780s, his opinions, until recently, in demand in some government and court circles, he kept his distance from the militant goals of the extreme royalists. Mallet's aim, at least by editing his journal, was to present an image of France whose flaws and vulnerability would persuade the European states that they were not dealing with an invincible enemy. Exiled in London because general Bonaparte had demanded his expulsion by the Swiss authorities, Mallet saw the situation in terms of international politics, less worried by the domestic issues in France, however wider their relevance actually was, and more concerned by the impact that France's political system spread by its military force could have on the rest of Europe. His appeal had to be both broad and pragmatic so that the states able to oppose France should take heed.

The exiles' perception of the moral flaws of the revolutionary regime, and implicitly of their own being in the right, varied according to their different kinds of outlook and expectations. The articles in *Mercure Britannique*, particularly those in the first volume, discussed the developments in terms of the proper relations between states. This was a rather different kind of argument from the ultra-royalists' who reasoned in terms of the proper hierarchy in one country (but with claims to universality), and the importance of tradition for the legitimacy of the royal dynasty. As Mallet regarded the stabilized revolutionary administration in his periodical through the prism of the French invasion in Switzerland, he could make a credible case without straining the argument too much. The extreme royalists, on the other hand, had an uphill struggle to put across a convincing argument. This may explain the different emphasis and shape of the discussion between Mallet's journal, on the one hand, and *Mercure de France* on the other. Mallet invoked tradition because he found there a more democratic form of government than the French had imposed in his country. The other exile faction was keen to discover evidence in the past of the normality of the *ancien régime*. This entangled the ultras in laboured arguments about the relationship between sovereignty and monarchy, definitions of the nation and the significance of contract.

The use made of philosophy and history in these discussions implied that they lent themselves to different purposes, the émigrés having more recourse to history because it could be used according to need. The ultra-royalists justified their position in theological, juridical and historical terms. Mallet confined himself mainly to history with the emphasis on the proper international relations and what he saw as the common sense of tradition. It appears that the extreme royalists were keen to prove their case by means of an idiosyncratic use of history but also by theoretical efforts of their own, and so they felt compelled to consider suitably vague concepts and assemble them in plausible arguments. Mallet du Pan tended to state his empirical points one by one, among outbursts against the flights of abstraction in Paris, and to leave it at that. The appeal was in one case to faith and authority, while in the other to experience as a guide.

Moral Sphere with a Difference

Before proceeding to the next sequence of the analysis it would be useful to point out a couple of aspects which, even if obvious, need to be restated here as particularly relevant to what follows. Although a prudential choice in most cases, exile is not a convincingly rational one; suspicion, fear, lack of information played a decisive part. A person may not be subjected to a legal decision or physical expulsion. Yet the inconvenience of remaining in the country outweighs that of exile to such an extent that the issue becomes clouded and there can hardly be a question of equably contemplating the alternatives. Therefore the arguments produced in exile are hardly elaborated from an intellectually serene position. An element of bias is suspected of entering the émigrés assessments, analyses, solutions. To this is added the drive to justify oneself in order to change the image of being in the wrong. The exiles are compelled by the circumstances to provide a defence of their stance. Placed in what they considered an unfair situation, free to act, and used to articulating their views, they are led to furnish a demonstration of their rightness.

Paradoxical Morality

Other things being equal, a moral value in fairly undisturbed circumstances may be taught, commended and practised. The circumstances of exile however constitute an extreme case. The attributes ascribed by the émigrés to themselves articulate a moral justification *sui generis*. It is an argument that arises when normal circumstances do not obtain. Forced to leave their countries and perceived as having lost in a political encounter, the exiles react by providing their own explanation. This kind of explanation implies or expresses certain moral attributes as part of their defense; it is an account that tends to be biased or irrational simply because the relationship between the exiles and those who drove them abroad does not have a rational basis: force is answered by rhetoric. Neither the authorities' power—or the fear they inspire—to drive their opponents abroad, nor the émigrés' rhetoric responding to that power rely on reason. This implacably confrontational relationship characterizes the framework of the exiles' arguments.

The justifications present in these arguments have two paradoxical features. First, this defence relies on a moral attribute that claims to have a general quality, yet cannot be extended to all and sundry (taught or practised). Second, the strength with which this attribute is invoked is equalled only by the strength of their purpose that would cancel it. There is a temporary element about this attribute: the intention of the émigrés is to return home which means abandoning the quality claimed exclusively in exile to affirm their moral advantage. In other words, although they assert their moral rightness by appropriating a suitable attribute, their objective is to cease assuming the position of self-styled representatives of their nations, thus giving up the very moral trait employed to redeem them.

An argument resorting to this kind of moral attribute is characteristic of exile because the validity of the argument is not meant to last beyond the period of banishment (even when referred to in later discussions at home). The "liberales" can return home and put and end to their exile only when their convictions may be expressed openly in Spain, which in their opinion would mean being expressed by the vast majority of the population. The nation would therefore manifest and assert itself and there would be no longer any need for a restricted group to constitute the nation's entity in exile. A similar process would occur when it becomes possible for Mazzini and his adepts to return home: once the population grows aware of their forming and belonging to a nation, Mazzini's claim of representing the nation, the moral attribute that would dismiss the stigma of exile, would become unnecessary. Even in the case of the French émigrés this moral attribute would have its temporary dimension; although upon their return the ultra-royalists may still claim that they constitute the real nation (a claim they apparently dropped when they did come back), this assertion would be made as part of a restored hierarchy, and not as a justification for dismissing the guilt of being exiled.

The point here is that while there are moral attributes that would keep their validity after the refugees' return, there is one such attribute discussed above whose validity as understood by the émigrés would cease when they stopped being émigrés. To the extent to which this moral weapon loses its efficacy when banishment is at an end, to that extent is it a particular weapon devised only for the exiles' arsenal since it redresses the ascribing of guilt implied by the act of banishment.

The periodicals contain a level of straightforward political arguments: the merits of the divine right of kings, constitutional monarchy, liberalism or the national implications of radical political changes. These arguments rest on a rational basis, they marshal evidence in order to prove the other side wrong. There is hardly a dialogue going on, but at this level the exiles appeal to logic. This would be the kind of argument developed by the political opposition at home were it allowed to function.

Parallel with this potential conflict of political opinions marked by reason, there is the tension between the force (or fear) that ejected the émigrés and the rhetoric that they respond by, a tension where reason does not feature. It is as part of this irrational encounter that the moral attribute of constituting the nation emerges. I suggest that it is at this second level that the exiles try to reject the blame attached to them by expulsion. This level, where reason is absent, depends on the former. The moral attribute is occasionally claimed as part of a political argument, but when the claim is spelled out it becomes obvious that the tone changes, and the author ceases to make a political point crossing over into the rhetoric of morality. The outlook of the émigré is thus established and the claim need not be repeated.

Defendants as Judges

The values emphasized by the émigrés derived from the background and contemporary concerns of their countries: hierarchy, limitation of royal power, unity, independence, and republicanism. These values and concerns structure their arguments and are part of the reasons for which they were banished or fled. The choice of particular values was considered wrong by one side and right by the other. The criteria of rightness were political, social, economical, having also clear moral implications to do with justice and fairness. However, there were new values to be taken into account, particularly one that concerned directly their situation. This was the growing belief that a nation possessed a quality of its own. Since Herder's prize-winning essay of 1770 on the origin of language and his later work on the philosophy of history, the idea of the unique attributes of a nation rooted in its language, culture and history had been spreading apace. For the refugees who argued in these terms, in addition to others such as national liberation and unity, Herder's hypothesis must have been of immediate interest. His explanation could be used in morally charged political arguments, thus acquiring a dimension initially absent. In addition, the increasing awareness of national issues afforded the exiles a topical area which could be employed in order to re-establish their moral credibility damaged because marked by banishment. This is the second chief point of this final chapter: a new quality which did not carry an emphatically ethical dimension was accommodated by the émigrés to their own systems of morally-infused values in order to firm up their case; furthermore, the sense of condemnation accompanying the decision of banishment was counteracted by claims of being the proper representatives of the nation.

This is a case of modifying an idea in order to use it for one's own purposes. The need to do this was due to the relevance of this new value to the refugees' predicament. Those French émigrés who claimed that the royalists and the high aristocracy embodied the nation because they carried its culture received extra aid from a new theory defining a nation in these terms (in this particular case, the importance of folk ballads and such like was glossed over). During the eighteenth century the French aristocracy had increasingly included culture among its defining features, which earlier had rested chiefly on martial and political criteria. The Spanish liberals in exile who stated that they were the only part of their people free to express themselves and, therefore temporarily, articulated the opinions of the nation as their representatives could also draw support from the new hypothesis. And those who fought for the independence of their nation like Mazzini received an obvious backing from such a theory. In each case the existence of a particular quality in a nation was transformed into a part of an argument that evaluated and approved a state of things. On an individual level there were further moral implications to do with the value of belonging to a nation, feeling pride in its history, and showing loyalty to one's co-nationals.

Which Nationalism, What Nation?

This is not a study of nationalism. The background to this complex and elusive phenomenon needs to be sketched here only to provide the wider context of changing notions which the exiles could relate to or distance themselves from. The émigrés' claims concerning their nations differed from the standard ones beginning to emerge at the time. Their claims arose from an antagonism between themselves and some of their own fellow-countrymen, as ever, with the partial exception of Mazzini. These claims were meant to reverse the exclusion to which the refugees had been subjected. That is why they are not part of the unfolding of nationalism and of its rhetoric. The French and the Spanish émigrés were trying to wrest from the authorities at home the prestige of representing their nation or articulating their position. (The Italians, Mazzini above all, assumed the role of the nation's representatives simply because of the absence at home of the necessary awareness and practical conditions.) The French referred to cultural and generally traditional criteria, and the Spaniards to censorship and persecution at home. It was a political issue being turned into a moral confrontation where aspects of budding nationalism became part of the special pleading in exile. That is why such claims must be seen in terms of the factors the refugees related to with nationalism as an edifying background but not of overwhelming importance in the matter.

The word ("natio," "nation") has migrated from being a peripheral term describing distant and amorphous groups ("populus" being the name for the proper community) to the central position held today, passing through the use referring to more definite groups (clergymen, students, the higher aristocracy).[24] It has been argued that initially "natio" was not a genuinely collective concept like "populus" and that as late as the fourteenth century "noblece de nation" meant the birth status of an individual, while the use grouping various kinds of persons persisted throughout the period between the fourteenth and sixteenth centuries. At the same time the concept of "nation" became increasingly a political one beginning with the sixteenth century. Herder's work brings together "people" and "nation" where the people are no longer subordinated to an exclusive "nation" but becomes the nation itself, a change established by the French Revolution culminating in the meaning used in the Declaration of the Rights of Man and Citizen. During the first decades of the nineteenth century the meaning of "nation" is linked to the authority of the monarch as the "founder" of the people, while liberal conceptions of

---

[24] For detailed discussions of the history of the relevant terms and concepts see Aira Kemiläinen, *Nationalism: Problems Concerning the Word, the Concept and Classification*, Studia Historica Jyväskyläensia 3 (Jyväskylä: Jyväskylän Kasvatusopillinen Korkeakoulu—Jyväskylän Yliopistoyhdistys, 1964) 13 ff., and Reinhart Koselleck et al., "Volk, Nation, Nationalismus, Masse" in *Geschichtliche Grundbegriffe: Historisches Lexikon zur politisch-sozialen Sprache in Deutschland* (1992), the latter with a noticeable German emphasis as, in fact, the subtitle indicates.

nationalism acquire a new dimension in the 1830s through a certain international solidarity with the movements in Greece (already in the 1820s) and Poland.

Whether one can talk about one or more kinds of nationalism, whether a nation precedes and produces the phenomenon or is created by it, whether language, culture, a common history, economic circumstances, the will to set up a state characterize the group and the process, the definitions and explanations vary with a particular author's outlook and preferred causal factors. The approaches range from no *a priori* definition of a nation, to a cautious one, while some scholars doubt that there is such a type of community at all.[25] Nationalism has been seen as having a weak and a strong version depending on the conditions available for a nation state, as a "cultural phenomenon" taking a political form, as caused by the industrial age which requires an increased homogeneity and a political framework to protect it, or as emerging "out of" and "against" cultural phenomena such as "the religious community" and the "dynastic realm."[26] In quite a few definitions one of the common denominators is the overlapping of the ethnic and political boundaries.[27]

Other attempts at defining the phenomenon have taken as a decisive criterion the role played by nationalism in particular historical contexts. "Risorgimento" and "integral nationalism" are the two chief types estab-

---

[25] E.J. Hobsbawm, *Nations and nationalism since 1789. Programme, myth, reality* (Cambridge: Cambridge UP, 1992) 8. The cautious approach where "historically evolved relations of a linguistic, cultural, religious or political nature" lead to coherence and common interests is provided by Peter Alter, *Nationalism*, trans. Stuart McKinnon-Evans (1985; London: Edward Arnold, 1990) 17. Ernest Gellner considers that it is nationalism that "engenders" nations, *Nations and Nationalism* (1983; Oxford: Blackwell, 1992) 55-56. Benedict Anderson sees the nation as "an imagined political community" limited and sovereign, *Imagined Communities* (London: Verso, 1983) 6.

[26] Eugene Kamenka, "Political Nationalism—The Evolution of an Idea," in Eugene Kamenka, ed., *Nationalism: The nature and evolution of an idea* (London: Edward Arnold, 1976) 15-16; John Plamenatz, "Two Types of Nationalism" in Kamenka, ed. (24); Gellner 40, 140-41; Anderson 12. Hans Kohn has distinguished between a Western and an Eastern kind of nationalism in his *The Ideas of Nationalism: A Study in its Origins and Background* (New York: Macmillan, 1946) 329, 574, a classification accepted by Kamenka and discussed at length by Kemiläinen (115 ff).

[27] For instance, Gellner (1) and Kamenka (15-16), while Hobsbawm (9) contents himself with Gellner's definition.

lished in this respect: the former implying "liberation from political and social oppression" while the latter containing militaristic and extreme characteristics (Alter 29, 37-38). More sociological efforts, still accompanied by historical criteria, have found two kinds of nationalism: "individualistic-libertarian" and "collectivistic-authoritarian." Further distinctions between civic and ethnic types of nationalism offer an extended range of permutations.[28]

Various suggestions about the emergence and historical evolution of nationalism have been determined to a large extent by the defining criteria. Where its roots are regarded as cultural and its growth is connected with the decline of religion and the prestige of monarchy, as well as with the development of "print-languages" facilitating communication and hence the process of imagining, then its dawn is placed in the eighteenth century.[29] If other conditions need to be ripe—a degree of complexity, mobility and the need to communicate—then the relevant time sequence starts at the turn of the century, and in many cases well into the nineteenth century (Gellner 140-142). It has also been suggested that among the conditions necessary for early nation-formation there are the growth of the secular state and decline of the clerical authority, while one of the chief scholars in the field, looking at the early emergence of nations, finds relevance in "the more permanent cultural attributes of memory, value, myth and symbolism."[30] On the whole, apart from references to the ancient Greeks' loyalty to their *polis*, to the virtue of Roman patriotism, or to the importance of national unity as envisaged by Machiavelli, most scholars date the beginnings of nationalism to the latter half of the eighteenth century.[31] It has also been argued that what appeared at that

---

[28] Liah Greenfeld, *Nationalism: Five Roads to Modernity* (Cambridge, MA: Harvard UP, 1992) 11.

[29] Anderson 12, 44-45. On chronology being conditioned by the choice of the defining circumstances, see also Anthony D. Smith on the "modernists" in *The Ethnic Origins of Nations* (Oxford: Blackwell, 1986) 8-9.

[30] Boyd C. Shafer, *Faces of Nationalism: New Realities and Old Myths* (New York: Harcourt Brace Jovanovich, 1972) 29. The quote comes from Smith (3-4).

[31] Some historians distinguish between national consciousness and nationalism, the former emerging in the twelfth century (Kamenka 6), and remaining "nationalism in the weak sense" (15). On the same distinction and on the ancient roots of "patriotism" and "devotion to the community" see Plamenatz in Kamenka, ed. (24).

point was the concrete form imbued with an idea that dates from the times of the ancient Hebrews. Significant for the present discussion, nationalism has also been seen as developing a new kind of morality with its own sanctions and rewards while another account has claimed that nationalism was an ethical force for Herder; however, Herder's outlook is qualified by the observation that nationality, particularly in its later sense, would not have carried for him the "highest value."[32]

In general, the scholars who assumed that there were such entities as nation, national consciousness, nationality waiting to be brought into being were able to talk about an historical development and examined earlier centuries and millennia for suitable signs that would confirm their theories. These historians have been called "perennialists" (Kohn being a good representative). Then there are the "modernists" (e.g., Gellner): they believe that nations and nationalism have been occasioned by social and economic developments, and analyse the decisive factors, without finding much relevance in the historical background.[33]

Exile Redefined

The emergence of nationalism offered new possibilities of displaying one's moral rightness. Whether it was based on civic rights or culture, a nation was a good thing, belonging to it was the proper condition of any citizen or culture bearer, and showing loyalty and affection to it was morally commendable. To be excluded or to seem to be outside could be perceived as so much more of a punishment than exile had been regarded before. The opposite also became possible, the new idiom could be seized and used for the exiles' own moral and political benefit.

---

[32] "It [nationalism] developed a morality with rewards and punishments, virtues and sins, rituals and symbols, and a missionary zeal ... a great number of religious terms passed into the domain of politics during the French Revolution, and many of these had to do with the fatherland and patriotism" (Shafer 133). See Kohn (440, 430) for the remark on the value of nationality.

[33] These categories have been suggested by Anthony D. Smith, *Nationalism and Modernism: A critical survey of recent theories of nations and nationalism* (London: Routledge, 1998) 16-24. Other terms used by Smith are "historians" and "social scientists." For a critical view of Gellner's theory see ibid., ch. 2.

The French émigrés answered the rights-based national claims in France with an argument which contained traces of earlier political issues but which, in the main, acquired what in the late 1790s would have been a new theory of nations, Herder's explanation grounded in language and culture. Even that was used selectively by the French exiles who emphasized a certain cultivated tradition and toned down the popular one. The significant point here is that the rights-based nationalism, let us call it Rousseau-derived for the sake of the argument, was noticeably charged with moral value, while Herder's was not: an individual simply belonged to a community speaking a certain language which allowed a particular cultural expression, but there was nothing especially commendable in the phenomenon as such. Being expelled by the revolutionary authorities from a nation to which it was morally right to belong, the émigrés answered with another version of nation, one that initially did not contain a moral dimension, but which in the process was invested with one. It should be remembered that the French exiles also played on a pre-herderian, medieval meaning of nation, but there again they invested with moral value a "natio" which otherwise had been an ethically neutral entity.

The forms of nationalism that some of the exiles claim or distance themselves from vary. The French royalists have to take into account a comprehensive redefinition of the nation and of the quality of belonging to it. Not only did every individual inhabiting the French territory become a citizen of equal importance (in principle), but the degree of commitment to this new kind of nation was also raised to a new pitch of intensity. Membership of such a nation comes very close to a form of political commitment. In France one witnesses a version of nationalism that has to do with a more proper relocation of power from monarchy to an assembly representing the people. Simultaneously we see a transformation of the status of a large number of people, possibly a majority, who insist on constituting that entity where power has been relocated. Having been outside the sphere of civic rights and dismissed by the aristocracy as being members of "le peuple" rather than of "la nation," most Frenchmen discover that their loyalty to the nation and to the new political order coincide. The conclusion that a majority of the citizens should have a share in sovereignty becomes a moral statement, and the consequent measures a moral gesture. The French ultra-royalists oppose the rights-based nationalism with its accompanying kind of sovereignty by means of a culture- and tradition-based national spirit. The émigrés realize that they have to match the morally infused nationalism developed at home, and ascribe a moral charge to their own version of culture-based national claims, a quality that Herder would have hardly recognized.

The Spanish refugees articulated their claims to represent the nation after a period when almost the entire population had been brought together in their collective opposition against the French invader. The "afrancesados" were to be found among intellectuals and the higher aristocracy, neither very numerous, and not among the people at large. This period of war and attempted political reforms was followed by repression. The "liberales" abroad were able to refer to a moment of glory, a glimmer of political hope quickly suppressed by an arbitrary ruler, and they could particularly play on the monarch's unhonoured promises. Being exiled under these circumstances, both the French and the Spanish émigrés had the opportunity of counteracting the guilt attached to them: the ultra-royalists could easily shift from a political dispute where they could not redeem the stigma of exile to a duel of claims about the proper nation where a still remembered tradition could show that they were in the right. The "liberales" could always make assumptions about the silenced nation who had recently showed signs of welcoming their new constitution with all its subsequent benefits. Only Mazzini was able to make a direct appeal to an increasingly recognizable form of nationalism. Unlike the established states of France and Spain there was no Italian state, and Mazzini's claims of national awareness and militantism questioned more successfully the actions of those who had banished him.

When placing the exiles' response in its context it is proper to bear in mind the manner in which the outlook on the nation was articulated at home. It must also be said that there is a difference between the straightforward nationalist statements and the claims made by the exiles. By the time their justifications are expounded in the periodicals a certain distancing from nationalism as such has occurred. The topical problems of nationalism fade away as the émigrés' idiosyncratic, rhetorical explanations combine aspects of cultural history and political doctrine couched in relentless diatribes against the powers at home, all that intended to absolve them from guilt.

The object of the present analysis is not so much the individual moral norms of behaviour; the moral dimension in these periodicals is related rather to the nature of a nation as claimed by the various émigrés. Their arguments deal with the proper ways of holding and exercising power framed in terms of the exiles' relationship to their nation, and also in terms of the quality, role, and identity of the nation itself. Whether it is the specific quality of a nation based on its language and cultural productions, or the location of sovereignty based on the "rights of man and citizen," the refugees defined their position with the help of norms and qualities derived from beyond the individual sphere. This is a morality extracted from the significance of a community (the nation) but applied to the individual cases of groups of émigrés. It is an *ad hoc* set of ethical attributes for use in extreme circumstances.

Taking the existence and manifestation of a nation as the criteria from which to derive moral norms, the good in this case means belonging to, representing, being (indeed embodying), the nation. The manner of holding and exercising power would then have to be agreed upon, taking into account the criterion of the specific national quality in the shape given to it by the exiles. The refugees' arguments about political issues would consequently be accompanied by the way they relate themselves to their nations, a self-proclaimed, or implied, morally advantageous position which would also reflect on the political solutions advanced by them. Thus, what was initially a cultural and linguistic hypothesis becomes integrated into political arguments that apparently refer only to justice and fairness, but in fact ascribe a moral dimension both to the solution and to those who present it. The ultra-royalists' claim that they are the nation is also a claim that they are both morally and logically right, and that their political solution is correct. The same point, somewhat modified, could be made about some of the Spanish liberals and also about Mazzini.

A form of the embodiment of the nation in the monarch is in fact mentioned by Herder in a discarded draft of his chapter on political organization in *Ideas for a Philosophy of History* (1784-91). Herder explains the appearance of hereditary monarchy suggesting that "[t]he person of the first elected monarch was, as it were, the abstracted symbol of the whole nation; all honours and distinctions that were conferred upon him were insignia, by means of which external recognition could be given to the collective values of the political artefact which the hereditary monarch represented."[34] The recognition granted to the collective values of the nation occurred through the monarch. Even if they originated in the community, something easily overlooked by the royalists, they could insistently point to the place where they were symbolically concentrated and visible. The French royalists used their argument about the king embodying the nation while in France *la nation* and *national* were replacing *le roi* and *royal*.[35] As they were about to get rid of the king and having forced his successors to flee, the revolutionaries were linguistically and conceptually in the process of prising off the attribute that the monarchy used in defining itself. Not surprisingly, the émigrés stubbornly emphasized this very attribute in their arguments.

The social order is endowed by Burke with morality. Its destruction is therefore equivalent to destroying morality: "The truth is, that France is out of itself—the moral France is separated from the geographical … If we look for the *corporate people* of France … they are in Flanders, and Germany, in Switzerland, Spain, Italy, and England. There are all the princes of the blood, there are all the orders of the state, there are all the parliaments of the kingdom" (qtd. in Parkin 62). This is one of the series of distinctions that the exiles seize upon and develop, eager to spell out in what way France was "out of itself." The wider good is further defined in terms of harmony between will and judgement, lower and higher human nature, people's demands and the solutions of the aristocracy or its replies. Accepting the existence of a particular quality that defines a nation, the French exiles, inspired by Burke, attempt a redefinition, chiefly by retaining the aristocracy's contribution to tradition and discarding the folklore.

The argument was tempting enough for other refugees to resort to and adapt to their own circumstances. The nation need not be regarded

---

[34] Quoted in F.M. Barnard, ed., *J.G. Herder on Social and Political Culture* (Cambridge: Cambridge UP, 1969) 320, n. 15.

[35] See Jacques Godechot, "The New Concept of the Nation and its Diffusion in Europe," in Otto Dann and John Dinwiddy, ed., *Nationalism in the French Revolution* (London: Hambledon Press, 1988) 14-15.

in terms of its initial development; its chief characteristic could be seen in terms of a latter-day crystallization. The emphasis could be laid on the role of the aristocracy and monarchy, or on an active and vocal political group such as the Spanish "liberales." Here the refugees consider that they embody all the previous qualities of the nation plus the latest desire of a liberal, constitutional system, which only they can articulate in exile. A distinction is made here as well, and, as always, one of the elements outlined has an emphatic moral dimension. In the case of the Spanish exiles, the moral quality is achieved by the contrast with the absolutist monarch, as expected, but also with fellow-countrymen who failed the true cause, the "afrancesados." There is also a sense in which the appeal to the ancient constitution is in fact an invocation of a culture-based national value. The desirability of bringing back the qualities of this ancient document acquire a moral quality that reflects on those who militate for it as one of the nation's greatest achievements transformed in time into one of its symbols. When the ancient constitution becomes the issue, the political element—limiting the monarch's power—is combined with this particular attribute of the nation: the age invoked is "golden" because it was then that this value could manifest itself unimpeded.

An important element that should be clarified is the kind of moral attribute the exiles invoke in their articles. If a moral attribute is commendable the expectation is that it ought to be possessed by as many individuals as possible. The case of moral justification in exile nevertheless alters the nature of this expectation. A self-delimited moral space arises cancelling any universalist dimension of the moral attributes invoked within this sphere. The quality that the émigrés ascribe to themselves, constituting the nation, cannot at the same time be possessed by the individuals at home, be they rulers or the ruled. The polarization caused by banishment brings along a similar ethical polarization creating a particular case of morality. As it becomes impossible to extend this moral attribute to the people back home, any moral option in this respect seems excluded. From the exiles' point of view, the chief attribute that redeems their moral position cannot manifest itself outside their enclosed space. Yet, with the exception of the French ultra-royalists, there is a way in which the fellow-countrymen of the exiles can acquire this attribute, namely by joining the exile community. It is here that the

Spanish writer or politician can articulate his views which implies voicing the people's views, convinced that temporarily it embodies its will, and turning exclusion from the nation into an impossibility. For lack of a more nuanced opposition, anyone who is against despotism is considered a liberal, and that amounts to most of the nation, according to the "liberales." The ability to articulate openly political opinions becomes a way of manifesting the existence of the nation, and that becomes possible only in exile. Also, Mazzini's fellow-conspirators who realize the need for unity and independence can display their intentions only in exile. They acquire thus the quality of the proper representatives of the nation, and so cancel the disgrace of banishment.

In each case the issue must be granted a certain complexity. This would allow distinctions which produce the necessary ethical implication linked to the nation-defining quality. The sovereignty of the people plays a larger role in the Spanish exiles' arguments; the effort to ascribe a moral quality to this political concept is far less strenuous as the issue is more clear-cut. Mazzini rests his argument both on the unique cultural quality of the nation and on the people's right to sovereignty. By the time he is arguing his case in exile these issues are less striking and he emphasizes the role of each nation according to its particular gifts. For the French aristocrats the Revolution may have appeared as an aberration and at the time it may not have been completely absurd to insist on the role of monarchy as an embodiment of the nation. Four decades later the accent was bound to shift: the social changes and partly successful militant movements enabled Mazzini to look forward to a realistic part that various nations, soon to be independent as he thought, could play.

The move away from a morally neutral value occurred as it was being adapted to the particular outlook of this or that wave of émigrés. The reasons that had driven them abroad differed and so did the uses and the moral implications derived from the specific quality attributed to a nation. Above all, the use changed with the changing contemporary conditions, and the course followed by the countries to which the exiles belonged. The wider good envisaged by the refugees varied: the royalists saw it in maintaining order and the hierarchy, Mallet and the Spaniards considered it as being a constitutional monarchy, Mazzini regarded it as achieving his country's unity and independence as well as the emancipation of its citizens. These arrangements were seen as the proper ones containing the necessary values, which would satisfy the great majority. Their materialization also meant that the exiles' position was vindicated. And in all cases an important component was the degree to which the nation was reflected in the exiles.

The first sections of Mallet's periodical are in fact a morally charged reply to the introduction of French institutions in Switzerland. The imposition of a constitution from Paris is a moral gesture in the name of the revolutionary principles, according to him: "ils [the French revolutionaries] s'érigent en précepteurs de la morale & de liberté republicaine …" (1: 7). Irrespective of the Directory's intentions, this is how Mallet perceives them and he sees his answer as a moral riposte. He does not enter a purely ethical debate; he narrates at length the history of his country, dwelling particularly on its democratic tradition. Through this narration he matches what he considers to be the unwelcome French teaching about morality and so his reply is placed in a moral register within the context of the argument. He ascribes to Swiss history the ethical values that he needs in order to dismiss the French attempts at bringing over their own version of desirable values. (The first chapter of his long piece on Switzerland is called "État Moral & Civil de la Suisse, spécialement de Berne, avant & depuis la Révolution de France" [1: 11]).

Herder grounded his hypothesis in language and culture. A different criterion granting particular validity to a nation was based on a theory of rights materialized in the Declaration of the Rights of Man and Citizen proclaimed in Paris in 1789. The individuals of the French nation (although the point was valid in general) were re-defined as citizens, each endowed with reason and having an equal significance within a re-arranged system of loyalties—relating themselves no longer to corporations, guilds, landowners, monarchy, and the Church, but to one another in equal measure, and also to the overall community which they made up, namely the nation. And it was within this entity that sovereignty had its natural place. Since the Revolution had only occurred in France it was only the Frenchmen who re-discovered themselves as co-nationals according to the newly proclaimed principles. In the rush of enthusiasm where the nation and "la patrie" took on new dimensions leading, predictably, to an emphatic patriotism, the revolutionaries were not inward-looking: it was considered desirable and valuable to carry the radical ideas to other countries with the main aim of urging fundamental political changes, and with the possible incidental effect of making other nations aware of the inherent quality of their existence.

Herder was hardly mentioned in revolutionary Paris. Anything that brought the citizens together was rather derived from Rousseau's solution to the organization of the community and the process of decision-making. The distinctive note of French revolutionary nationalism was political rather than cultural; it had to do with rights-based sovereignty rather than with cultural specificity. The exiles hardly mentioned either, possibly referring to Rousseau only to ridicule and dismiss him. Yet the rightness of their opinions and desirability of the implied values rested on a cultural foundation, whether it meant a particular tradition or the role of the nation and its ability to make a certain contribution to the world. The way the émigrés developed their arguments against this background shows how they contributed to a particular level of intellectual history.

There was a paradox about these two varieties of nationalism, which may tentatively be formulated as follows. The nationalism based on the possession of reason and equal rights claimed, quite rightly, universality but it appeared threatening and remained emphatically local, confined only to France. The idea of the unique quality of a nation, although valid in the case of each people, according to the theory, was strongly tied to local circumstances, yet it had a wide (possibly universal) appeal. It may be argued that the former was threatening because its emergence would tamper with political, social and economic structures, while the latter was flattering and intriguing, basically outlining a sphere, current, stream of tradition, culture, or the potentialities of a language. All the refugees discussed here found themselves in exile because of their attitude to political structures. Their choice of one version of nationalism, an implicit or explicit option, was bound to be biased. Most of them opted for a tacit resort to the quality outlined by Herder; what was happening in the process was also an integration of a plain hypothesis into an existing arsenal of existing moral arguments. A few Spanish liberals did include in their argument elements of the first variety. But on the whole, the elements emphasized in the exiles' texts throughout all these decades shape the strand of intellectual history that I want to draw attention to.

Being an exile in these circumstances had a significance which had not existed earlier, and would not be encountered later when nationalism would be taken for granted as part of the general moral ammunition in debates. In exile, as the new quality had just been outlined, it would be more advantageous to appropriate and conveniently re-interpret it. In their own way, the French, Spanish, and Italian émigrés claimed to represent the real nation. (Perhaps Mazzini less, but none of my points apply equally to all exiles.) The assumption was that they thus started with a moral advantage, at the same time dismissing the attribute of émigré, which implied exclusion and defeat. Their particular emphases varied in order to adapt the notion to the circumstances of exile, the reasons for their flight and banishment, and the spirit of the respective decade.

Finally, the tone of the debate at home, or just the tone imposed by the authorities, conditioned the arguments in these periodicals. Since the intensity of their commitment had driven them abroad, the discussions developed there were more often than not confined by the polarity of a political conflict. The polarization could manifest itself in other ways as well. For instance, Mallet du Pan, to a large extent a product of the philosophes' intellectual influence, and a former protégé of Voltaire, would be driven to point out the disadvantages of an overall rational approach in its more exaggerated form and praise the benefits of tradition. This was something which he may not have done in the course of his normal activity as a political commentator in Paris.

The refugees' commitment prevented them from exploring freely a range of political options or moral values. They concentrated not so much on analytical complexity as on rhetorical impact by conveniently exploiting any useful material. The solution was known in advance, the point was to convey it as forcefully as possible in a combative language that would also belittle the adversary, not only prove him wrong. It may be argued that, consequently, they chose concise, simple arguments from various sets of theories and explanations (Bodin's, Burke's, Herder's, Bentham's) in order to prove their point. These periodicals were hardly philosophical examinations of a problem—they were militant calls to oppose and change a system, and in order to achieve that they carved out a convenient issue from a body of texts and used it. Rather than being failed philosophers they were philosophically initiated propagandists.

Summing Up

The examination of these periodicals has been undertaken in order to outline a strand of intellectual history characterized by the manner of using ideas and concepts in the extreme situation of exile. Seven magazines belonging to three nationalities and published during four decades after the French Revolution are not representative of the entire world of exile. At the same time they constitute a sufficiently abundant material to require selection and concentration on just a few questions. I have examined mainly the political arguments produced by the émigrés paying particular attention to their claims that they were morally in the right, and to how they employed topical concepts in the process.

To the extent to which exile is the result of an implicit or explicit sentence passed by the winners in a political conflict, and to the extent to which such a sentence attaches guilt to the defendant, I have assumed that the émigrés would attempt to re-define the circumstances in order to reject the label of exile and dismiss this guilt. Whether French ultra-royalists or constitutional monarchists, Spanish "liberales," or Italian nationalists, most of them intended to change things at home in order to return. Excluded as a result of a conflict only temporarily resolved, they attempted to maintain the tension in the hope of turning the balance.

Those who resorted to using arguments in periodicals proceeded at two levels. While there was a level of recognizable political argument, which the opposition might have carried on at home if tolerated, there was another level where the force that imposed the banishment was answered by rhetoric and by a paradoxical moral argument meant to counter an accusation. The chief way in which the exiles attempt to shape their response was by reversing the roles and claiming to be the true nation despite being in exile. The arguments varied according to the historical and cultural tradition of the émigrés and to the changing significance of the concept of nation along with topical political ideas. The French extreme royalists rather improbably invoked an exclusive, medieval definition of the nation, a couple of decades later the Spanish liberals identified it with the contemporary, emerging political creed they supported, while almost ten years later Mazzini appealed to a future national entity. In each case a convenient interpretation of the concept would obliterate the condition of exile and, boldly, declare the other side of being variously the outsider, unable to express, or unaware of possessing, the quality of nation. This reversal of roles, paradoxical and highly unorthodox as it is, does show a different way of handling concepts in an extreme situation. What is of interest here is not so much the validity of the argument, but the way it is set up and its purpose under the circumstances.

The use of contemporary concepts both in exile and at home has been discussed here mainly in the case of the French émigrés. The fact that the exiles resorted to these concepts, and the manner in which they opted for a suitable sense in contrast with the meaning used at home, suggests a way of determining the degree to which a concept is "unsettled" in a period of transition. The social and political shifts in the 1790s meant that some concepts attached to earlier phenomena and ways of thinking went on being used even after considerable changes occurred. "Contract," "nature," "sovereignty," could be seized on by the émigrés and used according to their aims, while they may have acquired a different meaning in Paris. This was also part of the effort of not allowing the tension to decrease and of ensuring the survival of a certain interpretation of the historical developments.

The exiles discussed in this study had not set out to produce comprehensive philosophical systems. They were educated people at a time when education was still restricted to a few, and that placed them in a category which for lack of a better word could be called intellectuals. At the same time, they had sufficiently strong political interests (or an awkward social position) to end up in exile. Being among the relatively few who could draw on a store of ideas and concepts, and compelled by extreme circumstances to respond, they added their own contribution to intellectual history.

Bibliography

Primary Sources

Manuscript sources

Add. Mss. Windham Papers 38736, 38769 (British Library)

Periodicals

L'Ambigu. London, 1802-18.
Apostolato popolare. London, 1840-43.
El Español. London, 1810-14.
El Español Constitucional. London, 1818-20, 1824-25.
Mercure Britannique. London, 1798-1800.
Mercure de France. London, 1800-1801.
Ocios de Españoles Emigrados. London, 1824-27.

Other printed primary sources

[Blanco White, J.]. *Letters from Spain.* London, 1825.

Della Peruta, Franco, ed. *Scrittori politici dell'ottocento.* Milano: Ricardo Ricciardi, 1969.

Mallet du Pan, Jacques. *Considérations sur la nature de la Révolution de France, et sur les causes qui en prolongent la durée.* N.p., 1793.

Mazzini, Giuseppe. *Scritti editi ed inediti.* Vol. 19. Imola: Galeati, 1914. 94 vols. 1906-1943.

Mazzini, Giuseppe. *Doveri dell'uomo.* Palazzo di Montecitorio: Camera dei deputati, 1972.

Mazzini, Giuseppe. *The Duties of Man.* Trans. Ella Noyes. London: Dent, 1966.

Sayous, A., ed. *Mémoires et correspondance de Mallet du Pan pours servir à l'histoire de la révolution française.* 2 vols. Paris, 1851.

Thom, John Hamilton, ed. *The Life of Rev. Joseph Blanco White written by himself; with portions of his correspondence.* 2 vols. London, 1845.

Secondary Sources

Abellán, José Luis. *Historia crítica del pensamiento español.* 5 vols. Madrid: Espasa-Calpe, 1979-91.

Acomb, Frances. *Mallet Du Pan (1749-1800): A Career in Political Journalism.* Durham, NC: Duke UP, 1973.

Allison Peers, E. *A History of the Romantic Movement in Spain.* 2 vols. Cambridge: Cambridge UP, 1940.

Alter, Peter. *Nationalism.* 1985. Trans. Stuart McKinnon-Evans. London: Edward Arnold, 1990.

Anderson, Benedict. *Imagined Communities.* London: Verso, 1983.

Arblaster, Anthony. *The Rise and Decline of Western Liberalism.* Oxford: Basil Blackwell, 1984.

Artola, Miguel, ed. *Enciclopedia de Historia de España.* 7 vols. Madrid: Alianza Editorial. 1988-93.

Aston, Nigel. *Religion and Revolution in France, 1780-1804.* Basingstoke: Macmillan, 2000.

Asún Escartín, Raquel. "Blanco White, José María." *Diccionario biográfico.* Vol. 4 of *Enciclopedia de Historia de España.*

Aymer, Jean-René. "Un épisode de la Guerre d'Indépendance (1808-1814); le moine Concha entre la Résistence et 'l'afrancesamiento'." *Recherches sur le monde Hispanique au dix-neuvième siècle.* Lille: Éditions universitaires, 1973.

Baker, Keith Michael. *Inventing the French Revolution: Essays on French Political Culture in the Eighteenth Century.* Cambridge: Cambridge UP, 1990.

Baldensperger, Ferdinand. *Le Mouvement des idées dans l'émigration française.* 2 vols. Paris: Plon, 1924.

Barnard, F.M., trans. and ed., *J.G. Herder on Social and Political Culture.* Cambridge: Cambridge UP, 1969.

Bellanger, Claude, et al., eds. *Histoire générale de la presse française.* 5 vols. Paris: Presses Universitaires de France, 1969-76.

Bellenger, Dominic Aidan. *The French Exiled Clergy in the British Isles after 1789: An Historical Introduction and Working List.* Bath: Downside Abbey, 1986.

Bentham, Jeremy. Letter. *Morning Chronicle.* 14 April 1820.

Berkeley, G.H. *The Making of Italy: 1815-1846.* 1932. Cambridge: Cambridge UP, 1968.

Bleiberg, German, ed. *Diccionario de Historia de España.* 1979. 3 vols. Madrid: Alianaza Editorial, 1986.

Bowle, John. *Politics and Opinion in the Ninenteenth Century.* London: Jonathan Cape, 1954.

Bracalini, Romano. *Mazzini: Il sogno dell'Italia onesta.* Milano: Mondadori, 1992.

Burke, Edmund. *Reflections on the Revolution in France.* Ed. L.G. Mitchell. Oxford: Clarendon, 1989. In vol. 8 of *The Writings and Speeches of Edmund Burke.* Ed. Paul Langford.

Burns, J.H. Conclusion. *The Cambridge History of Political Thought: 1450-1700.* Ed. Burns. Cambridge: Cambridge UP, 1991.

Burrow, J.W. *Evolution and Society: A Study in Victorian Social Theory.* Cambridge: Cambridge UP, 1966.

Burrows, Simon. *French Exile Journalism and European Politics: 1792-1814*. Woodbridge: Boydell, 2000.

Callahan, William J. *Church, Politics, and Society in Spain: 1750-1874*. Cambridge, MA: Harvard UP, 1984.

Carpenter, Kirsty. *Refugees of the French Revolution: Émigrés in London, 1789-1802*. Basingstoke: Macmillan, 1999.

Carpenter, Kirsty and Philip Mansel, eds. *The French Émigrés in Europe and the Struggle against the Revolution, 1789-1814*. Basingstoke: Macmillan, 1999.

Carr, Raymond. *Spain: 1808-1939*. Oxford: Clarendon, 1966.

Cicero, Marcus Tullius. *De Re Publica*. Trans. Clinton Walker Keyes. London: Heinemann, 1948.

Colley, Linda. *Britons: Forging the Nation, 1707-1837*. New Haven: Yale UP, 1992.

Crocker, Lester G. *Man and World in Eighteenth Century French Thought*. Baltimore: The Johns Hopkins Press, 1959.

---. *Nature and Culture: Ethical Thought in the French Enlightenment*. Baltimore: The Johns Hopkins Press, 1963.

Cruz Seoane, María. *Historia del periodismo en España*. 2 vols. Madrid: Alianza Editorial, 1996.

Daudet, Ernest. *Histoire de l'émigration pendant la révolution française*. 3 vols. Paris: Hachette, 1904-1908.

Dann, Otto, and John Dinwiddy, eds. *Nationalism in the Age of the French Revolution*. London: The Hambledon Press, 1988.

Dechêne, Abel. *Contre Pie VII et Bonaparte: Le Blanchardisme, 1801-1829*. Paris: Firmin-Didot, 1932.

Dérozier, Albert. *Manuel Josef Quintana et la naissance du libéralisme en Espagne*. 2 vols. Paris: Les belles lettres, 1968-70.

Destutt de Tracy, Antoine. *Commentaire sur l'Esprit des Lois de Montesquieu*. Paris, 1819.

Dictionnaire historique de la langue française. 1992.

Doyle, William. *The Oxford History of the French Revolution*. Oxford: Clarendon, 1989.

Ellis, Geoffrey. *The Napoleonic Empire*. London: Macmillan, 1991.

Encyclopédie, ou dictionnaire raisonné des sciences, des arts et des métiers. 1751-1780.

Epstein, James A. *Radical Expression: Political Language, Ritual, and Symbol in England, 1790-1850*. New York: Oxford UP, 1994.

Ezquerra, Ramon. "Blanco-White Crespo, José María." *Diccionario de Historia de España*. 2nd ed. 1986.

Furet, François. *Revolutionary France: 1770-1880*. Trans. Antonia Nevill. Oxford: Blackwell, 1992.

Galante Garrone, Alessandro, and Franco Della Peruta. *La Stampa italiana del Risorgimento*. Roma: Laterza, 1979.

Gay, Peter. *The Enlightenment. An Interpretation*. 2 vols. London: Weidenfeld and Nicolson, 1967-69.

Gellner, Ernest. *Nations and Nationalism*. 1983. Oxford: Blackwell, 1992.

Gengembre, Gerard. *La Contre-Révolution ou l'histoire désespérante*. Paris: Imago, 1989.

Godechot, Jacques. *La Contre-Révolution: doctrine et action, 1789-1804*. Paris: Presses Universitaires de France, 1961.

---, ed. *Les constitutions de la France depuis 1789*. Paris: Garnier-Flammarion, 1970.

---. "The New Concept of Nation and its Diffusion in Europe." *Nationalism in the Age of the French Revolution.* Eds. Otto Dann and John Dinwiddy. London: The Hambledon Press, 1988.

Goodman, Dena. *The Republic of Letters.* Ithaca: Cornell UP, 1994.

Greenfeld, Liah. *Nationalism: Five Roads to Modernity.* Cambridge, MA: Harvard UP, 1992.

Greer, Donald. *The Incidence of Emigration during the French Revolution.* Cambridge, MA: Harvard UP, 1951.

Haakonssen, Knud. *Natural Law and Moral Philosophy: From Grotius to the Scottish Enlightenment.* Cambridge: Cambridge UP, 1996.

Hamilton, Bernice. *Political Thought in Sixteenth-Century Spain.* Oxford: Clarendon, 1963.

Hamilton, J.A. "William Wickham." *Dictionary of National Biography.* 1885-1903.

Hayward, Jack. *After the French Revolution: Six Critics of Democracy and Nationalism.* New York: Harvester Wheatsheaf, 1991.

Hearder, Harry. *Italy in the Age of the Risorgimento: 1790-1870.* London: Longman, 1983.

Herr, Richard. *The Eighteenth-Century Revolution in Spain.* Princeton: Princeton UP, 1958.

Hesse, Carla. *Publishing and Cultural Politics in Revolutionary Paris, 1789-1810.* Berkeley: University of California Press, 1991.

Higonnet, Patrice. *Class, Ideology, and the Rights of Nobles during the French Revolution.* Oxford: Clarendon, 1981.

Hobsbawm, Eric. *The Age of Revolution. Europe: 1789-1848.* 1962. London: Sphere, 1973.

---. *Nations and Nationalism since 1789. Programme, Myth, Reality.* Cambridge: Cambridge UP, 1992.

Holtman, Robert B. *Napoleonic Propaganda.* Baton Rouge: Louisiana UP, 1950.

Hunt, Lynn. *Politics, Culture, and Class in the French Revolution.* Berkeley: University of California Press, 1984.

Kamenka, Eugene, ed. *Nationalism: The Nature and Evolution of an Idea.* London: Edward Arnold, 1976.

Kaplan, Stephen. *Farewell, Revolution.* Ithaca: Cornell UP, 1995.

Kemiläinen, Aira. *Nationalism: Problems Concerning the Word, the Concept and Classification.* Studia Historica Jyväskyläensia 3. Jyväskylä: Jyväskylän Kasvatusopillinen Korkeakoulu—Jyväskylän Yliopistoyhdistys, 1964.

Kennedy, Emmet. *A Philosophe in the Age of Revolution: Destutt de Tracy and the Origins of "Ideology."* Philadelphia: The American Philosophical Society, 1978.

Kohn, Hans. *The Idea of Nationalism: A Study in its Origins and Background.* New York: Macmillan, 1946.

Koselleck, Reinhart. *Critique and Crisis: Enlightenment and the Pathogenesis of Modern Society.* 1959. Oxford: Berg, 1988.

---. *Vergangene Zukunft.* 1979. Frankfurt am Main: Suhrkamp, 1992.

---. *Futures Past.* Trans. Keith Tribe. Cambridge, MA: MIT Press, 1982.

---, et al. "Volk, Nation, Nationalismus, Masse." *Geschichtliche Grundbegriffe: Historisches Lexikon zur politisch-sozialen Sprache in Deutschland.* Ed. Otto Brunner et al. 8 vols. Stuttgart: Klett-Cotta, 1972-97.

Kulstein, David. "The Ideas of Charles-Joseph Panckoucke, Publisher of the *Moniteur Universel,* on the French Revolution." *French Historical Studies* 4 (1966): 306-319.

Lefebvre, Georges. *Napoléon.* 5th ed. 1965. Trans. Henry F. Stockhold. 2 vols. New York: Columbia UP, 1969.

Lehec, Claude, and Jean Cazeneuve, eds. *Oeuvres philosophiques de Cabanis.* 2 vols. Paris: Presses Universitaires de France, 1956.

Leroy, Maxime. *Histoire des Idées sociales en France.* 3 vols. Paris: Gallimard, 1946-54.

Levy, Darline Gay. *The Ideas and Careers of Simon-Nicolas-Henri Linguet: A Study in Eighteenth-Century French Politics.* Urbana: University of Illinois Press, 1980.

Lloréns, Vicente. *Liberales y románticos. Una emigración española en Inglaterra: 1823-1834.* Madrid: Castalia, 1968.

---. *El Romanticismo español.* 2nd ed. Madrid: Castalia, 1989.

Lynch, John. *Bourbon Spain: 1700-1808.* Oxford: Blackwell, 1989.

Lyttleton, Adrian. "The national question in Italy." *The National Question in Europe in Historical Context.* Eds. Mikula Teich and Roy Porter. Cambridge: Cambridge UP, 1993.

MacIntyre, Alasdair. *A Short History of Ethics.* London: Routledge, 1967.

---. *Three Rival Versions of Moral Enquiry.* Notre Dame: Indiana University of Notre Dame Press, 1990.

Mack Smith, Dennis. *Mazzini.* New Haven: Yale UP, 1994.

Mandelbaum, Maurice. *History, Man, & Reason: A Study in Nineteenth Century Thought.* Baltimore: The Johns Hopkins Press, 1971.

Martínez Ruiz, Enrique, et al. *La España moderna.* Madrid: Istmo, 1992.

Maspero-Clerc, Hélène. *Un Journaliste Contre-Révolutionnaire: Jean-Gabriel Peltier, 1760-1825.* Paris: Société des Études Robespierristes, 1973.

McPhee, Peter. *A Social History of France: 1780-1880.* London: Routledge, 1992.

Morelli, Emilia. *Mazzini in Inghilterra.* Firenze: Felice le Monnier, 1938.

Moreno Alonso, Manuel. "Las ideas políticas de *El Español.*" *Revista de estudios políticos* 39 (1984): 65-106.

Morrow, John. *History of Political Thought: A Thematic Introduction.* London: Macmillan, 1998.

Murphy, Martin. *Blanco-White: Self-banished Spaniard.* New Haven: Yale UP, 1989.

Palmer, R.R. *The Age of the Democratic Revolution: A Political History of Europe and America.* 2 vols. Princeton: Princeton UP, 1959-64.

Parkin, Charles. *The Moral Basis of Burke's Political Thought.* Cambridge: Cambridge UP, 1956.

Popkin, Jeremy D. *News and Politics in the Age of the Revolution: Jean Luzac's Gazette de Leyde.* Ithaca: Cornell UP, 1989.

Roberts, James. *The Counter-Revolution in France: 1787-1830.* New York: St Martin's Press, 1990.

Roberts, J.M. *French Revolution Documents.* Vol. 1. Oxford: Blackwell, 1966-.

[Robespierre, Maximilien de]. *Le Comité de Salut Public à la Convention Nationale. Rapports faits en son nom par Robespierre.* Paris, 1794.

Rousseau, Jean Jacques. *Du contrat social. Écrits politiques.* Paris: Gallimard, 1964. Vol. 3 of *Oeuvres complètes.* 4 vols. 1959-69.

Sabine, George H. *A History of Political Thought.* 3rd ed. London: Harrap, 1964.

Salvemini, Gaetano. *Scritti sul Risorgimento.* Milano: Feltrinelli, 1961.

Sánchez Mantero, Rafael. *Liberales en el exilio.* Madrid: Rialp, 1975.

Shafer, Boyd C. *Faces of Nationalism: New Realities and Old Myths.* New York: Harcourt Brace Jovanovich, 1972.

Shafer, R.J. *The Economic Societies in the Spanish World.* N.p.: Syracuse UP, 1958.

Sherwin-White, A.N. *The Roman Citizenship.* 2d ed. Oxford: Clarendon, 1973.

Shubert, Adrian. *Social History of Modern Spain*. London: Unwin Hyman, 1990.

Sidgwick, Henry. *Outlines of the History of Ethics*. 1886. London: Macmillan, 1946.

Sieyès, Emmanuel. *Qu'est-ce que le Tiers état?* 1789. Genève, 1970.

Smith, Anthony D. *The Ethnic Origins of Nations*. Oxford: Blackwell, 1986.

---. *Nationalism and Modernism: A Critical Survey of Recent Theories of Nations and Nationalism*. London: Routledge, 1998.

Soboul, Albert. *La Civilisation et la Révolution Française*. 3 vols. Paris: Arthaud, 1970-83.

Staël, Germaine de. *Des circonstances actuelles qui peuvent terminer la révolution et des principes qui doivent fonder la république en France*. Ed. Lucia Omacini. Genève: Droz, 1979.

Stephen, Leslie. "White, Joseph Blanco." *Dictionary of National Biography*. 1885-1903.

Sutherland, D.M.G. *France 1789-1815: Revolution and Counterrevolution*. London: Fontana, 1985.

Tabori, Paul. *Anatomy of Exile*. London: Harrap, 1972.

Tulard, Jean, and Benoît Yvert, eds. *La Contre-Révolution*. Paris: Perrin, 1990.

Valbuena Prat, Ángel. *Historia de la literatura española*. 8th ed. 3 vols. Barcelona: Gustavo Gili, 1968.

Varela Suanzes, Joaquín. "Un precursor de la monarquía parlamentaria: Blanco-White y *El Español* (1810-1814)." *Revista de estudios políticos* 79 (1993): 101-120.

---. "El pensamiento constitucional español en el exilio: el abandono del modelo doceañista (1823-1833)." *Revista de estudios políticos* 88 (1995): 63-90.

Vidalenc, Jean. *Les Émigrés français: 1789-1825*. Caen: Association des Publications de la Faculté des Lettres et Sciences Humaines de l'Université de Caen.

Vingtrinier, Emmanuel. *La Contre-Révolution: première période, 1789-1791*. 2 vols. Paris: Émil-Paul frères, 1924.

Watson, J. Steven. *The Reign of George III: 1760-1815*. 1960. Oxford: Clarendon, 1985.

Weiner, Margery. *The French Exiles: 1789-1815*. London: John Murray, 1960.

Wicks, Margaret C.W. *The Italian Exiles in London: 1816-1848*. Manchester: Manchester UP, 1937.

Woolf, Stuart. *A History of Italy, 1700-1860: the Social Constraints of Political Change*. London: Methuen, 1979.

Index